Speaking through the Silence

•••Speaking

through

the Silence

Narratives, Social Conventions,
and Power in Java

LAINE BERMAN

New York   Oxford

Oxford University Press

1998

Oxford University Press

Oxford   New York
Athens   Auckland   Bangkok   Bogotá   Buenos Aires   Calcutta
Cape Town   Chennai   Dar es Salaam   Delhi   Florence   Hong Kong   Istanbul
Karachi   Kuala Lumpur   Madrid   Melbourne   Mexico City   Mumbai
Nairobi   Paris   São Paulo   Singapore   Taipei   Tokyo   Toronto   Warsaw

and associated companies in
Berlin   Ibadan

Copyright © 1998 by Laine Berman

Published by Oxford University Press, Inc.
198 Madison Avenue, New York, New York 10016

Oxford is a registered trademark of Oxford University Press

Library of Congress Cataloging-in-Publication Data

Berman, Laine.
Speaking through the silence : narratives, social conventions, and
power in Java / Laine Berman.
p.   cm. — (Oxford studies in anthropological linguistics ;
18)
Includes bibliographical references and index.
ISBN 0-19-510888-4
1. Javanese language—usage.   2. Javanese language—Address, Forms
of.   3. Javanese language—Social aspects.   4. Speech and social
status—Indonesia—Java.   I. Title.   II. Series.
PL5169.B47   1998
306.44'5982—dc21   97-29990

9 8 7 6 5 4 3 2 1

Printed in the United States of America
on acid-free paper

Preface

On Thursday, 21 May (Kemis Legi) 1998, President Soeharto relinquished his absolute hold over the people of Indonesia when he resigned the presidency he had held for over three decades. He seized power when Indonesia was in crisis, and in crisis he vacates it. His legacy of silencing criticism and stifling debate, banning all "political" activity, instilling ideologies of development and sacrifice, and requiring submission and conformity to his oppressive order (which included massacres and disappearances of so-called dissidents) will not be simply shaken off.

I had written this book initially to expand our scholarly knowledge of the Javanese language. I wanted to argue that our dominant associations of the Javanese language and culture with refinement and grace were inadequate because they did not account for what they hid: the silences that disguised an institutionalized suffering and inequality in everyday social interaction. Silence in Java is cultivated not just as the suppression of speech, but also through the control of knowledge at all levels of society. Silence in Java is defined as a noble acquiescence, which has greatly assisted successive absolute rulers. With the tides of change sweeping the country now, my intention is that the people of Indonesia recognize how they have contributed to these abuses of power, and that their everyday language practices are essential sites for political and social reform.

Melbourne   L.B.
22 May 1998

Acknowledgments

This book is the result of cooperation from many people and organizations that all helped to shape my understanding of Javanese as a people, as a language, and as a way of being. Without their sincere generosity and interest in me and my work, I could never have been so rewarded professionally or personally. I am especially grateful to Deborah Schiffrin, Heidi Hamilton, and Clare Wolfowitz for their patience, time, and support in guiding me through the writing of my dissertation at Georgetown University. Their suggestions proved essential in developing my own insights and giving me rich perspectives on and alternative possibilities for narrative and what it means to be Javanese. Rom Harré and Deborah Tannen provided the foundations for much of my thinking about language and identity. These ideas were shaped by discussions with Pamela Saunders, Rebecca Freeman, Patricia O'Connor, Christina Kakava, and Minako Ishikawa.

I also owe a great deal of thanks to John Wolff, Dede Oetomo, and Paryono, who gave me the opportunity to study Javanese at SEASSI, Cornell University, and to discuss the questions that would later shape my fieldwork. Also at Cornell I was to meet Ben Abel, Astri Wright, Gigi Weix, Susanne Brenner, Ben Anderson, and the students of SEASSI, whose stories of and experiences in Java were profoundly influential on my own.

From across vast distances during the various writing phases, I was greatly assisted directly and indirectly by John MacDougall and his Indonesia-L, David Bouchier and Wendy Miller. Thank you, John, for insisting that I get on the Net and become involved.

I wish to express my deepest gratitude to the Indonesian Academy of Sciences for its support and permission to conduct linguistic research for two years in Central Java. The Universitas Sanata Dharma, my local sponsor, provided office space, computers, the research staff at PPSD, and a wonderful opportunity to discuss Javanese notions of history, identity, culture, language, and politics. In particular, I must thank the resident spaceman, Mas Idaman, who taught me everything I needed to know about Javanese computers and politics.

I owe a lifetime of gratitude to Sri Sultan Hamengko Buwono X; Rama Joko; Rama Cokro; Rama Riya; Rama Barsono; my mother, Ibu Lindur; and the members of Krida Mardawa for permission to record their voices and learn about Javaneseness. For nearly two years, Wednesday became my favorite day of the week, the day to *sowan mlebet*. The Budiharjo family took me in and made me one of their own, presenting me with life's most valuable lessons. Pak Budi got me started in my Javanese interpretations by teaching me how to tell jokes and stories, and his daughters honored me with their stories, their trust, their humor, and their friendship. Mas Ratno introduced me to Javanese spiritualism as a way of life and gave me the opportunity to convene with my patron saint, *Kangjeng Ratu Rara Kidul*. Ibu Lindur and Ibu Sastra taught me the joy of *pasrah* (acceptance, surrender) and to never be afraid of the spirits of Java. I also wish to express my deep affection for Mas Didid, Mas Kirik, and the Keluarga Besar GIRLI (the street children of Yogyakarta) who provided their thoroughly new versions of Javaneseness and a sense of freedom and humor despite all the hardship. Mas Widodo transcribed my cassettes, and Pak Untung made my ordeals with the local intelligence police almost pleasurable.

With the national election of 1992 and the birth of a protest movement called *Golput*, my developing insights into Javanese language and identity were radically altered. The sensationally powerful statement made by the removal of all red and green banners, flags, and posters throughout the city over the course of one night, on 21 May, suddenly warned me of the significant role and potential impact of silence in an oppressive society. Athonk was my guide into this new world as he answered my questions and taught me how to return the trust and the love. He showed me that I was not imagining it all then, and he continues to teach me wonderful things now. Endy (Belanda), Mas Seno, Mas Safe'i, Mas Sulis, and others at DMPY (Dewan Mahasiswa dan Pemuda Yogyakarta, the Yogyakarta Student and Youth Council); Garuda 22; and ISI—Yogya, the GIRLI kids, Mas Adi, and the gang on Malioboro shaped my burgeoning activism and literally gave me a home. Most important were Mbakyu Ireng, Mbak Emmy (Bausasran), Mbak Kus, Si Yu, Ibu Tari (Juminahan), the community of Ibu-Ibu of Harjowinatan, Mbak Elly and Rifka Annisa, Sunarti (SBSI), Mbak Sri Gading, Ibu Sugeng, Ibu Harto, Ibu Lurah (Keraton), and the many women who trusted me with their words.

I also wish to express my deepest gratitude to my parents and my brother, Carl, whose selfless support, despite the tears, the miles, and the usual chaos, gave me the strength to continue.

During my two years of field research in Yogyakarta, Central Java, I was eventually to learn that beauty is not what you see but what you feel in your heart and bring others to feel. I am, and will forever remain, indebted to those who showed me Java.

Contents

A Note on Transcription
Conventions and Translations

This presentation of Javanese social interaction takes some bold new steps in transcriptions that need explanation. Rather unique in linguistic studies, I have chosen to present a *visual* key rather than the usual word-by-word gloss common for the speech levels of Javanese. My main reason for this is that such glosses focus the readers' attention away from the flow of the discourse and attract too much attention to the individual words. Example 1 shows the standard means of glossing Javanese discourse.

Ex. 1

Ibu	Asmoro	wingi	maringi	aku	foto	lawas
ki	name		ki			
kt = mother	name	yesterday	give	pn = I	photo	old

Ibu Asmoro gave me an old photograph yesterday.

Key: ki = *kråmå inggil*

　　 Ø = *ngoko* or no lexical variant

　　 kt = kinship term (see below)

　　 pn = pronoun

Such glosses stress the uniqueness of Javanese and its multiplicity of vocabulary terms. Example 2 illustrates the intricate variants that make up the Javanese language.

Ex. 2

Kulå	badhe	sowan	mlebet	kalih	putrå	penjenengan
k	k	ka	k	m	ki	k
pn = I	will	visit	inside	with	son	pn = you

I will visit inside [the palace] with your son.

Key: [xxx] = brackets give information omitted through ellipses, and so on.

　　 k = kråmå

　　 m = madyå

The goal of this book, however, is not to illustrate the complexity of the language by focusing on the *speech levels* and the ways in which they are used as indexes of formality. My goal is to show how the language functions through the *speech styles* of day-to-day interactions of native speakers. Thus, rather than direct attention to speech levels, that is, the *kråmå* or *ngoko* of each word, making up a stream of discourse, I instead wish to focus attention on the speech *act* that is achieved by the discourse as a whole. To this effect, I mark levels in a way that enhances a speaker's stylistic choice while not inhibiting the natural flow of the discourse. Example 3 shows a basic Javanese sentence with honorifics that express the speaker's respect for the person being spoken about:

Ex. 3

IBU Asmoro wingi **MARINGI** aku foto lawas.   Ibu Asmoro gave me an old photograph yesterday.

And Example 3 shows how a sentence in full *kråmå* would look:

Ex. 4

Kulå <u>badhe</u> <u>SOWAN</u> <u>mlebet</u> kalih <u>PUTRÅ</u>   I will visit in [the palace]
<u>penjenengan.</u>   with your son.

Both examples show how level markings are achieved through a method that highlights all non-*ngoko* variants. In brief, all markings beyond the basic font symbolize movements up the respect scale, with *ngoko* speech in plain font, **madyå** in bold, **<u>kråmå</u>** in bold with single underline and **<u>KRÅMÅ INGGIL</u>** and **<u>KRÅMÅ ANDHAP</u>** in bold caps with a single underline. The transcribed Javanese discourse is presented on the left with interpretations on the right, again to keep the flow of the conversations smooth.

In terms of the presentation of discursive examples, I initially present the stories marked for level shifts. As we move through the analytical discussions, level markings will be replaced by markings for the specific purpose being presented. For example:

→ 461. ASMORO: Aku wis ora sinden kok.   I don't sing any more y'know.
462. HARTO: Ning **<u>mboten wonten</u>**
    <u>IBU</u> nikå,   But when you aren't there
    <u>sami</u> gelå lo Bu   everyone is so disappointed mum.
    <u>NUWUN SEWU</u> menikå.   please excuse me.

Later, when the text is analyzed for its use of repetition and text boundary indexicals to clarify idea units, it will be presented like this:

→ 461. ASMORO: Aku wis ora sinden <u>kok</u>   I don't sing any more, y'know.
462. HARTO: Ning mboten wonten
    Ibu <u>nikå</u>,   But when you aren't there,
    sami gelå <u>lo Bu</u>   everyone is so disappointed mum
    nuwun sewu <u>menikå</u>.   please excuse me.

Transcription Conventions
Adapted from Schiffrin (1994)

Symbols for discourse transcription:

Units
   Intonation unit   {carriage return}
Speakers
   Speaker identity/turn start   NAME:
   Speech interruption   //
   Turn continuation   =
Transitional continuity
   Falling intonation and noticeable pause   .
   Slight rise and slight pause   ,
   Rising intonation and noticeable pause   ?
   Lengthened syllable   :
   Animated tone   !
Pause
   Long   ....
   Short   ..
Vocal noises
   Laughter, speaker   hehehe
   Laughter, participants   [hehehe]
Transcriber's perspective
   Researcher's comments, explanations   ( )
   Ellipses added in translations   [ ]
   Code switching   italics, <L2>
   Transcription doubt   (?)
Speaker's perspective
   Ngoko (no lexical variants) in plain font   Aku ra dong.
                              I don't understand.

   Madyå in bold font   "Nek aku piye" **ngaten**.
                              "So what about me" [he] said.

   Basic **kråmå** in bold font with single   **Kulå** melu.
   underline   I [want to] come along.
   Kråmå honorifics, either **KRÅMÅ**   Aku arep **SOWAN**.
   INGGIL or **KRÅMÅ ANDHAP** in bold   I will visit.
   caps with single underline
   Indonesian in italics   "*Saya juga*" ngono.
                              Me too, [I] said.

Orthography

Orthographic representations are phonemic. Apicodental /d/ and /t/ are in contrast with apicoalveolar /d/ and /t/. The latter is spelled [dh] and

[th] respectively. The open syllable [a] is pronounced /ɔ/ and here spelled [å] for those unfamiliar with Javanese pronunciation. The final [k] is pronounced /ʔ/, but spelling remains standard.

Translations

In most cases I give only a free translation from the Javanese except where word-by-word gloss is necessary.

Some classes of kinship terms are extremely common in Javanese and cannot be adequately translated into English while maintaining a natural speech flow. These terms are maintained in the original language. Those that appear in the texts are as follows, in order of descending formality:

RÅMÅ, Bapak, Pak = father
IBU, Bu, Mak = mother
Mbakyu, Mbak = elder sister
mas = elder brother
Adhi, Dhi, or Dik = younger sibling, unmarked for gender

All of these kinship terms are broadly used as polite vocatives in definite and indefinite terms and as indexicals of anyone sharing the general trait in reference to age and gender.

Glossary

abdi-dalem	servants in the service of the sultan
alus	smooth; refined; elegant
bapak	father; term of respect for elder males
båså	language (lit.) but is often used to refer to non-*ngoko* speech
båså kedhaton	language used in the palace for speaking with royalty
cårå Jåwå	the "way" of the Javanese
dhik	younger sibling; general term for younger person
gamelan	Javanese percussion orchestra
GBHN	*Garis Besar Haluan Negara*, State Policy Guidelines
ibu	mother; term of respect for older woman
Idul Fitri	feast celebrating the end of the fasting month of Ramadhan
ikhlas	a detachment from the material world
jarik	a tightly wound, ankle-length cloth; a batik sarong for women
jilbab	head scarf worn by Muslim women
kampung	usually lower-class urban community
kasar	rough; crude
Kedaulatan Rakyat	the local Yogyakarta newspaper
kodrat	essential nature
kotor	dirty
kråmå	the term for all forms of non-*ngoko* Javanese
kråmå andhap	humbling vocabulary
kråmå inggil	honorific vocabulary
kraton	the sultan's palace
Kridå Mardåwå	the section of the palace's bureaucracy that manages performances
krupuk	shrimp crackers
laras	harmony
londho	the general term for a white-skinned foreigner
madyå	middle Javanese speech level
mas	elder brother; term of respect for elder males

mbak	elder sister; term of respect for elder females
noda; dinodai	stained; disgraced
New Order	President Soeharto's regime
ngoko	basic or ordinary Javanese, often called low Javanese
nrimå	acquiescence
oleh-oleh	gifts brought back from a trip
Pancasila	the state ideology: belief in one supreme God; just and civilized humanity; national unity; democracy led by the inner wisdom of unanimity arising out of deliberations among representatives; social justice for the whole of the Indonesian people
Pembangunan	development
pesindhen	female singer in the *gamelan* orchestra
PKK	*Pembinaan Kesejahteraan Keluarga*, Family Welfare Guidance
priyayi	blood ties to royalty; the upper classes; people displaying exemplary behavior and demeanor
Ramadhan	the Muslim fasting month
sabar	the absence of eagerness, impatience, and passion
sowan mlebet	term used by *abdi-dalem* to visit inside the palace walls, but "serve" is a more appropriate interpretation
suci	pure
tåtå tenterem	calm orderliness
tukang becak	pedicab drivers
tumbal	a sacrifice to ensure the success of people or places and events
weton	the conjunction of the five-day and seven-day cycles in which a person is born
wong cilik	the "little" people; the ordinary people; the poor; the working classes
wong gede	the "big" people; the opposite of *wong cilik*

•••PART I

SETTING THE SCENE

one

Introduction

Untold Stories

It was already quite late on the last night of the fasting month of Ramadhan, 1993. I was sitting on the bottom bunk bed alongside Sari and her youngest brother, Otong. She had asked me to come and sit there because she had something to tell me. We were staring at the old ceramic block roof of her home, laughing at the rain that was pouring through its many holes. She repeated our old joke about my needing an umbrella to sleep there.

I had been here since early afternoon, enjoying the warmth and gaiety of my adopted family in Java and helping in the preparation and celebration of Idhul Fitri. Since 6:00 P.M., however, we had been anxiously awaiting the arrival of Pak Budi's younger brother. He was driving with his family to Yogyakarta from Surabaya to *mbukå påså* ("break the fast") with us and celebrate the end of the fasting month. It was past 10:00 P.M. on a wet, chilly night when they finally did arrive. This was the cue for us to prepare trays of hot tea and snacks for these special guests.

Before and after assisting in the preparations, I remained in the shabby structure of cracked cement, plywood, and woven bamboo that is the Budi home to receive and chat with the stream of visitors. This is when neighbors, friends, relations, and even new acquaintances can beg forgiveness for all sins past and present, intentional or not. This was a time I had especially looked forward to since I was certain to have committed numerous errors in my own ignorance as a newcomer to the rigorous formalities of Central Java. For over a year and a half I had been a frequent member of the Budi household, a well-received member of the *kampung*, and an expected participant in local activities that ranged from formal meetings to the most intimate gossip sessions. With not much more to go on beyond following the lead of the four Budi daughters, I shopped in the market for Ibu Budi, served tea at the local meetings, and lent a helping hand whenever and wherever one was needed. My status as a foreigner was naturally one of privileged outsider. But as a speaker of

Javanese, albeit far from perfect, and as a woman with no pretensions of Western superiority or fear of getting my hands dirty or saying the wrong thing, I managed to alter my position in this compact community to that of an odd child.

Early in our relationship, the Budis were eager to answer my linguistic questions and to explain and correct my speaking and behavioral errors. When I first began "getting my hands dirty" by helping the Budi women, Pak Budi asked me to stop. This was not the behavior of a guest. I persisted, however, and the women all giggled in embarrassment mixed with glee as I strained the tea, added far more sugar to one glass than I personally use in a year, and carried it out to other guests in my clumsy attempts at Javanese humility. In time, instead of just listening at village meetings, I started to speak, and at home, I started to do the dishes, sweep, or grate coconut. My education as a female child who needed to know what *cårå Jåwå* ("the Javanese way") meant from the inside was an accepted, although often humorous, fact of life, especially as I began to show signs of improving. But my eagerness to be positioned as a "child" needing to be socialized (because this is specifically what I *felt* like), contrasted and occasionally conflicted with my differences. My foreignness, age, and status as university lecturer also permitted me a certain freedom to ask difficult questions, speak about unmentionable topics, and be trusted with intimate secrets. Thus, precariously balanced between odd insider and privileged outsider, I went about my business of learning *cårå Jåwå*, fully trusting in the theater of life that was the Budi family's daily routines.

Pak Budi emerged from his younger brother's elegant home in front of the Budi's cramped, windowless shack; sat down on the torn plastic and iron chair; let out a sigh; and tossed a small plastic bag of raw shrimp crackers (*krupuk*) onto the table. He must be feeling exhausted from the month-long fast and the wait for his brother to arrive, I thought. I looked at him and the bag he tossed and asked in formal Javanese, "Menikå menåpå Pak?" ("What's that, Pak?"). He answered briefly, "Oleh-oleh." It was the gift brought by his brother. I looked again at the expressionless smoothness of Pak Budi's face, then at the bag, and I immediately burst out laughing. Pak Budi, always one to love jokes, sat up with a grin and waited for my explanation. The joke lay in the rudeness. I said, "Kok, uthil tenan, Pak! Oleh-olehe mung sakbungkuse krupuk mentah!! Åpå meneh, sesuk di balikke wis mateng nggo sarapane!" ("How extraordinarily cheap and selfish, Pak! [All you get for] *oleh-oleh* [is] a measly bag of raw *krupuk*—which [they know darn well Ibu Budi] will cook and serve right back [to them] for tomorrow's breakfast!")

Somewhere between shock and reality, my comments struck deep. The whole family burst into laughter until tears actually were visible on tired faces. After the laughter subsided, Pak Budi smiled at me, shook his head and said, "Mbak Lina, Mbak Lina. Matur nuwun, anakku."[1] ("Thank you, my daughter"). He then stood up in the tiny, cramped sitting room;

stretched and sighed; and went out into the night rain, back to the spacious house his brother owns but rarely occupies.

It was then that Sari motioned me to follow her into the sleeping area, partitioned off from the sitting room by a thin, sagging plywood board. After commenting on the ugliness of her home, made all the more obvious to her by my presence in it, Sari introduced her story by reiterating what I already knew: the Budi family were descendants of *priyayi*, members of the wealthy, noble classes. But she added that in generations past, *priyayi* families had a tradition of sacrificing one of their children in order to ensure the success of the others (a practice called *tumbal*). Usually decided at birth because of a duplication in the date (*weton*[2]), gender, or position in the order of birth, that child would be symbolically "thrown away" to separate it from the other children. The baby would then be accepted back as a foundling, not as a full-fledged member of the family but rather as a servant. Pak Budi, she said, suffered this fate, and that is why he received no inheritance from his family. His three brothers, each with university degrees and important positions, received one-third of the huge parcel of ancestral land within the fortress wall that surrounds the sultan's domain. Yet, her father was allowed only a minimal education and was found a low-level civil servant's position as a family favor. Despite carrying much of the weight in the office, he was not awarded the promotions he deserved since he was not of *real priyayi* lineage. To this day, and as I saw very clearly for myself, Pak Budi and his family are still treated as unpaid servants by the better-off siblings.

Ibu Budi, Sari went on to explain, not only bore most of the burdens of the family's poverty but also suffered the same *tumbal* rejection her husband did. Women earn their status from men, Sari explained. She told me about the times her family went hungry because her mother would cook snacks (*jajan*) to sell on the streets for money, only to have them stolen by her uncle's children. She also told me that for years her mother had only one *jarik* (sarong) and one *kebaya* (traditional-style blouse) and that every night she would very diligently wash them; hang them to dry; and wear them again, dry or not, the next day. Sari also told me about the times her mother would miss her own family and walk the five kilometers south to Bantul to visit them. Never was she treated as family or as a guest; never was she invited into the house. Rather, she was always told to wait outside, given a cup of tea, and treated as nothing more than a common beggar. Sari stressed the fact that her mother never asked her family for anything. Sari explained that she had accompanied her mother on some of these journeys and saw for herself how her mother was treated. Her mother, Sari explained, never said a word or expressed any disappointment to anyone. This is the fate of women, she added abruptly.

When she had said enough, Sari's only comment was, "Kudu ngerti, Mbak Lin" ("[You] need to know, Mbak Laine"), and she got up to help her mother. Meanwhile, Otong, who had been sitting silently on my left, listening to these stories, visibly trembled as he murmured, "Kok, aku durung tau weruh. Kok, piye, Mbak? Aku åpå ki? Ra dong aku ki." ("Why did I never know. What do I do, Mbak? I don't understand any of this.") He had tears in his eyes. I did not know what to tell him.

THE VOICES OF THE POOR and the marginalized in third-world contexts are hidden in whispers and resonant silences. The voices of urban, poor Javanese women are perhaps hidden behind even deeper layers of silence because of the "traditions" that specifically define their access to, and styles of speaking in, everyday social interactions. This book attempts to uncover these silences by tracing the patterns they weave in the lives of a few Javanese women.

The Politics of Social Interaction

Cårå Jåwå is defined literally as "the Javanese way." The word *cårå* means "style," "manner," "method," "fashion," or "tradition," but *Jåwå* does not mean simply "Javanese." It means what one must know to be a member of Javanese society. In essence, this means to know one's place in the social order. Thus, *cårå Jåwå* entails not just speaking Javanese but also putting into practice all the behaviors that index one's social or hierarchical place.

Cårå Jåwå has long been of great interest to both linguists and anthropologists. At the center of that interest has been the elaborate system of speech levels and the interactive presentation of self associated with them. Clifford Geertz's (1960) famous book, *The Religion of Java*, set the focus for much of this interest by linking the stratification of language to that of the society. In its most simplified and idealized form, Javanese society recognizes *priyayi* as the educated elite, the noble class whose high status is apparent in the refined use of the most formal styles of Javanese language and the gracious, elegant behavior that must accompany it. At the other end of the social order, lacking the social refinements and linguistic abilities of their betters and making up most of the population of ethnic Javanese, are the *wong cilik*.[3] These are the ordinary people, the working classes who look up to the *priyayi* as models of the ultimate art of refinement.

From even this highly simplified but arguably realistic model we could conclude that the factors that separate and stratify Javanese society are indexed, as well as enforced, by the use of standard Javanese. To know one's place in the intricate nuances of Javanese social positioning and to have the sensitivity to signal this awareness through everyday social interactions is a sign of being truly Javanese, of self-knowledge and self-control, where inner harmony is the key to preserving an orderly society. As Joseph Errington (1984:284) explains, proper behavior for the Javanese is essentially a matter of exercising restraint, of not doing things that stem from and make apparent one's baser, selfish instincts. Maintaining harmony in society, then, is a sign of inner strength and mutual awareness. Awareness appears at both the social and discursive levels as participation in a tacit moral and ethical agreement through which speakers mutually preserve and guard equanimity by relegating self to the higher needs of that social order.

Taking such basic and broadly accepted explanations of the Javanese language and society into account, how, then, can Sari's story facilitate an understanding of Javanese identity in practice? For one thing, she warns us to recognize the silences that resonate as a result of what is locally considered to be an ethical and moral social inequality. The stories she told me were not known to other members of her family, as shown by her brother's response. Pak Budi never verbally resented being passed over for promotions, nor did he seem to resent cleaning and guarding his brother's huge empty house while the eight members of the Budi family lived in a tiny, windowless, leaking shack. Sari's mother told no one of the rejection she had received from members of her own family. Despite this victimization and poverty as a result of social inequality in practice, the Budi family never outwardly complained, never renounced the cruelty or unfairness of their fate. In fact, in their daily practices, the Budi family members demonstrated just the opposite. Through example, the Budi children were taught to behave in exemplary Javanese fashion, always carrying themselves calmly and with great humility through perfect mastery of linguistic etiquette. The family succeeded in showing their world that they did indeed deserve respect, and they obviously received it in abundance within their own *kampung*.[4] Yet, through such ideal Javanese behavior, the Budi family members also succeed in reproducing and even glorifying the very meanings that marginalize and victimize them in the wider social order.

The analysis of talk within Javanese contexts, then, requires a focus on more than the immediate conversation. Following George Herbert Mead (1934), I take communicative interaction to be the site within which self, meaning, community, and culture are all constituted through social acts; hence, all are interrelated and interdependent. The meanings and significant symbols accepted by members of a community, what Mead (1934:89) refers to as the "universe of discourse", are not *givens* but rather a type of social or political prize to be negotiated and sometimes fought over. In this respect, the social meanings that shape Javanese realities and become generalized as their institutions are the key links in a chain that reflect back on, and radiate out from, their social interactions. Thus, the institutions of a society are organized forms of group or social activity—forms so organized that the individual members of society can act adequately and socially by taking the attitudes of others toward these activities (1934:261). In this manner, communities "control" their members, and through this reflexive acceptance of shared meanings, socialized individuals emerge as persons precisely because they belong to a community. Since meanings, like other influences in people's lives, are social and, hence, larger than themselves in origin, human agents *control* themselves while they *create* themselves (Stark, 1996:11).

In Javanese contexts, institutions are hierarchical in their means of shaping all aspects of social interactions, from local conversations to the structures of the community and the very circumstances of culture itself. Since conversation is not separable from the larger social order that frames it, issues of *control*, and particularly *self-control* are basic in recognizing Javanese ways and means of negotiating social meaning. Within the framework of Javanese linguistic interpretation used here, *reality* is based on culture as clusters of symbolic acts and identified through the analysis of social discourse (cf. Geertz, 1973). The negotiation (and hence interpretation) of meaning, then, takes place at a three-way interaction among the social representations in peoples' minds (such as socially shared knowledge, beliefs, attitudes, and ideologies), the macro-level structures (generally of power and authority) that shape them, and the micro-level social interactions through which they all merge as subjective reality and become identifiable (van Dijk, 1994). Within the theoretical foundations of critical discourse analysis, social interaction is the arena in which speakers display their shared mental strategies and representations as a basis from which they can monitor the production and interpretation of their discourse (i.e., exercise their *self-control*). The aim of this book, then, is to develop a strategy for recognizing presupposed beliefs held by speech participants and to identify how such knowledge affects the structure of discourse (1994:108). Thus, it is my task to display how, and identify why, the shaping of reality in Javanese contexts is a site of political struggle.

In his book *From Grammar to Politics*, Alessandro Duranti (1994) defines political struggles as a linguistic problem. Based within the physical, hierarchical, and contextual limitations of a Samoan *fono* (the council meetings in which the titled members of the village meet to discuss political matters), Duranti shows how political negotiation is about "how to tell or, in some cases, *not* to tell a story, how to mention or *not* to mention a given event or its agent" (1994:3; emphasis in original). Stories about events that affect an entire village are regulated by not just an "information flow" but also a "moral flow." Yet it is this moral element that wields the power to shape information, which Duranti explains as a progressive and cooperative framing of characters and events in terms of their values to the community.

Duranti's "moral flow hypothesis," as well as his notion of politics as a *discursive* conflict, does indeed offer many clues for understanding Javanese social interaction, in which responsibility to the social order most certainly does constrain when, where, and how stories can be told. Through his analysis, Duranti sets a foundation for recognizing *context* rather than *individuals* as the source of the illocutionary force of utterances. Specifically relevant for my own goals here, Duranti shows how stories and their meanings are coconstructed as strategies for constituting or mitigating responsibility and its consequences.

In Javanese contexts, the framing of discursive responsibility is also negotiated through positions of power, but by adapting Mead's (1934) concepts of communication, all incidents of conversing include contests over meaning. For Mead, conversation is made up of gestures and adjustive responses within social acts that bring out the relationship that exists between interactants. Reified positions of power and hierarchy can determine who in a group of conversants will need to adjust to the other. But what needs to be clarified is the basic fact that all members of society belong to more than one universe of discourse, meaning that all kinds of combinations and permutations of positions and meanings are possible. In this respect, we begin with a far broader conception of politics than that through which Duranti (1994) explains Samoan discourses. In modern Java, "politics" is an entity that intrudes heavily on everything and everyone.

Even though we will not look directly at formal political discourses, the everyday interactions of common, working-class, urban Javanese women inevitably reflect these pressures, be they political or cultural. It is through these "political" filters, such as the ideologies of social hierarchy or gender, that identity is constructed in line with the expectations of the community. To give my picture of women's lives an intimate perspective, I have focused on the stories they tell among their family and friends. Yet, even within the presumed intimacy and boundaries of their own natural social networks, these stories will show how the framing of social positions needs to be recognized as an extremely potent factor in the social construction of not just the stories but meaning and social identity as well. It is by interpreting the *said* within the broader contexts of the *unsaid* that we are able to account for how members make sense of reality, how they think about the world, and how they identify and attempt to solve problems. To interpret the discourses of these working-class Javanese women, the values of the wider social order, the community, and the immediate contexts of interaction are all essential ingredients, precisely because of their strength and ability to weave a tightly constricting web around members and the social order they each support. Even though I begin here with the mundane stories told by close friends, the traditions of hierarchical domination and patronage in modern Java loom as intentioned intertextual forces. They are the institutionalized frames that shape and give meaning to the women's stories. Such constricting structures, effectively controlled by those with the power to do so, can reinforce social hierarchy as a dominant societal discourse through which to ensure that these institutions do not change. Social meaning is thus preserved in the conversations of the *wong cilik* as a type of "moral flow" and is revealed by recognizing the weight of social responsibility for sustaining the self-repressive values of hierarchy as the foundation for harmony.

Mead's (1934) image of conversation as comprising gestures and adjustive responses is easily applied to Javanese speech levels. Relations of power are reflected by the ways in which speakers adjust to others, displayed through talk as a highly flexible interactive strategy for constituting or mitigating responsibility. As Duranti (1994) specifies by his "moral flow hypothesis," this focus on responsibility in social interaction labels it as not simply a means through which meaning is coconstructed but also a highly potent and potentially dangerous reflection of how speakers make sense of the consequences of their speech actions. Social responsibility *is* very dangerous within the climate of control recognized in modern Java. Thus, where and how do we learn to read the silences in Javanese speech practices that are so important for the maintenance of social harmony but that standard structural analyses cannot account for?

With a political system based on metaphors of patronage and stability, President Soeharto's New Order government promotes its benevolent authoritarianism as the true path to modernization and harmony. Social equality and an equal share of the fruits of development are the eventual goals. Meanwhile, the *wong cilik* faithfully, silently, and often enough fearfully submit their minds, bodies, and souls to the authority's absolute terms and maintain their meager existence. Where one stands in the social order shapes a person's access to "individual interpretations" and the power to impose such an interpretation on others. As Alison Murray (1991:24) describes it, "The ruling elite invokes the patron-client model to foster an ideology of dependence, and justifies exploitation by encouraging alleyside people (i.e. urban poor) to think of themselves as the little people (*wong cilik*) who fatalistically accept that they are unenlightened."

This, then, is New Order harmony: a power-laden, absolute control over the social order and the specific roles, rights, and obligations of the players within it. With a massive work force of *wong cilik* at their disposal, the New Order promotes definitions of Javaneseness as a means through which to glorify the acquiescence of self to the greater good of the whole. Such a glory is alternatively interpreted by many as human rights abuses. For example, low salaries for women are not locally evaluated as an example of unfairness and inequality. In fact, low salaries are seen as a comparative advantage in that they bring overseas investors into the country. This is thoroughly compatible with the industrialization of Indonesia as the ultimate goal of the government's development policy. Hence, women are heroically and correctly doing their part in the development of the state.[5] The fact that women's salaries are 40–60% lower than men's is easily accepted in Indonesia, where women's income is recognized as a second, or support, income and where women are permanently tied either to parents or to a husband.[6] The widespread praise women receive through the state ideology for their sacrifices in the name of family harmony and national development assure them of their worth.

At least in terms of the urban poor, where is the dividing line between traditional definitions of Javanese elegance and modern political oppression? This analysis of Javanese social interaction investigates how such power elements actually function within the most mundane of day-to-day interactions. Yet, as I was to learn, these power relations are reproduced by the widespread enforcement of styles of discourse and the strength of class boundaries that in Java, more than perhaps most other places, is tied to the legitimacy of the existing social order. The boundaries that separate tradition, culture, and oppression blur when we begin to question how and why one group would permit another group or social institution to exercise control. This discourse analysis of actual Javanese conversations moves the inquiry into questions of social cognition:

> Such power is based on access to socially valued resources such as force, wealth, income, status or knowledge. Besides forms of force or coercive power, such control is usually persuasive: acts of others are indirectly controlled through influencing such mental conditions of action as intentions, plans, knowledge or beliefs. It is at this point where power relates to both discourse and social cognition. (van Dijk, 1994:108–109)

At this juncture of discourse and social cognition, we are about to embark on an exploration of social identity among Javanese working-class women as both a reflection and a construction of relations of power.

Language and Power in Java

Studies of Javanese discourse have barely skimmed the surface of these issues of social power and inequality, opting instead for a focus on the elegance and the spiritual beliefs that underlie rituals of self-control. Sari's stories alert us to recognize the intense power of language and harmonious self-presentation as a way to manipulate one's place in the world. But they also show that in practice knowing one's place requires more than self-knowledge, self-control, and a perpetual state of harmony. It also requires vast silences, extremely sensitive adjustments in speech practices, and presentations of self that reflect the community's power to shape or control a speaker's identity. These very complexities of social control over the presentation of self in day-to-day interactions warn us to reach outward from individual speakers as ideal models of communication. To understand the stories of the urban, poor women with whom I lived, I had to first learn to locate the most basic of referential information in Javanese utterances. In practice, this meant I could never lose track of the context of others and community. The key to interpreting *cårå Jåwå* lies in always balancing the inward with the outward. To know oneself requires one to know others.

Descriptions of the complexity of *cårå Jåwå* are well served in scholarly works by such noted linguists and anthropologists as Joseph Errington (1985, 1988), John Wolff and Soepomo Poedjosoedarmo (1982), and Nancy Smith-Hefner (1988, 1989). Errington's studies of the language of *priyayi* society illustrate its legendary fame through images of grace and refinement in language, behavior, and philosophy. Wolff and Poedjosoedarmo also quite accurately present these linguistic ideologies of harmony when they state that "all Javanese values are justified as a means of achieving or maintaining *tåtå tentrem* (*tåtå* means 'in proper order, everything in its proper place', and *tentrem* is 'peace and calm'). In these terms, humility, indirection, refined bearing, and other modes of conduct are all valued behavior" (1982:14). Smith-Hefner presents an even closer look at Javanese values of humility and refinement by describing how women readily sacrifice their own public positions of power and control in order to socialize children into a hierarchically manufactured community. By using more polite speech than they receive, women are not displaying subservience but rather the politeness and refinedness of their maturity.

Javanese speakers highly value consistency and stability of social demeanor, including the acceptance of fate without resentment and, most certainly, without unveiled ambition. Despite extreme hardship, abandonment, hunger, and illness, many of the poor, working women I knew in Yogyakarta, Central Java, maintained their public presentation of self in a thoroughly refined manner.[7] By translating such beliefs into everyday interactions, Javanese (the Budi family is a perfect example) do indeed earn respect and position from their neighbors and acquaintances. What should be emerging here is the strong connection between language and identity as the undeniable ties that bind localized versions of reality to social interaction.

We now examine what is meant by *good* Javanese to see what it can tell us about *good* or *ideal* Javanese identities.

The Javanese Language: Speech Levels

The thesis underlying Wolff and Poedjosoedarmo's (1982) monograph on spoken Javanese in Yogyakarta is that by examining everyday code choices, the researcher may lay bare the cultural foundations of a community and its social structure. Their focus is on speech-level variations as the means through which "the society organizes itself and perpetuates its cultural traditions" (1982:1). Cultural traditions as well as scholarly traditions all focus on the Javanese speech levels as a symbolic and social index of local organization. Before we can begin to challenge some of these definitions, or at least attempt to redefine them within different contexts, we must first recognize their power. It is here that the force of language as practice, or rather language as it is used in everyday interactions, reveals itself as both an extremely potent philosophical entity and a means of social control.

The Javanese language has uniquely adapted to the Javanese concept of person by exhibiting the most elaborate use of speech levels of any known language in the world (Keeler, 1987:19; Smith-Hefner, 1988:537). The term *speech level* conventionally refers to the five types of vocabulary classes, which in their various forms function as indicators of the degree of respect or formality a speaker shows to an addressee.[8] The highest of these is *kråmå*[9] (high Javanese), the refined, distant, polite speech of all nonintimate encounters. It includes approximately one thousand lexical items plus inflections.

Kråmå madyå (middle *kråmå*), comprising roughly 35 distinct lexical tokens, structurally incorporates aspects of both *kråmå* and *ngoko*. The highly fluid structure of *madyå* proves the speech levels to be a continuum with few clear-cut distinctions in actual use. With its broad range of flexibility, *madyå* is described as moderately polite and moderately formal for use with persons of familiarity but not intimacy, such as a neighbor.

Ngoko (low Javanese), distinctively harsh, abrupt, and direct, is broadly indicated in vocabulary, intonation, loudness, stress, and attitude. It expresses no respect on its own and may only be used with very close friends. *Ngoko* is the base language on which alternative levels have been superimposed. When no socially meaningful alternatives exist for a particular lexical item, *ngoko* as a level becomes neutralized.

In addition to these three main levels, there are the two honorific vocabularies called *kråmå andhap* (humble *kråmå*) and *kråmå inggil* (high *kråmå*). *Kråmå andhap* is made up of about 30 words, which function to humble speakers and their actions and are directed toward an addressee or third party. *Kråmå inggil* (high *kråmå*), about 30 words functions to honor those spoken to or about, as well as their possessions and actions. These highly ceremonial vocabulary items may be used in any utterance of any of the three levels to express specific respect relationships and, hence, create more respectful discourse. Although they are traditionally termed a speech level, they are actually used independently of the levels, where they function to augment any of the three. Thus, for example, a *ngoko* sentence can be made to show respect by the inclusion of honorifics.

This complex of levels tends to be simplified by Javanese speakers, who describe their own language as James Siegel (1986) does. Siegel claims that Javanese is made up of two distinct languages: *båså* or non-*båså*. *Båså* means language, but it generally refers to "polite" language, meaning the whole range of *kråmå* forms including *madyå, kråmå, kråmå andhap,* and *inggil*. The counterpart is non-*båså*, meaning *ngoko*. Siegel, however, introduces a polarity between these two languages by suggesting that they are separated by "translation." He presents the *priyayi* view, in which he states that *kråmå* "protects" its speakers from their "natural inclinations to speak spontaneously" (1986:3–12). High Javanese distances speakers from their own feelings, intentions, or animal urges and is often referred to metaphorically as a "mask" (see also Anderson 1990:131).

The translation model proposed by Siegel (1986) suggests that Javanese is not just one language but two. *Ngoko* (low Javanese) requires no social refinement or abilities; it is the first language children learn. Pure *ngoko* is language devoid of all sensitivity to status, formality, or the prestige of others. It is used for thinking, talking to oneself, and expressing anger. At the other extreme, pure *kråmå* (what Siegel calls high Javanese) is not reflective of a speaker's intentions as a set of communicative acts but rather of a speaker's sensitivity to the relative status of his or her interlocutor. Word selection is not based on communicative needs but on recognition of the social order of things, that is, "the nature of the world":

> The ability to speak High Javanese is assumed to be the ability to read signs inscribed in the world itself. To speak High Javanese, then, is constantly to uncover the unchanging nature of the social world. . . . Furthermore, to speak High Javanese is to demonstrate that one has the ability to read such signs and therefore has a place in society. (1986:19)

High Javanese, then, is a link to the ascetic purity of the spiritual world, maturity, and awareness, whereas low Javanese is the world of childish, animalistic urges and human feelings.

With such a foundation of scholarly work on the Javanese language as my starting point, I entered the field assuming that a study of identity in Javanese would be open for analysis only in *ngoko* and that *kråmå* speech could not be removed from the spiritual concepts and expectations that surround it. Joseph Errington (1984) tackled these metaphysical concepts through his extensive fieldwork among *priyayi*, dealing specifically with why the Javanese conceive of refineness as a sign of power. These forms of etiquette have long been used to mark stratified social roles in an elite court society that few working-class Yogyakartans feel has become obsolete. Thus, recognition of the social structure is marked by a display of one's knowledge of and respect for the traditional forms of social conduct, which still reflect Javanese conceptions of self-awareness and sensitivity. The ultimate goal of refineness is the achievement of awareness, awareness of self, of God, and of others through perceivable signs and hidden meanings that appear in social interaction as a prescribed relative detachment (1984). Speakers index not just immediate contexts but also a vast range of beliefs and values that serve as protection from the dangers of one's own egotism, which can hinder one's awareness of others.

Javanese linguists such as Maryono Dwiraharjo (1991) make similar claims. The Javanese speech levels specifically index the relationship that exists between interactants through *lexical* choices that must reflect social relations as close, middle, or distant. This demonstrated etiquette is both lingual and nonlingual. Behavior and conversation take their form directly from the speech event, in which both must combine to display harmony. According to Dwiraharjo's description of his native language, these speech levels, directed by social-contextual factors in the speech event, signal identity as a reflection of social relations. In his terms, speech can only reflect the immediate context; it cannot create it. He states that language clarifies *såpå wonge*, who the person is, through comparison of word choice, thus defining Javanese identity as comparative social status.

Who or where one is within the hierarchy should never be invisible. The practice of weighing oneself in relation to another in order to select the appropriate speech level in conversation (*unggah ungguhing båså*), if properly applied, creates a discursive etiquette that at its best must reflect a very old and very highly civilized culture. Discourse, as well as its accompanying behaviors and appearances, should be beautiful, distant, and gracious and should reflect all the hierarchical social factors existing within the speech situation. Speech must reflect social contexts by clarifying who the participants are relationally in the social order.

The Javanese language, as scholars describe it, is a form of high art whose inherent decorum and graciousness create a world of intense beauty (*mamayu hayuning jagad*). With its focus on elegance and decorum rather than content, competition, politics, and social inequality, refined language is a way of avoiding all conflict, where speakers compete to praise and bestow a calm graciousness on their interlocutors rather than express their own personality and feelings, that is, "preserve the mask" previously mentioned. To the Javanese, conversation forms the basis of life's principles through its display and maintenance of the noble character of its speakers.

In accordance with Javanese ideologies, identity is constructed through discursive choices, which include aspects of hierarchical position only. Soeroso (1990) explains the steps required for the application of *unggah ungguhing båså* as

1. *Mawas dhiri*, or introspection; that is, what is my social position relative to my interlocutor?
2. Choose the appropriate language for this social position; that is, do I need *kråmå, madyå, or ngoko*?
3. Choose the appropriate words: are honorifics needed?
4. Apply the correspondingly appropriate behavior as respectful or relaxed.

While only steps 2 and 3 are lingual, steps 1 and 4 are essential factors in speaking Javanese and are automatically included in descriptions of the language. They are, thus, an essential part of social interaction in that they display *identity*.

Dwiraharjo (1991) further describes the role of Javanese speech as synonymous with linguistic etiquette.

1. The teaching of linguistic etiquette is a cultural inheritance that still lives and holds strong.
2. Linguistic etiquette is a part of Javanese life that cannot be removed or separated.
3. Linguistic etiquette is taught so that Javanese respect and honor others.
4. Linguistic etiquette guarantees communicative ease for Javanese speakers.

The lofty values geared toward *mamayu hayuning jagad*, or creating a world of beauty, are thus composed of a conscious linking of the rapidly changing, uncertain present with the memories of a far more civilized, romanticized past. In the Javanese context, such a past is associated with superbly elegant courtly behavior; clear and orderly hierarchical positioning of all members of society; and above all else, the preservation of the state of calm orderliness (*tåtå tentrem*) in all social interactions. Since my own research involves not only the urban poor but also women, my concerns lie in the use of such terms as *elegance* and *refinement*, terms often denied to women and the poor. Where, then, is the role of power and inequality in Javanese theoretical discussions?

Yet, although all of the studies of Javanese etiquette use *priyayi* as the model for standard, refined behavior, few studies have observed these behaviors in use. Nor have any attempted to locate how such conceptions of language, power, and identity have been adapted into working-class discourses and philosophies. Returning to identifiable patterns of language use, Joseph Errington's *priyayi* informants considered *madyå* speech "bad *båså,*" a "least-favored speech level choice" to be used with "outgroup" members (1985:124–127). Reminiscent of William Labov's (1972) studies of social dialectology in New York, linguistic variables were correlated systematically with the speaker's social class (i.e., Geertz, 1960; and even brings to mind Bernstein, [1970] 1972). Expanded to lexical and stylistic choice in Java, Errington's informants considered *madyå* a low-valued speech level, signifying the crudeness of the working class while justifying and preserving the social values of hierarchy. Just as Seigel's (1986) translation model requires clear-cut extremes where they do not necessarily exist, studies of the Javanese language tend to glorify the powerful while they omit the language styles of the majority of the population.

Previous studies of Javanese focus on the surface values of speech *levels* while neglecting the possibilities of *style* variants. Whereas sociopolitical and economic changes are altering the Javanese conceptions of social class and linguistic etiquette, scholarly inquiry has not yet turned its gaze toward the psychological salience of etiquette as a code of ethics that guides social identity in all classes. How and where the lines should be drawn to separate the refined (*alus*) from the crude (*kasar*) beyond the surface guides of speech levels require a more micro-oriented analysis than has previously been undertaken. Interview approaches to discourse with elite native speakers raise questions about the separateness of one language or level from the other. At the individual token (i.e., lexical) level, this is not a problem. But people do not speak with individual words; they coordinate them into utterances. This is where the tradition of measuring Javanese linguistic values needs to turn toward *style* as a means of recognizing social action as practice.

The preceding description of the Javanese speech levels reveals the strength of local attitudes that embrace the principles and functions of linguistic etiquette in the face of, and even in spite of, modernization. Its proper use among members of any class elicits real feelings of pride toward the language itself and the people and culture it represents. Contextually appropriate speech is thus a major creator of social harmony within the confines of the given speech event. Dwiraharjo (1991) further states that *worsuh*, or level mixing (what he describes as *kråmå,* moving "downward" toward *ngoko*), usually reflects "emotional" behavior. Emotion here is a type of interference that disturbs the harmony of the Javanese linguistic etiquette that is invariably exercised in *kråmå*.

Modern research on Javanese language and culture adhere to these same traditional categories of hierarchical interpretation as a controlling measure in creating harmony (*laras*). Yet, conversely, hierarchy is also *created* by harmonious behavior, where those low on the social scale humbly adhere to these rigid scales of human worth. Geertz referred to this avoidance of potential disharmony as the combined values of *iklas*, *sabar*, and *trimå*. *Iklas* is a detachment from the material world; *sabar* is defined as the absence of eagerness, impatience, and passion; and *trimå* means "to acquiesce," referring to the inevitability of fate, class, hierarchy, gender, and event. These three prized characteristics lead to "emotional equanimity, a certain flatness of affect" (1960:240–241).

Keeler also describes refined Javanese in terms of these same characteristics as "the behavioral style of potency," which, he states, displays "the restraint and calm indicative of disinterestedness and self-control" (1990:132). He goes on to explain that the individual who wishes to project high status must express total control discursively and behaviorally through "avoidance of spontaneous or extreme feelings, as evidenced in speech and gesture" (1990:133). These include suppressing all signs of excitement, anger, jealousy, hilarity, or even hunger, thirst, pain, or exhaustion, what Joseph Errington (1988:223) refers to as "the avoidance or muting of indexically communicative behavior." In terms of modern Indonesian experience, *iklas* means that everything one experiences in life, whether happy or sad, is the will of God and thus not part of an individual's action or effort.[10]

From these descriptions of Javanese language and behavior, we should begin to piece together a picture of a people who value above all else an external display of self as calm and graceful. How this self-control translates into the day-to-day lives of real people and their successes and failures is what we will investigate. Yet, these social rules of harmonious order and calm acquiescence already hint at the existence of numerous issues that grind away in silence beneath serene surfaces. As Sari had once explained, when her father learned to accept his fate[11] as being beyond his personal control, he quite naturally returned to his Javanese roots and the family was reunited in peace. When I asked if his reconciliation with the family and his fate involved a verbal phase, Sari said no. It was never discussed as far as she knew. When her father began sleeping at home, going to the mosque regularly, and turning over his salary to her mother, they all knew that their prayers had been answered.

Toward a Community-Centered Approach

The studies discussed in the previous section have all presented highly valuable and extremely astute descriptions of the subtleties of Javanese linguistic behavior in the shaping of social identity. From the essential foundations they have offered, others can now expand their knowledge of Javaneseness by focusing on natural social interactions. Instead of the almost exclusive focus on the ideals of formal *priyayi* speech patterns, it is appropriate now to examine the everyday experiences of the *wong cilik*, or lower working classes.[12] Informal conversations among any group of Javanese in practice rarely display *level* indexes linked to respect or hierarchy alone. This in no way means that Javanese values are absent. It does mean that alternative relational indexes need to be found in line with a more context-oriented approach. Only by examining Javanese discourse in practice are we able to locate the illocutionary force of utterances as emergent meanings.

Clare Wolfowitz (1991:51–57) begins to bridge the gap between structural analyses of the speech levels and the social constructionist requirements of Javanese interactions argued above. Through her research on the Javanese of Suriname, Wolfowitz proposes a much more person-centered ideology of speech choice in contrast to the bipolar model of a formal/informal, more polite/less polite continuum. Wolfowitz's three-way model of Javanese stylistic oppositions proposes a respect style, which is capable of combining with either the formal or the informal ordinary style (*ngoko*). In this model, there are four diacritic features of basic polite styles: (1) vocative kinship term,(2) crooning intonation, (3) formal lexicon, and (4) syntactic completeness with monotone intonation. Of major significance here is Wolfowitz's observation that there is a vast difference between formality and respect and that respect can be indexed in ways other than through formal lexicon, or *kråmå*.

This model introduces a needed alternative for speakers who frequently show their respect without honorifics or deferential speech levels and who still strive for "a dignified social distance" (Wolfowitz, 1991:50). The model remedies the problems of oppositional values, which are central to current descriptions of standard *priyayi* values. But in this modern world where boundaries and values are quickly changing, more flexible approaches are still needed to account for actual speech. Even real *priyayi* do not always use formulaic honorific phrases in everyday interactions. Similarly, the Central Javanese working classes also require linguists to develop alternative models to understand speech styles in practice. For any social class of speakers, linguistic models must account for how actual speakers display in natural contexts their own interpretations of social requirements as they themselves see fit. Javanese models of refinement impose too narrow a set of expectations, which may possibly have prevented recognition of alternative styles and meanings. In nonformal speech, level oppositions as indexes of formality are simply not a major part of the daily repertoire. As Wolfowitz has already shown, this by no means should lead us to evaluate such discourses as unrefined or nonstandard.

The conflicts raised here, then, center on the imposition or domination of idealized *priyayi* values and elitist expectations on all speakers of

Javanese. In consideration of the socioeconomic disparities between groups (not to mention social variables of location, e.g., rural or urban or gender), this study attempts to describe the discourses of the poor, urban working class in their own terms and through their own words. My focus on speakers in this class should in no way lead readers to assume that they are unable to speak in glorified, formal Javanese terms. Quite the contrary, all the speakers in this study are fully capable of speaking extremely formal levels, including *båså kedhaton*, the language specifically used in the palace for speaking with royalty. I have heard them all give exquisitely formal speeches in high Javanese with no preparation. I simply choose not to focus on these formal interactions in favor of the most mundane, naturally occurring conversations between friends because it is here that the most significant social work takes place, that is, that of the social construction of identity and meaning for everyday contexts.

Yet, despite my own contrary expectations, hierarchical values are very clearly retained among the speakers in my corpus, even in the stories they tell as a natural part of conversation. I had expected stories would appear in *ngoko* only and emerge as a free and relaxed form of signaling a speaker's identity and intimacy. Instead, I found stories between close friends and even siblings to be full of hierarchical markers of position, status, deference, and self-consciousness, where *style* variations were the salient markers of social relations. Additionally, my Western-based expectation of what a story would be among friends only rarely appeared in my observations or my transcripts. Because of the natural consistency and limitations of context, I found that natural interactions between friends could, however, illustrate how speech styles adapt to varying interpretations of power relations. Yet, despite intimacy between participants in a given conversation, the descriptions of Javanese stratification and elegance cannot be removed from the equation either. Among the working classes, as well as *priyayi*, recognition of greater powers than oneself in the determination of social class, action, and identity is the foundation for the calm orderliness and humility that for so long has been defined as essential to Javanese interaction. But within the real-life dramas that affect the women with whom I lived, striving for harmony also emerged. Not only was it the "normalizing" cultural filter through which these social actors played out their roles on a day-to-day basis, but I also could see it as a potent tool for the centralized control and political domination that upheld the women's oppression.

With everyday speech practices as the guide, I introduce a wider dimension to the traditional description of Javanese discourse as an index of social refinement. I present this glossy picture of refined elegance in conjunction with the modern political structure of control. In other studies on Javanese, power is located in the cultural and spiritual centers of royalty (the *kraton*). In this study, power is never *elsewhere* but rather right *here*, as we speak. Power is located within everyday experience as a *given* among community members. It is reflected and reinforced as the hierarchical order that structures all social interaction between speakers, within families, and within the wider community of familiars.

It is the goal of linguistic and anthropological analyses to be sensitive to the interactive displays of a people in conjunction with the ways in which their society organizes itself, factors that we take to be tightly interwoven. Focusing on natural, everyday social interactions, I show that the ordinary Javanese do not adhere to traditions of *priyayi* refinement in their speech *levels*. Rather, we see that their speech *styles* do, in fact, maintain high Javanese values and that *ngoko* is not the level of that which research refers to as the true, weak, wholly human self. These working class women's stories will illustrate what daily speech practices do achieve and how they do perpetuate the traditions of calm orderliness (*tåtå tentrem*). These may not be the exalted values of *cårå Jåwå* the Javanese would prefer to be associated with their ideals of tradition or modernity, but it is a way of living and acting that grows out of their own socially constructed limitations to access and privileged interpretation.

Approaches to the Study

To investigate modern Javanese conceptions of language and its role in the construction of meaning and identity, I work from conversational narratives as a means of identifying the voices and interactive goals of a select group of Javanese women. I focus on narrative because it is a central component of the meaning systems that form human experience, as well as the communicative style that organizes experiences into meaningful episodes (Polkinghorne, 1988:1). Through a discourse analysis of the public and private narratives that occur daily in contemporary Javanese society, I aim to locate the ways in which the encoding of meaning in narrative reflects how aspects of social identity and perspective are constructed through a language traditionally and politically viewed as highly constricting of both.

I employ an ethnographic approach to both the collection and interpretation of conversational data, from which I take the discourse it contains as being constitutive and reflective of social culture. This method requires the recording of spontaneous, social interactions within natural social networks, which then form the basis of analytical discussion of social activities or practices (Duranti, 1994; Geertz, 1973; Mead, 1934). Native speakers here are seen as social actors whose conversations contribute to the creation and maintenance of local meaning. It is the role, then, of the ethnographic linguist to become involved and aware enough to take part in, record, and analyze these conversations, as well as to take part in everyday rituals from the sacred to the most mundane. From these firsthand experiences, the ethnographic linguist learns how to "read" meanings, be they uttered or *not* uttered, as anchored within a much broader context than the immediate speech event.

Soon enough, however, it will become evident that Javanese women's narratives present a very different structure and function from other descriptions of narrative. For me even to locate stories within the transcripts, I had to locate and define patterns of indexical elements as they are used in the narratives. Indexicality, as used here, implies a highly contextualized, socially interpretive description of how classes of words function in specific people's lives and spoken contexts. Indexical elements, such as pronouns (*I, you*, etc.) and demonstratives (*this, that, here, there*, etc.), all provide frameworks for tying the word to dimensions of time; space; and, as I stress, responsibility. This is the property of indexes that holds a particular speaker morally responsible for his or her utterances and for any consequences that may arise in relation to them. Indexical location within a moral order of rights and obligations is composed of both fairly static and dynamic "locations" from which to speak and be heard. Status, role, age, and gender provide speakers with a complex background of experiences, discourses, images, and so on, which interact with others in a dynamic process. These social positions further depend on how far responsibility for an action in a particular culture is diffused throughout the community to which a speaker is indexed at a moment of speaking (Benveniste, 1971; Hill and Irvine, 1993; Mühlhäusler and Harré, 1990). As we see, women are expected to carry most of the responsibility in Javanese communities.

With the inclusion of responsibility as an indexical location, agency is not just a linguistic category but also a social one. In consideration of the ways in which the women in my corpus maintain stratification in their own social networks, we need to identify and measure natural social positions by how they are indexed. This includes those features that signal the styles of discourse the speakers draw on, each of which carries its own weight of assumptions, explanatory frameworks, and particular relevancies (Davies, 1990:32; Davies and Harré, 1990). Social identity is then a range of socially indexed personae that must include the flexibility of contextual changes in status, role, position, and any other relevant community identities that speakers take up, either willingly or not, in the course of negotiating meaning.

Rather than recognizing Javanese speech-level elements as indexes of hierarchical place or respect or even as the standard norm, this approach takes meaning to be interactively produced and verified *only* by the ways in which it is recognized in actual contexts. Indexical elements, of which speech levels are only one, should serve to mediate between the micro levels of face-to-face interaction and the macro levels of community and culture. The tie to contextual particularity, however, will inevitably be at odds with the psychological salience of the Javanese speech levels as I have described them. My research goals were not to measure levels of refinement or linguistic choices but rather to investigate the negotiation of meaning among a nonelite group, a novel enough approach that should be spared the stigma of class and gender prejudices. I also expected to see how and where the depersonalized ethic of *tåtå tentrem* was replaced by a more agentic, self-indexing, informal discourse—presumably speech in *ngoko*. What I found instead was that even among a disempowered, working-class community of women, relations of power in determining relative positions are the fundamental means through which individuals and their stories are constructed.

With community and the mundane conversations of everyday practice as the setting for data acquisition, my primary attention was directed toward the relationships and the connections people forge in their daily social settings. The women whose stories appear here are friends, family members, and neighbors and thus meet regularly and naturally for a variety of social reasons. The conversations reproduced here are the actual social interactions that tie roughly a dozen Javanese women to their social networks, communities, and culture.

The speakers whose voices make up the body of this study are not faceless, ideal native speakers, extracted from a population at random. The voices presented belong to women whose words and experiences are rooted in the everyday practices of their community, and thus their voices are shown to be constructed in accordance with its norms. It is that community, whether in the form of an interacting partner, an underlying code of ethics, or topics of conversation, that plays a central role in the shaping of identity—an identity that is not a constant in the lives of the speakers but a repertoire that varies according to how a speaker is positioned relative to others.

As we see in chapter 3, the narratives that I found through the recordings did not resemble standard notions of narrative structure because almost without exception the stories were embedded in conversations. Furthermore, they were rarely indexes of a particular speaker and her experiences. This embedding, I argue, is an index of the ways in which the speakers themselves are embedded into their immediate contexts and broader communities. Narratives among these women are not action-oriented personal accounts, as Western definitions prescribe, but rather a means through which the speakers in a community jointly construct meaning and reinforce their own social boundaries, even the oppressive ones. These conversational narratives, despite being spoken mainly in *ngoko*, contain structuring elements that I identify as doubly indexical; that is, they locate narratives within the stream of conversation, as well as speakers within a matrix of hierarchical rights and obligations. These relative positions clarify the multistructured layers of self-other-community-culture that shape social interaction.

The stories I focus on, then, can be taken as models for a unified linguistic analysis (Linde, 1993), a style of linguistic analysis that is not bound to lexical choices, sentences, or even discursive text. Instead, it specifically attempts to link a speaker's words to the negotiation of social identity and belief systems and to the social construction and reflection of a community's perception of culture itself. This approach illustrates how narrative structure is related to the storytelling event and, hence, both reflects and constructs the context in which it is told. This theoretical basis is well supported by previous work on narrative, as I show in chapter 3, and thus poses no surprises. But if what appears later turns out to be a different style of storytelling than that which forms the basis of these standard expectations, could those differences be taken as evidence for a different social context, including all the identity and identity-constructing elements associated with social interaction?

Analysis of women's conversational narratives in this third-world setting illustrates a localized practice of negotiating meaning that should help us to reevaluate conceptions of self, the collective consciousness, and agency (cf. Mohanty, 1991). Such a perspective contributes to the linguistic study of narrative by expanding existing work on both the structure and the function of conversational narratives. It additionally presents a means of suggesting how the story structure is related to the social function of the storytelling event itself. Furthermore, whereas studies of narrative are common in non-Western languages, these studies are primarily limited to performance and written genres. By presenting data from adult peer groups in informal contexts in their natural social networks, we are able to gain an intimate glimpse into the social functions narratives serve in the negotiation of identity and meaning within the narrow constraints of a stratified society.

From the very start, however, it is essential to warn that none of these defining factors are as simple to describe in practice as they are in theory, and identifying the context of an interaction is no easy task. The fact that these stories occurred in the Javanese language, famous for exhibiting the most elaborate use of speech levels of any known language in the world (Keeler, 1987:19; Smith-Hefner, 1988:537), only further complicates the task. The very existence of these fantastic elaborations has almost exclusively blocked any other focus in studies of Javanese by both Javanese and non-Javanese scholars alike. Furthermore, since this analysis was located in the words and lives of present-day people, it needed to account for the overwhelming conflict in ideologies of tradition, religion, magic, modernization, materialism, and development ringing throughout Indonesia, including the Central Javanese city of Yogyakarta, known as the "center" of Javanese "traditions."

In Yogyakarta (also called Yogya), one may still find two palaces (*kraton*) and two sultans and all the pomp and ceremony associated with them. Both of these palaces (in particular the *Kraton Hageng*, or Large Palace) are still widely revered as sources of mystic power and highly potent bases of traditional religious and magical practices. But these beautifully maintained oases of serenity are surrounded by a frenetic, third-world version of modernization, heavily influenced by rapid industrialization, rampant materialism, new and expanding channels of communication, and the widening rift between the privileged classes and the ordinary people (*wong cilik*).

How, then, do the traditions of hierarchy and harmony interact with modernity and how are they to be interpreted and applied to studies of modern Java and its language? The indigenous, mystical interpretations with their calm, romanticized elegance strive to fit, or be fitted, into the everyday practices of modernization. Both tradition and modernity, however, are shaped by dominant powers, and both are reflected in the ideologies that shape our field interactions and subsequent studies. The reasons and the means through which all of the above are enacted are best seen in the ways in which "traditional" and "modern" affect the voices of the people. Thus, location, intimacy with the community, and proficiency with the language all had to be carefully considered.

Field Stories

What is broadly known as standard Javanese is firmly anchored in the traditional centers of cultural, religious, political, and spiritual power—the palaces, which have for more than two hundred years been widely regarded as the ultimate models of Javanese culture and refinement.[13] Javanese at its best and most beautiful is said to exist only within these royal seats of power in the Sultanates of Yogyakarta and Surakarta (also called Solo), about 65 kilometers apart. I chose to base my research in the city of Yogyakarta, the larger and more "modern" of the court cities,[14] to find out where these ideals of Javanese language and culture stand at this moment in relation to the personal experiences of those who live them on a day-to-day basis.

My own personal experiences of living in Yogya were already extensive since I had taught at the teacher-training college there in 1983 to 1984 and had visited frequently while teaching in other parts of Asia and the Middle East until 1989. On 16 September 1991, I arrived again in Yogyakarta for the sixth time, no longer as a tourist who spoke fluent Indonesian and had an extensive network of friends and acquaintances, but as a researcher. I had to evolve into this new role by constructing and projecting my own identity as a single, white woman and understanding its inherent limitations. Regardless of an accumulation of more than three years of residence prior to this study and a large number of old friends, I was a trespasser. Speaking Javanese rather than Indonesian radically changed my interactive styles and, hence, my relationships with others.[15] But speaking a language does not directly imply understanding the force of its speech actions or knowing how to manage the discourses of respect and intimacy just because I knew *kråmå* and *ngoko* variants. I had to learn how to interact in a manner that would lead to trust and real friendship, something I wanted as a person and not just as a researcher. I needed a *family* to become my haven from the chaos and a ready source of support and understanding as I underwent the socialization process.

The Budiyanto (henceforth Budi) family, the poor cousins of the wealthier family I was boarding with, were far more accepting of a *londho* (the general Javanese term for a white-skinned foreigner) than were my own hosts. Perhaps this was only because they were too poor to make a fuss over me and had no preconceived notions of what a foreigner should be like. During the initial adjustments and confusion of the first few months of my residence, the Budi family listened to and corrected my Javanese[16] and kept me strong and healthy both spiritually and physically.

My relationship with the Budi family began shortly after I arrived to stay for two months with the Wando family, wealthy *priyayi* with close ties to the royal family. The situation was not comfortable, however, as the family regarded me as a status symbol of their own modernization and as someone with whom they could practice their English. Unhappy in their house, I began to spend more and more time wandering around the neighborhood. The ugly hovel behind the six-foot-high fence and barbed wire that surrounded the Wando estate was always bright and noisy at any time of day or night. Thus, despite warnings from the Wandos— W*onge apik, ning dudu priyayi* (they're good people but they're not *priyayi*)[17]—I soon found myself craving the lively comfort the Budi family exuded in abundance. Not only were there four adult daughters with whom I could associate, but also Pak Budi was very interested in my research project, offering tales, descriptions, folk theories, advice, and loads of assistance. The Budis became and still remain my family.

The Budis are a large family with *ibu* and *bapak* (mother and father), four grown and unmarried daughters, and two sons. The Budi children ranged from the eldest, Atik, 29, and Sari, 27, down to the youngest, Atong, 16. Pak Budi took it upon himself to teach me what Javaneseness meant through stories and legends and detailed and often humorous explanations that united the whole family in boisterous good cheer for many hours into the night. The two eldest daughters, Atik and Sari, became my best friends and frequent companions with whom secrets and vast amounts of time were shared. Ibu Budi's cooking was the best I ever had in Java,[18] and her home remedies, whether *jamu* (medicinal herbs) or *kerok* (scraping the skin with the side of a coin to allow the "wind" to escape), always seemed to cure what the doctors never could.

The Budis knew exactly what my purpose in Java was and became actively involved in helping me solidify research ideas by openly discussing, asking, and willingly answering. By becoming an accepted part of the lives of the Budi family, I was able to achieve exactly what I had hoped for, to feel at home in Java. The trust we developed soon led to Pak Budi's suggestion that I use his family as my recorded informants. Providing they were given power to erase any tape that could prove dangerous or embarrassing, I had full permission to record frequently and openly. With their support I accumulated over one hundred hours of chatting, joking, discussing, and gossiping among family members, neighbors, friends, and guests. From their suggestions and insights, I grew to understand that shared knowledge is essential in interpreting the texts. The unspoken information that shapes Javanese interactions takes the form of ellipses and what early on in our relationship looked like unclear references. For these women, however, what is *known* need not be *said*. Thus, I focus on the same speakers in a variety of interactions in order to identify these "silences."

The stories that make up much of this corpus were recorded in the shabby sitting room of the Budi's house, which was built originally as a warehouse for chairs. As mentioned earlier, Pak Budi's brothers gave it to him nearly 25 years ago out of charity and embarrassment. Since the warehouse was off the street, they had hoped their poverty-stricken brother would not be such a visible disgrace. The warehouse had a rough cement floor, a wooden and ceramic roof that leaked badly in the rain, no plumbing, no doors or windows, and rarely enough electricity to read by.

My other family was Ibu Asmoro, the eldest and highest ranking of the active palace singers, who has since the age of 12 been a central figure in Javanese court music. I met her quite by chance during my first weeks in Yogya while performing the required registration rituals at all the levels of New Order bureaucracy.[19] While engaging the district head in conversation, we eventually spoke of my interest in the Javanese *gamelan* (the traditional Javanese orchestra) and my hope of finding a singing teacher. He immediately told me about Ibu Asmoro and suggested I contact her directly as she lived just around the corner. She was not what I had expected.

When I met Ibu Asmoro, she was 77 years old and living alone in a tiny bamboo shack, with no electricity or plumbing, on a palace salary, which after 64 years and having achieved the highest rank possible, was $10 per month. The *kampung* she lived in was a labyrinthine mass of extremely narrow passages between low wood, bamboo, and cement houses on *kraton* soil, densely populated by those who serve the court. She has been alone there since her last husband died over thirty years ago and is haunted in her decline by those she believes wish to do her harm.[20] In her prime, Ibu Asmoro was one of the great singers, a favorite of three sultans and their families and now the trusted elder (*pengirit*) of the female singers (*pesindhen*). When she had wealth, it was prodigious— and it was squandered on her love of extravagances, including drink and gambling. But Ibu never let go of a strong set of moral principles that guided her throughout her long life and now form the underlying topic of all her stories.

I became a daughter to this lively old woman, a willing and grateful audience for her stories. Through Ibu Asmoro I also became an *abdi-dalem*, a servant of the royal court. Each Wednesday for close to two years I would *sowan mlebet* (visit inside [the palace walls], but "serve" is a more appropriate interpretation), dressed in full court attire as a singer in the *gamelan*. Over time, my status among the *kraton* officials, the servants, and the musicians and singers of *Kridå Mardåwå* (the division of palace bureaucracy devoted to traditional forms of entertainment) changed from that of foreign oddity to friend. By visiting the *abdi-dalem* at home and helping in the fields, selling snacks with them in the street (*mbakul*) or in their food stalls (*warung*), cooking, and minding babies (as any other intimate might), boundaries of nationality, education, age, and other stereotypes gradually diminished.[21]

I recorded 20 cassettes in Ibu Asmoro's home and another 30 cassettes in the hidden recesses of the sultan's palace where the aged servants gather to work, gossip, meditate, play music, nap, or receive a meager meal and a cup of weak tea ("Not sweet enough!" was the usual complaint). Recording talk inside the palace grounds required very special efforts of several different types. I needed to master the protocol of palace etiquette, as well as the styles of Javanese appropriate for meetings with true royalty. As the protégé of Ibu Asmoro, I was allowed certain privileges. And as a foreigner who was seen to be diligently attempting to speak a language that most Javanese care about immensely, I was eventually offered opportunities to record whenever I liked. In the early months of my *sowan* (entering the palace as a servant), the *abdi-dalem* would also frequently comment on my learning the linguistic elements and behaviors that conflict spiritually with their stereotypes of Western belief, meaning, and self-presentation. Before coming to terms with these comments, I had actually attempted to record inside the palace grounds twice while permission from the sultan was pending. Both times (and on only those occasions in two years of constant use) my new recorder jammed. After receiving permission, no further problems ever occurred, and I learned to take subtle hints far more seriously.[22]

The stories selected for this analysis[23] represent the lives and thoughts of these diverse communities of speakers as they construct meaning through the most important means or channels they have access to, that is, each other. For me, then, the narratives evoke loving memories of friendships and histories of interactions that developed into trusting and shared experiences. The sounds and the words evoke scents and sights: the smell (and my fear) of the chickens at the Budi house mixed with the aromas of cooking and the flower gardens planted to hide its ugliness. The palace stories evoke recollections of incense and jasmine, magic and spirits, ancient legends, and the profound faith of the aged servants. The vast social inequities are invoked through the musty charcoal scents of these poor women who awake long before sunrise to cook and clean and then walk miles to serve in the palace because they cannot afford the bus fare. These stories are mixed with the smells of the seasons and the mildewed stone, the feel of the hot sand that burned my bare feet but not those of the old women who had no shoes. These stories invoke my pride as I excelled in pulling my short hair into the hairpiece (*sanggul tekuk*) I actually found in auburn and the great care I took to hand-crease the narrow folds (*wiron*) that graced the front of my *jarik* (a tightly wound, ankle-length cloth; a *bathik, or* "sarong"). Sitting cross-legged on the outdoor palace stage (*pendåpå*) without moving for hours (and sometimes all night long) in a tight *jarik* was agonizing for the first year I served in the palace. In time, however, through the guidance and influence of these old women I learned to deal with and even control the pain in still silence. This lesson, it turned out, was of major symbolic importance for my beginning to understand the Javanese language and its related concept of self for lower-class women.

The Mask Metaphor

Underlying theories of Javanese language and interaction are the socially opposing speech levels (*ngoko* and *kråmå*), but remember, I use the terms *speech levels* to refer to purely lexical categories, and *speech styles* to allow for the possibility of nonlexical pragmatic variations. These speech levels reflect more than the hierarchically ordered society that forms the very foundation of Indonesian national stability. They also reflect a "dualism in the Javanese mind" (Anderson, 1990:131). *Ngoko* is seen as the language of the "true," weak, wholly human self, whereas *kråmå* is "a little like a mask" through which an idealized, timeless, greater-than-human world is portrayed.[24] Several questions immediately arise. To what extent does the social hierarchy influence or even shape social identity? Is *ngoko* speech really open, honest, and direct, and if so, is *kråmå* speech indirect and "masklike" or just the opposite of *ngoko*? Does this variation in "languages" constrain the types of identities speakers may present? Are we really looking at a "mask" behind which Javanese speakers may hide their sense of self in the exalted name of refined harmony, or is a Javanese self more accepting of the ebbs and flows required by the innumerable possibilities and challenges of social interaction? How do these different identities manifest themselves in everyday interaction? Yet, if we return to questions of power relations, we must also ask if the "mask" then refers to speakers' accommodations to structures of power and social status. Is this really a "mask" we are looking at, or is it a label for aspects of a highly flexible social identity we do not yet understand?

As the rest of this book illustrates, a speaker's ability to control the complexities of the Javanese speech levels is not the only means through which the hierarchy and its symbolic harmony are preserved. The "mask," then, needs to change its shape several times before we can understand what it conceals—if indeed, it is hiding anything.

The Javanese world and the language that maintains it have been subjected to the extensive and inevitable pressures of time. Yet the values that sustain them are still visible in everyday social interactions. Where yesterday's *priyayi* were considered the model of refinement and correct language use, they are today's civil servants devoid of the elegance and grace of royal or Dutch patronage.[25] Where the ninth sultan was known to have used *kråmå inggil* (the most honorific of Javanese styles) to all, this picture of powerful benevolence has given way to his son's reign, which is conducted primarily in Indonesian. If the powerful center of Javanese refinement no longer sets the standard, what occurs at the peripheries, where the *wong cilik* dwell?

Studies of Javanese social interactions must account for these inevitable changes. The values ascribed to *cårå Jåwå*, that is, hierarchy and its speech style attributes, have been altered, although perhaps not equally, by the shifting tides of history, politics, economics, religious doctrine, and eventually scholarly inquiry. The well-established descriptions of speech levels do not yet acknowledge much of the corpus I analyze here, which reflects *wong cilik* voices rather than those of the *priyayi*. Despite the fact that the interactions recorded for this study were mostly informal meetings between friends, family, and old acquaintances, the Javanese themselves discredit the speech as slang or bad Javanese precisely because of its lack of lexically refined language. Such a self-critical attitude sustains beliefs in mask metaphors while it doubly preserves the glorified acquiescence that gives the mask such an elegant countenance.

Organization of the Book

This study analyzes the Javanese concept of self by examining how the self is constructed through conversational narratives. To achieve such a task, I have divided the book into three parts, each of which deals with different aspects of social and scholarly investigation. Part I covers some of the community-based information that forms the backdrop not just for the study but also for native speakers' "cultural" knowledge. I have tried in this part to set the scene by introducing the speakers and a bit of their worlds. Chapter 2 identifies the role gender inevitably played as the underlying guide for how I interacted with Java and how the study took its shape. I have also tried to expose the realities of gender ideologies and their role in the positioning of women as subordinate to men in this community.

Part II presents the theoretical framing of the Javanese conversational narrative. I work from actual narratives in order to define what a Javanese oral narrative is, devise a methodology for locating one in a stream of conversation, and show how its structure is reflective of practice-based functions that themselves reflect immediate social values and needs. Chapter 3 compares Javanese conversational narratives to the framework devised by William Labov (1972; Labov and Waletsky 1967) to locate where and why expectations of structure require functional reassessment in a Javanese paradigm. Chapter 4 proposes four indexical features that assist in the location and definition of Javanese oral narratives. This chapter also presents evidence for multiple indexicality by suggesting how the structure of the narrative mirrors the structure of the community. Thus, we must recognize the cues that expose the hierarchy as an essential step in interpreting the story and the social meaning it creates.

Part III presents an ethnographic trilogy of stories told by the same speaker in three different contexts. Through analysis of these sequences of narratives in actual speech situations, I demonstrate how the concepts proposed in Parts I and II are grounded in social practice. This section is centered around Sari's experiences of abuse and cruelty as a seamstress in a garment factory, and it illustrates how the traditional and modern definitions of Javaneseness collide within the real-life confines of a moral dilemma. By comparing the various ways in which speakers encode participation in relation to the three different speech situations, these three chapters offer evidence for the role of the various "others" in the shaping of Javanese social identity.

two

Ideologies of Gender and the Social Positioning of Women

This chapter introduces the broader community into the analysis of Javanese women's discourse and identity. Initially, we examine the role of ideology as a tool of power, after which we look at the official Indonesian ideologies on women and their roles in the state. To see how the ideological positioning of women functions in practice, I discuss how language conventions assist our understanding of gender. Then, we explore in brief how women are portrayed in the mass media. By focusing specifically on themes of violence toward women, we see how cinema, literature, and the press frame gender roles in terms of responsibility. In conjunction to the media representations of women, I present excerpts from letters written by rape victims to a women's crisis center to show how the ideological positioning of women has framed their perceptions of self. Finally, this chapter shows how both gender and class ideologies combine to marginalize the urban, working-class women whose narratives make up the corpus on which this study of language and identity is based.

Gender Ideologies: Macro Levels of Controlling Female Identity

As discussed in the previous chapter, the theories of George Herbert Mead underlie the position that culture is a "system of symbols and meanings," and just like the universe of discourse, it is a manifestation of communicative interaction (see also Stark, 1996). Mead (1934) has also argued that social meaning is not a given but rather a prize to be struggled for. Thus, those with the power to control discourse are those who shape reality. In this chapter we investigate a notion of power as a contest for the control and definition of symbols and their meanings. Control of these social meanings filters down into the linguistic interactions through which communities make sense of their realities, and it is there that we can see discourse as a symbolic means of inducing cooperation (Stark, 1996).

This analysis of Javanese women's stories strives to achieve several broad goals that all link notions of language to relations of power. Initially, it allows for an intimate view of the processes of identity construction in a non-Western language. In this capacity it attempts to identify the "reflective self" that emerges within everyday, organized activity.[1] It also attempts to show how these everyday activities are organized into universes of discourse, or systems of common, shared meanings. But particular universes of discourse may be made dominant either through coercion or consent. For our needs here, we focus on consent as it is produced from within the community of marginalized women themselves. Thus, consent *and* disempowerment need to be recognized as active processes of (re)articulating the ideological positioning of particular meanings as a "universal" symbol. In this respect, ideologies are understood as the dynamic process of creating the patterns of meaning or commonsense assumptions that guide people's behavior in a particular society (Freeman and McElhinny, 1995:220; see also Fairclough, 1989).

Conversely, ideologies and the values they shape are major instruments in the construction of power and political hierarchy in everyday and ritual talk (Gal, 1989:345). All languages and all societies stratify in one way or another, and recent studies have shown that we are not always conscious of how we rank each other (e.g., Fairclough, 1989; van Dijk, 1994). Studies have also shown how control over language is exercised and how this affects the way language is evaluated, giving evidence for the distribution of social power at all levels of society (Nichols, 1984). Power is the ability to define social reality, to impose visions of the world. Such visions are inscribed in language and, most important, enacted in interaction (Gal, 1992:160; 1989). Talk is not simply a comment or reflection of activities but a practice that actually constitutes the social order through ideological structures that are linked to human agency. Agency and structure have been addressed in sociolinguistic studies, but only recently have they been located within a larger system of inequality. So it is this recognition of the role of the state and the power structures as they constrain agentic choice that needs to be considered in understanding the relationship among identity, culture, and power. The works of Burke (1969), Mead (1934), and Gramsci (1971) present varying notions of cultural hegemony central to this line of thought from which to question the role of authorized voices in definitions of social and cultural life—without loosing sight of the ways in which they serve the interests of their own dominant classes. But before we can discuss what the effects of New Order ideologies are on Javanese women in practice, we need first to deal with the ideologies.

Ideologically speaking, the New Order government seems to distinguish its people along several lines of demarcation. Not only are women and men considered to hold separate and very different roles in society, but also differences between upper and lower classes also impede heavily on state discourses. Thus, it is not only women who have had almost no role in state politics but also the huge numbers of poor and working-class men. Working-class women in particular have been crushed by development "advances," which have turned their traditional agricultural and manufacturing jobs over to men with machines, and young women have been recruited to work in factories under grossly exploitative conditions (Blackburn, 1994; Logsdon, 1985; Norma Sullivan, 1994; Wolf, 1996). Furthermore, because of the government's views on women and their abilities to function productively in development programs, the special needs of women have also been targeted through training programs. These programs, of which PKK (*Pembinaan Kesejahteraan Keluarga*, or Family Welfare Guidance[2]) is the "most successful," are hierarchically structured[3] and based on a philosophy that sees women as unenlightened adjuncts to national programs. Poor women are "not yet ready" for development. In short, the New Order government is ideologically opposed to combating the subordination of women or its own discrimination against poor women (Blackburn, 1994).

The following official guidelines for state policy (GBHN, 1992) describe the role of women in the development of a modern Indonesia:[4]

a. as a wife and associate of her husband;
b. as the educator and cultivator of the younger generation;
c. as the controller/regulator of the household;
d. as a worker who adds to the family's income;
e. as a member of community organizations, specifically women's organizations and social groups.

Women's roles here are firmly affixed to that of men. Women's roles, despite full-time work in the civil service, fields, markets, cottage industries, and so on, are wife, mother, homemaker, and a worker who adds to the family income. In addition to all these requirements on their time and energies, women also must be members of the character-shaping women's social groups. Nowhere does it say that a woman has any prime role to play at all in the nation's development, except, that is, when focus is on the home and maintaining harmony within it. This powerful state ideology, which is meant to raise women's opportunities in Indonesian development, reflects the dominant image of state paternalism and Javanese feudalism. This notion of women, called *ibuism* (Djajadiningrat-Nieuwinhuis, 1987; Suryakusuma, 1996), merges the social, economic, political, and cultural aspects of the developing state's requirements with the traditional elements of upper-class *priyayi* values. It maintains a cheap underclass, while it not only commands women to serve their men, children, community, and state but also expects them to do so freely and without expectations of prestige or power (Suryakusuma, 1996:101–102).

Women are not recognized for their own potential as an intellectual, employee, or wage earner because their identity is based on their social affiliations to men. With the strict demarcation that exists between the public and private realms of social life, men dominate the public and political spheres, and given that the private and domestic spheres of everyday life are subordinate, this also gives men effective domination over the private and domestic world of women. Yet, as others have found (Sen, 1994; Norma Sullivan, 1994; Sunindyo, 1996; Suryakusuma, 1996), and as is often reported in the local news, social pressures and public discourses severely sanction women for breaking away from their expected roles, whereas men must be supported and understood when they fail in their capacities.[5] The strength of these relentless gender ideologies is best seen through the fact that women face the heaviest pressures to fulfill their domestic roles from other women themselves. With the exceedingly powerful ideologies of gender and class from which to shape their knowledge of the narrow worlds they are permitted to inhabit, communally accepted pressures prescribe that "women work energetically at maintaining their own subordination to males" (Sears, 1996; Norma Sullivan, 1994:184).

While ideological constructions are not always negative (i.e., see van Dijk, 1994), their function to change attitudes or actions for self-serving partisan needs through the use of words is blatantly apparent where state ideologies and women in Indonesia are concerned. Hierarchical positioning as a broad-reaching and highly constraining aspect of Javanese society already organizes all social interactions, whether in the family or in the public sphere. It also sets up the perfect foundation of power through which to impose attitudes and actions while restricting reflection and choice, what others have referred to as "psychological violence" (Ellul, 1973). Such ideologies, stressed as a "separate-but-equal" thesis, are an effective means of camouflaging the much deeper structural inequalities that exist between men and women, husbands and wives (Norma Sullivan, 1990).

The dichotomous roles that separate men from women and public from private realms of existence in Java are firmly drawn by gender ideologies that originate in the high offices of power as public, power-laden discourses that eventually seep down into everyday interactions. In this level of micro analysis, we see how such ideologies shape public and private perceptions of women.

Language and Gender

The study of language and gender has always been grounded in the elimination of social disadvantage (Freeman and McElhinny, 1995). But from the primarily Western perspectives such studies take, ideal notions of alleviating oppression or supporting women's emancipation in the third world have barely begun to scratch the surface. Beyond the question of what exactly it is that constitutes our definitions of third-world women, Mohanti (1991a:5–6, and 1991b) points out that such understandings are shaped by scholars (and documentaries, news releases, etc.), who mainly describe these women in terms of underdevelopment, oppressive traditions, high illiteracy, rural and urban poverty, religious fanaticism, and overpopulation. The majority of studies objectify women through fertility statistics as a social indicator of their status or through demographical shifts from rural to urban locations as a result of postindustrial booms in multinational factory employment. From such studies we learn very little indeed about third-world women, their perspectives or their sense of self. The emphasis for feminist scholarship in anthropology and linguistics is often on unequal relations of power and the social, cultural, economic, and political domination of women.

Before scholars can begin to challenge false assumptions about gender differences that often result in discrimination, we need to confront the knowledge that ties us all to particular worldviews with respect to sex, gender, class, race, and so on. As feminist scholars in the West have shown, the values, attitudes, and behaviors considered feminine in a given community must be documented and described first. Only then can we challenge their exclusive association with women and point out their value for all people (e.g., Freeman and McElhinny, 1995). In the same way then, we need to expose the constitutive nature of language in shaping our understanding of the social world, the relationships we have, and our own social identities. As Fairclough (1989) points out, we must recognize which and how discursive acts contribute to inequality as a necessary first step to changing them. Thus, to truly empathize with third-world women rather than merely celebrate their isolated acts of resistance, we need to first recognize how they construct their own communities. From this point we can better understand how women are disempowered by their own speech practices and, hence, their own communities.

Research on gender in the English language points to specific linguistic elements that create or reflect biases. Gender-marked male terms, which are used to index people in general, have been shown to attract more male attention in hiring and in the classroom and to reinforce male hegemony. Using male terms for generic reference is incorrectly considered unmarked. Frequently found examples such as "Each student is expected to do *his* best" or generic nouns such as *mankind, chairman*, and *brotherhood*, among many others, have been proven to affect readers in a multitude of ways. Graddol and Swann (1989) point out that if masculine terms are considered to be neutral, the terms marked as feminine often carry a sense of less significance. Words like *hostess, stewardess, actress, waitress*, and *seamstress* do not carry the same authority or sense of formality or permanence of career as *waiter, host, actor*, and so on.

The English language is changing as a result of feminist awareness of the ways in which naming conventions reflect inequality. The classic case of *Mr.* as the only form of address for a man, while women were forced to clarify their identity by *Miss* or *Mrs.*, suggested that a woman's defining characteristic was, in fact, her marital status. The term *Ms.*, now appearing on official applications as a third option, allows women to decide whether or not to disclose this information.

Neither Javanese nor Indonesian languages have pronouns that are marked for gender. The argument does not by any means stop there but rather points to a need to analyze other types of discourse practices to locate how gender positions are inscribed into local communities.[6] Recently, however, terms have been brought into common usage that do distinguish gender positions. Most of these are Sanskritic or Arabic loan words with gender-marked suffixes. Common endings are *-a* for both male and general usage and *-i* for female. *Pramugara* is defined in Echols and Shadily (1989:435) as an attendant on long-distance transport, and *pramugari* is a female attendant. *Mahasiswa* is a university student, and *mahasiswi* is exclusively a female university student. *Putra* is a prince, a male child, or a general term for child, and *putri* is princess, female child, or female. All of these examples are in common use in both Indonesian and Javanese discourse. The suffixes *-iman* for male and *-iwati* for female have not been long in common use,[7] but as all my informants insist, the gender markers are preferred. Is this a frightening new trend in a society that uses biased Western concepts of gender roles as its model (Norma Sullivan, 1994)? This trend does identify a place for research to expand its focus from lexical variants into the far more complicated, deep-rooted sexist ideologies that emerge from stylistic variants in discourse.

To widen our sphere for recognizing gender ideologies in everyday contexts, we examine Deborah Cameron's (1990) study on gender and language, particularly her analysis of a rape that occurred in England. Her point was to show that we need to look beyond labeling conventions and other lexically based analyses to understand how gender identities and gender relations are discursively constituted. Positions of power among actors in narratives are also apparent when analyses make clear *who* is represented as doing what, to whom, under what circumstances, and with what consequences. Through news media excerpts from a "quality" paper, the *Daily Telegraph*, and a "popular tabloid," the *Sun*, Cameron shows how the presentation of information shades an event.

> The *Daily Telegraph* reported:
> A man who suffered head injuries when attacked by two men who broke into his home in Beckenham, Kent, early yesterday, was pinned down on the bed by intruders who took it in turns to rape his wife.

> The *Sun* reported the same event:
> A terrified 19-stone husband was forced to lie next to his wife as two men raped her yesterday.

As Cameron points out, though the news is about a rape, the experience of the man is in the foreground. He is the grammatical subject, and it is he who "suffered" and "was forced." In the *Telegraph's* report, the woman's experience is mentioned third in a series of events, implying that the rape was less of a crime than the beating of the man. In both accounts, the woman is mentioned only as "his wife," which again subordinates her status as a victim and as a human being. Both these newspapers represent the rape as a crime primarily against the man through the sexist stance taken in the narratives, not through sexist naming practices (see Cameron, 1990:16–18).

With Cameron's approach and findings in mind, we look at Indonesia to see how gender identities and relations are discursively constituted in various types of narratives. In the next section we take a closer look at these sexist ideologies as they appear in everyday discourses of violence to understand how Indonesian women are socially and morally subordinated in everyday life. By analyzing the presentation of information in various public and private narratives, we see how the public discourses that define the inequality of women's positions in society are taken up by women themselves and thus become the means by which they define themselves.

Reproducing Ideologies of Gender

A woman's preference in selecting her own role is not really much of an option since Indonesian women are defined relationally to and are ultimately dependent on men for their status (Sears 1996; Norma Sullivan, 1994). Both ideologically and legally, state discourses position women as dependent wives who exist for their husbands, their families, and the state (Sunindyo 1996:121; Suryakusuma 1996:98). Beyond these powerful ideologies, which require a woman to be hard-working and responsible, we find that in everyday practice she is also expected to be pure, silent, passive, and monogamous. Not only does this section explore the concept of the "ideal woman," it also investigates the possibilities for variations available to women as it explores what happens when that ideal is lost. I wish to discover how a society that values restraint and harmony above any displays of human emotion deals with the tragedy of rape.[8]

Rape has been on the rise in Indonesia, although it is impossible to gauge whether the increase is in actual incidents or in its discussion in the public media. Since articles about actual rapes have been flooding the press, they are a striking means through which to analyze and compare the social construction of gender roles. More precisely, I hope to see how these roles are justified in scenarios that explicitly focus on gender inequality. For these purposes, I frame the ideological perspective first by briefly discussing representations of gender and rape in the Indonesian cinema. From there we look at newspaper articles from the local Yogyakarta press, followed by accounts of rape in popular Indonesian novels. Finally, we hear the words of the victims to see how they position themselves within the framework of the "ideal woman."

Rather than make broad generalizations about Indonesian languages or cultures, this section attempts merely to direct our gaze toward media representations of rape as one of the many threads in the interwoven fabric of the cultural construction of gender roles. My goal then is to isolate a few of these threads within a limited social context to demonstrate how they become accepted as defining discourses. Beginning with media narratives of authority and privilege, followed by the pleas for help from isolated victims, I combine these diverse voices to illuminate the hegemony of discourses of power in shaping gender inequality.

Krishna Sen's (1994) study of the Indonesian cinema is a perfect starting point for understanding gender ideals because, as she points out, these movies reflect the mainstream ideology of the sexual division of labor and gender hierarchy. Deviations from themes of women as dependent wives are rare and subjected to what Sen refers to as self-censorship. This mainstream ideological view of women is politically "ordered" through a constant narrative structure that moves from order to disorder to restoration of order. Disorder can often be depicted through criticism toward the working woman, who faced with a crisis suddenly realizes she has been neglecting or upsetting the "natural" male-dominated order of her own family because of her job. The narratives concern what the scenarios describe as sexually problematic women, meaning that they were raped, abandoned, or too independent and so must be repositioned back into order for the movie to have its happy ending. But the choices for resolving sexual conflicts are few: either through monogamous marriage or death. This restoration of the protagonist to her ideal femininity is always represented by silent passivity, in which ideal female types are beautiful and pure (*suci*), silent and loving.

The film *Halimun* (*Mist*) opens with a marriage. We soon learn that the wife, Awit, is pregnant by another man, who had drugged and then raped her. Inu, the husband, has only married Awit to save her "family from disgrace" until the baby is born, after which he will divorce her so he can be with Mila, the woman he loves. The film's scenario informs us that even though Awit is much more beautiful than Mila, Awit has been stained (*dinodai*) by this unwanted sexual encounter, thus making her utterly undesirable. Mila, however, is still clean (*suci*). Despite the emotional horror of rape, unwanted pregnancy, a mock marriage to a man who finds her "dirty," and her groom's constant abusive tirades, Awit remains silent, unquestioning, and alone. Despite a male's action—the rape—as the cause of the pregnancy, Awit alone is forced to bear all the responsibility in silence. Meanwhile, not only are all the narrative's actions focused on the men and their perspectives, but also Inu frequently throws tantrums and expresses his own anger and hurt feelings.

The central conflict for many of these narratives centers on the perversion of female nature and its inevitable correction. Awit is an unattached woman who carries the proof of her sexual "stain" in the form of her illegitimate child. Yet she exists within a moral order that cannot accept visions of female independence or sexuality outside of monogamous marriage. Only Inu can salvage her feminine essence through reconciliation and discovering his love for her as his wife. The happy ending results when the child's life is threatened and Inu realizes that Awit does truly care for the child. This occurs only after he again attacks her verbally for her behavior with men and for neglecting her child. His accusations are naturally false, but Awit does not defend herself since her role is to be *seen* and not *heard*. Instead, she faints. Inu miraculously discovers his love for her, the baby recovers, and we assume they live happily ever after.

Despite being billed as a film "for women, by women and about women," the narrative and the two women, Awit and Mila, are constructed and judged entirely from Inu's male perspective. Adult female protagonists are judged in relation to models of femininity, in which they are either in a natural state of perfection (*suci*) or degraded (*dinodai*), usually by the actions of predatory male sexuality. As Sen (1994:144) argues, when a woman's sexuality is aroused outside the sphere of monogamy, it signifies a crisis for the symbolic world. In other films also, for example, *Noda tak Berampun* (*Unforgivable Stain*) and *Bernafas Dalam Lumpur* (*Panting in the Mud*), women who have been sexualized or stained must bear the guilt for this condition, becoming "unforgivably stained." These ruined women respond with restraint, nonexpression, and the internalization of emotions.

In the film *Rembulan dan Matahari* (*The Moon and the Sun*), Ayu (literally "beautiful") is suddenly confronted by the father of her child, a man who had left her pregnant seven years before. Ayu had acted appropriately in accepting her fate after her lover left and she married a much older man to give her illegitimate child a name. The film constructs Ayu's quiet resignation as "the ideal of the speechless woman," gentle, utterly domesticated, and accepted by men and their society. Upon her chance meeting with her lover, the scenario reads: "Her body trembled, her hand covered her mouth restraining a scream. . . . She grew confused. Restraining her tears, she went inside the house" (Sen, 1994:143).

Whether or not cinema narratives present authentic performances of social actions and emotions can best be determined in comparison to other versions of the rape narrative. To this end, I turn my focus now to articles that appeared in the Yogyakarta newspaper *Kedaulatan Rakyat* (*KR*). One of these articles (18 October 1995, p. 8) is a response to the sharp rise in the local incidence of rape. As a half-page special contribution to the Wednesday crime section and under the title "Plucking Wisdom from Reports of Rape," the article is positioned as an authoritative voice, demanding that citizens study the "modus operandi" of these crimes in order to take appropriate preventive measures. The following three excerpts were presented as successive examples (emphasis in the original):

(1) Seorang siswi SLTA bertandang ke rumah rekan prianya. Maksudnya untuk belajar. Kenyataannya, siswi

(1) A female high school student visited the home of a male friend. The reason was to study. In fact, that

itu disuguhi minuman yang sudah dicampur pil koplo. Setelah teler wanita itu lalu *dikerjain.*

student was offered a drugged drink. After becoming intoxicated, that woman was then *done.*

(2) Seorang pelajar putri diperkosa seusai melihat kesenian di desanya. Ini terjadi karena ia pulang sendiri. Kemudian dalam perjalanan "disambar" lelaki dan selanjutnya dinodai.

(2) A female student was raped after watching a performance in her village. This happened because she went home alone. Then, during the journey, [she was] "seized" by a man and then disgraced.

(3) Seorang pemerkosa seperti Agt sesungguhnya tak punya niat hendak memperkosa. Namun ketika dini hari itu melihat Ny. Sn tertidur di emperan di kawasan shopping centre—dan kebetulan roknya tersingkap—lalu gairah kelelakiannya mencuat. Apalagi saat itu Agt dalam keadaan teler. Korban dan suaminya, keduanya pedagang sayur, ditodong. Si suami diperintah diam di tempat. Sedang si istri diseret ke tempat gelap, tentu, dengan todongan pisau. Ini benar-benar keji. Karena korban "digarap" tak jauh dari suami.

(3) A rapist like Agt actually never had the intention to rape. But one day he saw Mrs. Sn asleep in a shop front in the shopping center—and by chance her skirt had risen—so his manly desires sprang forth. What's more, at that moment Agt was in a state of drunkenness. The victim and her husband, both vegetable sellers, were threatened at knife point. The husband was ordered to stay put in silence. While the wife was dragged to a dark spot, certainly under threat of the knife. This is truly disgusting. Because the victim "was worked on" not far from the husband.

Just as in Cameron (1990), this sanctioned voice of authority is narrated entirely from the male point of view. Each narrative ends with the achievement of forced sex, whereas none of the consequences of the act for the woman are revealed. But here, in each of these cases, the rape becomes the responsibility of the woman because she put herself in a position to be raped. In (1), she went to visit a male friend in his home, in (2) it was *because* she went home alone, and in (3) some part of her body became visible as she slept on a shop front. Is responsibility for rape then borne by a woman alone precisely because she did not protect herself from predatory male sexuality? More importantly again, does this show us how gender responsibility in general is divided in society?

As the article goes on to describe, men cannot help themselves:

(4) Terjadinya kasus perkosaan terkadang "tidak selalu" dibarengi niat. Seorang lelaki boleh jadi berpikiran *ngeres* dan gairah kelakiannya mencuat setelah melihat wanita, yang mungkin berpakaian

(4) Cases of rape are "not always" the result of intention. A man may suddenly feel *discomfort* and his manly desires spring out after seeing a woman, who perhaps is scantily clad or with a fabulous body or some

minim atau bodinya aduhai atau faktor lain. Itu bisa terjadi di jalan, di gedung, di pasar, dll. Bisa terjadi pula, pikiran *ngeres* itu muncul di suatu tempat akibat tergiur wanita tertentu, lalu yang jadi korban wanita lainnya.

other factor. This can happen in the street, in buildings, in the market, and elsewhere. It can even happen that those *uncomfortable* thoughts arise somewhere triggered by arousal for a specific woman, but then the victim becomes some other woman.

While male agency in acts of rape is acknowledged in the article, it is seen as conditioned by natural desires that are beyond his control. The use of the Javanese term *ngeres* to describe sexual arousal hints at the understanding or sympathy the writer has for the necessary release of such manly needs. *Ngeres* is the kind of discomfort one feels when there is sand or grit in one's eyes or bed sheets. Thus, it can happen anywhere and at any time, and it is simply not the type of sensation one can just let pass. Is this basic, local knowledge, and does this mean that local culture recognizes a "boys will be boys" perspective and that women must remain vigilant?[9]

The male perspective in framing the narratives are never more apparent than when the writer comments on the "true brutality" of Mrs. Sn's rape: *si istri dikerja-in, boleh dikatakan, di depan suaminya* (the wife was worked, it can be said, in front of her husband). The rapist was sentenced to the maximum of 14 years because the crime involved theft also. But the truly contemptible nature of Agt's actions lie in committing rape in front of the husband, not in raping a woman who is no longer a virgin.

The words used here for forced sex are *digarap*, meaning "to work on something," and *dikerja-in*, a colloquial word for having sex, derived from the word for work. These terms emphasize the man's perspective and highlight actively "doing a job" while the women are silenced, objectified, and utterly controlled. This overwhelmingly male perspective presents no conflict to the ideal model of femininity, however, except for the woman's apparent display of sexuality outside of the permissible bounds of marriage. So the woman now bears the unforgivable stain. If male sexual urges cannot be ignored, who, then, are the victims here?

In my large collection of rape narratives from newspapers all over Java, only *Pos Kota* in Jakarta and *Wawasan* in Semarang have used the phrase "the victim and his wife" (*korban dan istrinya*). In all other examples, the women are labeled "victim." But as we have already discussed, the construction of gender roles and relations is not only found in lexical choices. Stylistic variants such as collocation, order of presentation, power roles and their consequences, and types of evaluation, among others, assist us in identifying women's roles—at least as depicted by journalists. In terms of Mrs. Sn's rape narrative, it was the experience of her husband that the writer considered "truly disgusting," whereas Mrs. Sn is barely mentioned.

This article from which the excerpts are taken was published as an authoritative warning, to inform women how they can avoid falling victim to rape. In each example, the woman was at fault for creating the opportunity for rape. There are no alternative interpretations since readers see only the rapist's vision of sexuality. As Sen (1994:116) notes with reference to the Indonesian cinema, sympathy toward male sexual aggression is constructed when a woman's sexual appeal is emphasized prior to the rape. Thus, we must take for granted that men have these uncontrollable yet natural urges and women are responsible for their own safety.

I was apparently not the only *KR* reader to be shocked by the alarming number of sexually violent narratives it prints. The following is an excerpt from a letter to the editor (15 December 1995, p. 4). The male writer offers a useful commentary on a woman's responsibility for a man's indecent acts against her. As the writer states, saleswomen who wear short skirts cause their own sexual harassment:

Dengan adanya seragam yang memperlihatkan bentuk tubuh wanita tentu akan semakin merangsang mereka membuat yang tidak senonoh. Betul, enggak?	With the wearing of uniforms that reveal the shape of a woman's body obviously this will stimulate them [men] to act in immoral ways. Right or not?

It should be pointed out that Javanese "national" dress is also very tight-fitting, to the point of being restrictive, and it very much exposes a woman's shape. The blouse (*kebaya*) is snug, transparent, and low-cut,[10] and the bottom (*jarik*) is a saronglike cloth that is wound very tightly from the waist down to a woman's ankles. Not only do they restrict walking (women must take small, "delicate" steps), but also, when women sit on the floor they are painful, as I have mentioned. Such costumes are not complete without the obligatory hairpiece. Male national dress is far more relaxed: a *bathik* shirt and regular trousers. Now many questions quickly come to mind here regarding the exploitation of women and their physical attributes. As the previous writer implies, such exploitation also seems to be used as a marketing device by shopkeepers. Attractiveness and youth are all that many sales positions require, so this is what many young women learn to offer. Even in the public sector, the Indonesian national rail system forces only female employees to sign guarantees that their employment will terminate either at marriage or upon turning 30.

Tineke Hellwig's (1987) analysis of depictions of rape in two popular Indonesian novels also assists our understanding of the "ideal woman" in modern Indonesian society. As she points out, popular novels in Indonesia are subject to trends and take the tastes and expectations of the public into account. Similar to Sen's (1994) characterization of cinema narratives, Helwig also notes thematic consistency in these novels, which deal with love and marriage, choosing a partner, sexual contacts, unwanted pregnancy, and substance abuse, usually among students from well-to-do families in urban settings. Happy endings follow the often illogical and violent developments required for the protagonists to finally "get" each other.

Hellwig's (1987) goal is similar to mine, that is, to break away from the dominant male perspective the novels invariably take to see how female characters are portrayed in relation to a rape and its social consequences. In both novels—*Karmila* (a woman's name) and *Kugapai Cintamu* (*I Yearn for Your Love*)—the main characters are ambitious female students whose careers are abruptly ended because of rape and the resulting pregnancy. Yet, what is much worse than the rape itself is that it might become known that each has lost her virginity and is expecting an illegitimate child. The only solution is to marry someone—anyone. In one novel the victim marries the rapist, and in the other she marries the village brute. Rape themes, as Hellwig illustrates, are first and foremost ways of enhancing women's roles as mothers. Everything, from her career to whatever versions of romantic love she may have imagined, becomes subordinated to her role as mother. A rape, then, is a perfect scenario for inculcating the silent acquiescence to feminine perfection on a broad scale.

These novels present the same patterns of gender characterization Sen (1994) has described for the cinema: silent passivity and motherhood as the ultimate goals for women. In the novels, "bad" mothers are those who "neglect" their mothering tasks for any reason. In *Karmila*, readers are made to sympathize with the rapist because he is "immediately converted to a better life, cured of his criminal behavior" and will not be forgiven by Karmila, who rejects him for destroying her life. Just as in the film *Halimun* (but from opposite gender positions), the child falls ill and Karmila realizes her errors, finding that she does love the child and his father after all. They live happily ever after.

As Sen (1994) notes, female protagonists are judged in relation to models of femininity, in which they are either in a natural state of perfection (*suci*) or degraded (*dinodai*), and narratives reach their conclusion either in happy marriages or in death. The novel *Kugapai Cintamu* covers all of these storylines. Widuri is "the prototype of the passive Javanese virgin," a pure village girl whose noble character and blameless behavior lead Irawati, the evil and promiscuous city woman, to arrange to have her raped. Widuri accepts her fate and marries to save her reputation (none of these "degraded" women consider abortion), sacrificing both the man she loves and her professional career to her (unwanted) motherhood (Hellwig, 1987:249). In this novel, Widuri is the heroine because of her acceptance of the roles forced on her by men. She finds happiness, whereas Irawati is forced into an arranged marriage with a man who hates her. But in line with Sen's dual choice for the happy ending, Irawati dies during the birth of her illegitimate child. Murtini, another young woman in the narrative, confesses that she is no longer a virgin and thus describes herself "a completely worthless person" (*saya tidak berharga sama sekali*; cited in Hellwig, 1987:249). Again, there is no discussion in any of these narratives of the psychological consequences of such behaviors on these women.

The novels, the films, and the news articles deal with rape as a theme of male nature, never as an expression of male domination or power over women. Instead, the focus is on a "boys will be boys" attitude that seems tied to an expected inability to control "manly" desires. Meanwhile, a woman's nature, in the words of President Suharto himself, is defined through her role "as the mother in the household and simultaneously as a motor of development. . . . We must not forget their essential nature [*kodrat*] as beings who must provide for the continuation of a life that is healthy, good, and pleasurable" (cited in Tiwon, 1996). Women are then dependent on men for their own completeness, the fulfillment of their natural destiny. There are no alternatives.

Since a woman's nature is to be loving and giving, she must accept natural male weaknesses, including responsibility for men's misdeeds and the loss of harmony in the family without demanding power and prestige in return. She is also responsible for protecting the image of her ideal femininity. As a victim of rape, she is further victimized by a society that sees female sexuality outside of monogamy as destructive. Her "hymen is her crown" (*KR*, 18 October 1995, p. 6), the narratives proclaim, and losing this evidence of her purity not only "destroys her future" but also eliminates her chances for romantic love. In these scenarios, whether in film, literature, the news, or real life, the woman is forced to marry any-one who will have someone so "disgraced" (p. 8), and this is quite often enough the rapist himself. Such a marriage will eliminate the family's shame at the time of the birth, after which the couple is free to divorce. Yet, such stories have happy endings when the passive, silent woman achieves fulfillment through motherhood. The emotional states of the woman are never an issue, and the psychological consequences of rape are not dis-cussed. Hence, it is precisely these silences, the widespread neglect of a woman's identity and aspirations, and the blatant inequality of ideologi-cal roles that remain the dominant factors in framing women.

These rape narratives allow us to isolate some of the discourses that structure and define the "ideal woman." The stories consistently show that men are the subjects, victims of their own nature, and women the silent objects. But rape involves at least two participants, so we now turn to the stories of several women. In light of the far more powerful discourses that shape public sentiment, these comparatively weak voices display their own views of rape as framed by the dominant discourses. All speak in similar terms and all are utterly defeated because they no longer fit in with socially acceptable definitions of femininity. The social constraints placed on women's self-expression, verbal or sexual, and the unforgivably negative value judgments on women's loss of virginity are imposed by structural factors in society and the dominant group's ability to control language, right down to the individual level.

In January 1996, I began regularly visiting the Women's Crisis Center in Yogyakarta. With good publicity through a Sunday advice column in *KR*, women's letters, describing their pain and suffering, flooded the center, although very few women have ever appeared in person to request shelter or assistance. The five letters received from rape victims that January outlined similar patterns. All had been raped by friends, neighbors, or relatives, and all described their reactions with the same vocabulary. Since none became pregnant from the ordeal, the women had never told anyone about the rape, including their own families, and it was only now, with their discovery of the center through the Sunday press, that they found a way to seek help. All the women used the term *dinodai* ("stained" or "disgraced") to describe themselves, and they described their loss of virginity in terms of being destroyed for life (*menghancur* or *merusak masa depan*):[11]

EN: 5 tahun yang lalu saya diperkosa oleh teman sendiri. Saat itu saya tidak berani bercerita dengan siapapun termasuk orangtua karena takut. Baru saat inilah saya baru sadar bahwa ternyata perbuatan teman saya itu sangat menyakitkan dan merusak masa depan saya.

Five years ago I was raped by my own friend. At that time I was afraid to tell anyone including my parents because of fear. Only now have I become aware that obviously my friend's actions were very painful and destroyed my future.

KADIYEM: Saya tak bisa mengungkapkan masalah ini kepada siapapun juga termasuk keluarga saya sendiri.

I cannot speak of this problem to anyone at all including my own family.

GADIS: Saya menyimpan sakit lair batin karena dinodai majikan lelaki (alias Bapak).

I am concealing an internal and external pain because I was disgraced by my male boss (alias Bapak).

While the pain and defilement of rape that each of these women is forced to bear alone and in silence is hideous enough, what I want to focus on are what each interprets as the social consequences of her rape. In particular, I want to show that the trauma is created not just by the rape but equally so by the socialization processes of the "ideal woman." In each case, the rape resulted in the woman's burgeoning awareness that she can never fulfill the ideal role. Since, in most of the cases documented here, the actual sex act occurred many years ago, long before she was fully aware of the consequences, the trauma and antisocial behavior began much later:

YOGYA UTARA: Saat itu umur saya 7 tahun, sehingga belum begitu sadar akan akibatnya.

At that time I was 7 years old, so [I] wasn't yet aware of the consequences.

RASTY: Saya waktu itu kan belum ngerti apa-apa. Akhir-akhir ini terlintas dalam benak saya.

At that time I didn't know anything. Lately this has been on my mind.

EN: 5 tahun yang lalu saya diperkosa oleh teman sendiri. . . . Baru saat inilah saya baru sadar bahwa ternyata perbuatan teman saya itu sangat menyakitkan dan merusak masa depan saya.

Five years ago I was raped by my own friend. . . . Only now have I become aware that obviously my friend's actions were very painful and destroyed my future.

The trauma is caused when the women become aware of what Sen (1994) described as "awakened sexuality," which refers to any physical state beyond that of *suci* (pure). When a woman's body becomes sexualized, through whatever means, she is forced to accept the guilt that leads to the "unforgivable stain." Thus, she tells no one. The fear is that the stain will become known:

SEMARANG: Sampai sekarang belum ada yang mengerti. Saya juga belum bilang sama orang tua saya. Karena takut jatu ke tangan polisi.

Up to this time know one knows. I also have not yet told my parents because I am afraid it will fall into the hands of the police.

As Hellwig (1987:248) explains, Widuri also tries to conceal the rape because she feels utterly helpless and is obsessed with fear that it will be revealed. It is for this reason that Widuri does not want to report it to the police.

This fear of public knowledge results in each of the women assuming guilt and horrible remorse for their awakened sexuality, to the extent that they avoid social contact:

KADIYEM: Selama ini saya slalu menghindari teman-teman yang bermaksud bersahabat lebih dekat dengan saya. Saya menghindari dengan berbagai alasan. Saya cuma tak ingin menyakiti dan mengecewakan apa lagi orang-orang yang saya cinta. Karena saya merasa sudah tak perawan lagi saya ngak mau menyakiti hati mereka, maka lewat rubrik ini saya berharap bisa menemukan jalan keluarnya.

Up till now I always avoid friends with good intentions to become more intimate with me. I avoid them with all sorts of reasons. I just do not wish to offend or disappoint anyone especially people I love. Because I am no longer a virgin I don't want to hurt them, so through this column I hope to find a way out.

RASTI: saya takut dan menyesal sekali atas semua kejadian yang menimpa dan telah saya lakukan. Saya merasa kotor, najis, menjijikkan, rendah. Saya tidak berani membina

I am afraid and very much regret all that happened to me and the things I have already done. I feel dirty, defiled, disgusting, and low. I am afraid to develop relationships with hubungan dengan orang lain (baik dalam taraf pertemanan atau pacaran)

other people (either as friends or boyfriends)

YOGYA UTARA: saya ingin sekali bisa bergabung, bergaul bersama teman-teman sebaya seperti halnya gadis lain, namun saya betul-betul merasa tidak bisa karena saya sudah kotor, tak suci lagi. Rasanya semua orang bisa melihat keadaan saya yang sesungguhnya.

I really wish I could gather, socialize with friends my own age like the other girls do, but I truly feel I cannot because I am dirty, no longer pure. It feels as if everyone can see my real state.

It is the fear that knowledge by others will most certainly lead to rejection and the personal responsibility the woman must assume for the rest of her life that have made her so afraid. Loss of virginity for young women like Kadiyem is offensive. Rasty and Yogya Utara avoid social contact because they know that as someone who is unmarried and no longer *suci* (pure), she is *kotor* (dirty), bears the stigma of her *noda* (stain), and will be forced to live with permanent rejection. Each of the young women states that she can no longer bear the suffering and has nowhere else to turn for help.

These five young women, between the ages of 17 and 20, have all mastered the dominant discourses, which brand them as "unforgivably stained." True to the power of such rigid ideological positions, none will forgive herself, and all suffer in the passive silence of the dominant fantasy of ideal femininity. In four of the cases, the rape occurred when the woman was very young, and each states that it was only later that she became aware of the consequences of the act. In these cases, it was not so much the rape that had traumatized her but her failure to live up to the male fantasy of "ideal woman" that society imposed on her. The fear and self-disgust emerge from her awareness that she is *stained*, no longer acceptable to others, and that she alone is responsible.

These narratives of rape have given us a very intimate look at how sex roles in Indonesian society engender far different values, expectations, and responsibilities. This inequality in roles is achieved and fortified through the reproduction of public discourse as a means of reflecting, expressing, and imposing social knowledge. "Ideal woman" ideologies have the power to engender the silent passivity that locks women into their roles.

Ideologies of Class and Gender

Dichotomous notions of gender roles are further plagued by the heavy burden of class. I have already hinted at the vast differences between socioeconomic classes by describing the homes and attitudes of the Wando and the Budi families. Inside and outside the *kampungs*, the upper class (*wong gede*) residents stand in stark contrast to the *wong cilik* in the design of their homes, lifestyles, means of interacting, access to resources, and recourse to spare time. Only minimal if any social interaction takes place across these boundaries because of the disdain and distrust of one for the other. Poverty is often referred to as a "cultural problem" by politicians who blame the poor for their "traditional" beliefs and their inability to grasp the essential concepts of modernization. Those in power at any level must attempt to educate and make decisions for others who are unable to do so for themselves.[12] The politicized traditions of social hierarchy as a glorification of elitist domination is the root cause of many modern social problems, bolstered by the fact that social hierarchy is an ingrained part of the public discourse. It has thus become the main ideological framework for the everyday construction of social and cultural identity.

This relationship between the authoritarian government of Indonesia and the *wong cilik* is the same as that described by Paulo Freire by the terms *oppressor* and *oppressed*. This relationship is one of *prescription* since it "represents the imposition of one individual's choice upon another, transforming the consciousness of the person prescribed to into one that conforms with the prescriber's consciousness. Thus, the behavior of the oppressed is a prescribed behavior, following as it does the guidelines of the oppressor" ([1970] 1993:28–29). With national stability as the main ingredient in the New Order's development policy, this *prescribed* glorification of social place within a hierarchy of rights and obligations is of primary significance in mobilizing a huge work force to the best possible extent. Through this patriarchal arrangement, the government is able to lure foreign investors by guaranteeing one of the lowest wage rates in Asia and a strike-free environment (Wolf, 1996).

Social rank in the family, the factory, the *kampung*, and the society is the way in which members discriminate among themselves along a scale of social worth. Discrimination is based on age, nobility, property, occupation, gender, behavior, and so on. Wolf has written a great deal on female factory workers in Central Java, in particular the fostering of patriarchal dependencies between managers and female workers. Thus, by way of age, gender, and occupation, the mostly male managers liken their relationship to their workers as that of father and daughter. However, as Wolf (1996:156) states, the patriarchal relationship is conditioned by the "ideal woman" ideology, which dictates that the woman's role is a subdued, shy, quiet, fearful, and submissive one. Daughters do not disobey or disagree with their fathers. This acquiescence is what managers attempt to cultivate in the factory (and government on a much broader scale) by disguising company (or national) self-interest as benevolent paternalism and familism.

One of the main reasons that the oppression of female workers—that is, keeping them docile, underfed, underpaid, and overworked—rarely emerges as a moral issue is because of considerable class differences and the stereotypes and expectations created by inequality and ideology. The working classes are seen by their factory managers as "too traditional," meaning that they are undisciplined, lazy, unreliable, ignorant, and in need of control. The larger factories then hire former military and police officials as their personnel managers to instill fear among the workers and bring "militarism, state power, and the hint of violence and oppression to the multiple hierarchies already existing in worker-management relationship" (Wolf, 1996:157). The values of class and gender permit industrialists to take advantage of workers' fear and "feminine" traits to maintain control over them and to ignore illegal and dangerous conditions in the factory (Kemp, n.d.; Wolf, 1996).

The extent to which public discourses determine who is in and who is out of the social order, as well as where one stands within it, is obvious in the widespread presentation and reproduction of socially labeling terms. The women workers described above sacrifice themselves dutifully and heroically, as members of the economic formal sectors are required to. Meanwhile, those in the informal sectors[13] fall into entirely different categories since they cannot be made to work for the development of the state in its patriarchal role. Terms that mark individuals or groups as either outside of or low within the system are not only used by those in power but also have been adapted by those so stigmatized. Yet what needs to be understood is the strength or power of such labels to position individuals in an uncompromising manner. For example, such terms as "subversive" (*subversif*), "hoodlum" (*preman*), "rebel" (*mbalelo*), "obstructer of development" (*penghambat pembangunan*), and "anti-*Pancasila*" (against the state ideology) all function to separate and stigmatize those who do not fit in with what the authority demands for national stability and its development policies. These words have the power to make those so labeled not only dangerous in public perceptions but also seen as criminals who can be subjected to legal action. Such "obstructers" are frequently factory workers and others who demand that the existing laws on minimal salary requirements, safety, and other basic rights be upheld.

On purely socioeconomic terms, the *wong gede* ("important" or "big people") are legitimized by having their voices reproduced in the mass media. Their commands are directed toward the *wong cilik*, here positioned as not just economically but also socially and politically incapable of enjoying the fruits of modernization and hence requiring the advice and patronage of their betters. Yet, every once in a while, a group of *wong cilik* takes offense at the patronizing nature of the term and publicly rejects such a marginalized position in the social hierarchy. In October 1995 a group of over one hundred pedicab drivers (*tukang becak*) protested to the district head of Sukohardjo, East Java. The drivers admitted that they earned a low income, but they rejected the term *wong cilik* because they said it stigmatized them as having no potential and ability to advance (*Bernas*, 3 October 1995, p. 1). What these men were protesting, then, was not the reality of their poverty but the term *wong cilik*, which branded them as being outside of the modern, developing society.

Not only have women's and men's "natural" roles been put to good use by state development planners and policymakers in Indonesia, but also they have been accepted without question.[14] The dichotomous roles of women in the private and domestic realms and men in the public and political domains are fully endorsed by local residents, social scientists, state ideologies, and government-supported and membership-required development programs. This separate-but-equal view of women is based on a culturally or traditionally supported concept of social stratification that maintains the normative order of *tåtå tenterem*. Widespread social consensus in defining reality is based on these prevailing ideologies of complementarity and thus has little to do with descriptions of everyday life or women's roles in it (Norma Sullivan, 1994). Redefining modern contexts through so-called traditional symbols is a major ideological tool used by the state to penetrate community life and harness its vast human resources for the achievement of political goals (Norma Sullivan, 1994:140; see also John Sullivan, 1992; Pemberton, 1989). Thus, state laws and ideologies promote advances for women while they in fact confine women in the private and domestic spheres even more narrowly than before this era of modernization. Previous views of women's roles included much more space for extrafamilial activities than now, when the current political regime and its development ideologies misleadingly stress the home as "a crucial area of development" (Norma Sullivan, 1994:80). The only difference is that now women—as underpaid workers, housekeepers, mothers, childbearers and child rearers, wives, and ultimately citizens— are formally acknowledged as participants in, and practical supporters of, male-conceived and male-directed development programs (1994:132).

While inequalities between gender and class boundaries are well recognized at some levels in Java and frequently appear in Western studies, as well as in the Indonesian press; in male-dominated seminars; and in the discussions of the primarily male, educated classes,[15] none of this publicity brings about any changes at all for women. In fact, what one finds most is that men, and the occasional woman in high office, direct and define women's roles. Between official government efforts to bring women into the national development process and the state ideology of the "ideal woman," women are safely confined to their domestic roles. Alternatives render women dangerous. Ideologies of gender are then strictly tied to ideologies of development, which have largely replaced the ideologies of liberation and reconstruction that predominated in the pre-1965 era (Norma Sullivan, 1994:137).

Consider a brief example. From the 1920s onward, the women's movement was an integral component of the struggle for independence from Dutch colonizers. Two months after the famous Youth Conference of 1928 released its Oath (Sumpah Pemudah), the first Indonesian Women's Congress was opened on 22 December, resulting in the formation of the Association of Indonesian Women (PPPI, Perikatan Perkumpulan Perempuan Indonesia). Aside from becoming a communications channel among the many already existing women's groups, it focused on such topics as the role of women in marriage,[16] polygamy, and education. Its achievements and influences were rewarded in 1959 when President Sukarno designated 22 December a national holiday: The Day of Women's Resurgence (Hari Kebangkitan Perempuan). In such organizations as Sukarno's Marhaen, and GERWANI (the Indonesian Women's Movement), the struggle for women's recognition and advancement focused heavily and effectively on the plight of the *wong cilik* (Hafidz and Krisnawati, 1989).

But history is often re-created for political purposes, and 22 December is now simply Mother's Day, in praise of the dedication and servitude of mothers. Modern women's groups strive to moderate and pacify, instilling New Order values such as servitude and sacrifice. Differences in class values and roles are officially denied, and struggling for specifically *wong cilik* causes often leads, ironically, to accusations of Communist affiliation.

Agency as Responsibility

This final section in the chapter deals with the highly complex notion of human agency. Agency is most simply defined as the assignment of personal responsibility in a discursive act. Agency as an aspect of human subjectivity is based on a capacity for critical reflection on one's own thoughts and actions. The emphasis on the separateness of people from one another and the individuality of the will has led to a conception of people as independent agents, individually responsible for their actions (Mühlhäusler and Harré, 1990:102–103). Individuality leads to notions of intentionality, which had long influenced linguistics,[17] as well as intellectual thought.

The term *agency* as I use it here, however, requires a different meaning. Not only are we dealing with the third world and all the hierarchical values and demands this involves, but we are also dealing with women. Feminist writers have strongly criticized definitions of agency as the right or responsibility of an actor to carry out various acts, claiming that such a view defines women as nonagents (Davies, 1990; Smith, 1987). Social theories that depend always on autonomous actors are misleading; also, in much of Southeast Asia, activity-oriented exertion carries a rather different implication—"a lack of spiritual power and effective potency, [which] consequently diminishes prestige" (Shelly Errington, 1990:5; Wolf, 1992:64).

In light of what we know of gender and class roles among the urban poor, we are in need of research methods that assist us in recognizing a scale of agency fitted to the lives and identities of third-world women. I attempt to accomplish this by locating how social needs are reflected in the structuring of stories, the presentation of information, and the types of information that can be presented by Javanese women. Thus, in this study, variations on agency refer to variations in discursive styles of acting as the means through which social meaning is constructed in a given community of speakers. But as I have already mentioned, the women whose stories we analyze rarely talk about themselves, their intentions, hopes, ideas, or any of the other speech types we may have associated with agency.

The issue here lies in what it means to be an agent and how this conflicts with the notions of agency demonstrated in Javanese stories. The stories are a means through which speakers index relationships and social norms in terms of responsibility to one's community. Thus, agency in Java is a social act of responsibility to one's community of others, not necessarily to oneself.

Duranti (1993; and see chapter 1) has already set a foundation for recognizing context rather than individuals as the location for the illocutionary force of utterances, showing how coconstructing stories and their meanings involves specific strategies for constituting or mitigating responsibility. Responsibility here takes on a significant weight because it includes responsibility for the consequences of speech as social action. The locus of understanding is not intentionality but the actual impact speech can have on the world.

Through the various strategies of participation that speakers take up, we see how the needs of social interaction at the immediate and broader levels of contextual knowledge shape identity. This is what I describe as *responsible agency* rather than agency. Responsible agency is a matter of choice demonstrated by the degree to which a speaker participates in a conversation and, hence, takes up its positions as one's own. Agency in these texts, then, is synonymous with participation, and it can be measured as indexes of a speaker's choice in being responsible to the group-constructed conception of meaning and harmony.

Other variations on agency among third-world women support my view, although not from a discourse-based perspective. While Mohanty (1991a:13) calls for the need to recognize "the complex relationality that shapes our social and political lives," she also posits a "dynamic oppositional agency" through which oppressed women can balance their systemic relationships with the directionality of power. In her study of female factory workers in Java, Wolf (1992) presents a notion of *female agency*, which attempts to expand the continuum between individual autonomy and victimized passivity. Wolf's assertion that agency is not synonymous with activity and that agency can involve choices, including passivity and acquiescence, supports definitions of social action as complex, varied, and nuanced.

Despite gender, poverty, and exploitation, Wolf shows how underpaid, overworked, and abused young Javanese factory women exercise agentic choices by preferring the relative freedom and prestige of factory work to the alternative available to them, the less free and less prestigious life at home. Oppression, like the social positions that enforce it, is relationally defined from both micro and macro levels of personal experience. From this perspective we see that when social identity is constrained by responsible agency, silence resonates powerfully.

This notion of agency as a set of behaviors that includes acceptance of oppression, repression, and often what we may see as a great deal of self-sacrifice, fits well with previous descriptions of life in the *kampung*. The social roles of these Javanese urban communities, or *kampung*, set up very specific rights and rituals of correct behavior (i.e., *cårå Jåwå*) amid the hierarchy essential to the physical and emotional proximity of one household that is literally leaning on the next. As Sullivan (1992) and Guinness (1986) have shown in their studies of urban Yogyakarta *kampung*, the families and people linked together in these geosocial units are highly interdependent. In such a densely populated and tightly linked physical and social space, this interactive communality is conducive to a notion of person that is very much subordinated to the preservation of the hierarchy in everyday interactions and to the community in New Order discourse (Hafidz and Krisnawati, 1989; Lette, n.d.; Weiringa, 1992), what Niels Mulder (1992) calls a recognition that one is neither alone nor self-sufficient in one's pursuit of life.

The perspective that I take by locating, defining, and analyzing conversational narratives is an attempt to mediate the positioning of individuals with reference to their communities. Speech draws an individual's narratives into the ultimately shared arenas of socially manifested propriety,[18] where identifying strategies of achieving conformity and sameness as presentations of social harmony are the means through which local conceptions of identity are revealed. Public discourses in the *kampung* are saturated with their own standardized forms, which are, in actuality, compounded by inherent dangers. Internal conflicts revolve around an external pressure to conform, combined with the very real fear of becoming gossip fodder. Whereas Coates (1989) describes gossip as nearly always pertaining to personal experience, young Javanese women seem overwhelmingly to prefer to talk about someone else.

Agency, as a concept used to describe the social activities of third-world women, must fully accommodate this flexibility of relational identities. In worlds where asymmetrical relationships are a purposeful and harmonizing dynamic, the maintenance of stability is expressed by learning the discourses of membership,[19] that is, *cårå Jåwå*. Looking at what these discourses are and how they index membership, we see that they all point to relational aspects of the immediate context and the community by showing how speaking styles are reflective of a responsibility to one's "others." Responsible agency preserves the harmony necessary for communal interdependence. Hence, even among the ordinary people living in the *kampung* of urban Yogyakarta, *cårå Jåwå*, without the perfect elegance normally associated with it, is the basic social contract, underpinning harmony, meaning, and identity.

Narrating Gender

The shaping of the fieldwork, my choices and outcomes, was the direct result of my being a woman and on my own in Java because of the strong cultural and physical constraints Javanese society places on women. Despite my skin and hair color—obviously marking me as a member of a different world, locally known for our vast riches, sexual and political freedoms, lack of politeness, and transience in their world—my ability to speak Javanese and my faithful associations with the Budi family and Ibu Asmoro gave me a great deal of acceptance in local terms. I feel free to use the term acceptance because of the way groups of women in the *kraton* and the *kampung* involved me in their gossip circles. Most importantly, in small groups they would often make a point of socializing me by gently criticizing or praising my language, dress, and behavior and teaching, demonstrating, and explaining what I needed to know to be a Javanese woman, something they all assumed I wanted to be. Through these processes of socialization and privileged intimacy, I slowly came to recognize the stringent constraints placed on these women. As a result, the context in which I not so much chose as felt confined to required my associating mainly with women. Thus, we need to discuss how and where women are placed—and place themselves—in the social order.

The focus I present here should explain some of the differences between a sociolinguistic approach to language in use and one of linguistic anthropology. Sociolinguistic studies tend to study the fundamental categories of man/woman, black/white, middle class/working class, and so on, whereas anthropology requires a much closer attention to interactions as social practice (see Freeman and McElhinney, 1995, for further discussion of these differences). Thus, one of the great motivating forces behind this study was precisely the desire to transcend "categories" in analyzing Javanese discourse, whether these be male/female, royalty/working class, or even *krämä/ngoko*. The further influence of social psychology and the use of discourse in recognizing the role of agency in the construction of social identities additionally moves this study away from isolating language from everyday activities, which is common in more formal linguistic analyses (see O'Connor, 1994, for discussion of a similar interdisciplinary approach). Formal language (or in this case, narrative) structure does, however, have an important role to play in locating a specific speech act in a bounded activity. But to locate the social function of the speech act, we need to first know what the internal, that is, contextual, obligations for accomplishing the act are. As we see, these obligations are almost entirely hierarchical, meaning that they are bound up in relations of cooperative power and role inequalities, all of which are located in the structural and functional domains of the event and thus must all be involved in analysis.

This book raises two important issues for studies of Javanese women's discourse in context. The first is that an understanding of power relations requires at least three levels of contextual awareness. These are the immediate micro context of the discourse act itself, the recognition of those people involved in the speech act, and the additional awareness of the macro contexts of community pressures that further constrain discourse practices in everyday contexts. These dimensions of context are discussed as the ways in which speakers signal their "cultural" knowledge of how and what to say in a given context. Thus, an understanding of what it means to be a member of Javanese society must be confined to specific interactive processes or activities as they are lived out by the speakers themselves. Instead of isolating language for linguistic analysis, this method isolates a social context and its defining activities as a basic unit through which we could come to a better understanding of diverse and fundamentally different ways of being.

The second, rather paradoxical, point to be presented is that the category of gender in language may not be very salient for this study. Even though the majority of speakers who appear on these pages are women, in particular working-class women, many of whom are obvious victims of gender oppression, I found it extremely difficult to pinpoint any of the discourses as gender-based. Categories of inequality of class and economic development are obvious issues, compounded and, as far as the speakers contend, resolved by their ability to maintain harmony. Thus, the most salient categories for these Yogyakarta speakers themselves are socioeconomic position and the expectations of fair play, that is, the harmonious resolution of problems through expectations that those in power will do the right thing. And if not, the laws of karma will ultimately equalize all ills. The women do not see gender as an issue.

But I do.[20] The fact that I could not locate specific gender styles of interacting is probably the result of limitations in my own analyses, compounded by the lack of research on comparative male discourses. Until parallel studies of working-class, male social interactions are conducted, the specifics of gender-based discursive styles can only be suggested. Although not from a discursive approach, the dichotomous notions of gender in Java have been studied from the perspectives of politeness, prestige, and refinement (Keeler, 1990; Smith-Hefner, 1988) or the macro levels of gender ideology and group membership, whether among neighbors, in the media, or within government-controlled women's organizations (Djajadiningrat-Nieuwenhuis, 1987; Sen, 1994; Norma Sullivan, 1994; Wieringa, 1992). These are the sites in which gender differences arise and through which gender learning and self-presentation sustain and enforce community boundaries. These are the classification schemes through which people learn to understand their worlds and their own roles in them.

With contextualized activities as the basic unit of analysis, the range of identities and positions individuals have access to becomes the focus, rather than stereotypes of gender, culture, identity, and so on. As others have also shown, individuals emerge through the processes of social interaction, not as a relatively fixed end product but as one who is constituted and reconstituted through the various discursive practices in which they participate (Davies & Harré,1990:46; Mead, 1934). This discussion will add to the dimensions of social identity by focusing on the roles of discourses of power in the construction of women's identity. Adapting a concept of the triangular relations among discourse, cognition, and society, we have explored how women are ideologically constructed as subordinate to men through media discourse. We also saw how public discourses impose social knowledge that can be directly located in women's speech. Such powerful discourses reproduce women's positions as inferior while they also constitute societal knowledge regarding women and their roles in society. In ideological terms, Indonesian women are defined relationally to men. Rejection or attempts at breaking out of gender boundaries are simply unacceptable, dangerous, equated with chaos, and seen as a threat to the state (Sears, 1996:19).

I am with the granddaughter of a past Paku Alaman sultan and her husband, a retired military officer, at the birthday celebration of the reigning sultan. We became very close friends during after the eight months I resided in their old palace (Kangjengan) in 1992.

Me as an *abdi-dalem* with some of the *pesindhen* of Krido Mardowo. Ibu Asmoro is on my left, and Ibu Umaya is on my far right. We are in the rear chambers of the *kraton*, waiting to participate in the public *gamelan* rehearsals. Men and women here are habitually, if not officially, segregated. It was here among these women that most of the palace tapes were recorded. We are sitting on a mat on the ground because *abdi-dalem* may not sit on chairs.

The Budi daughters: Sari, Atik, and Yati, relaxing on the veranda of their uncle's house.

Sari and Atik, sharing a bowl of rice and *krupuk* before we left for the picnic on Christmas Day. This is the bottom bunk bed, where Sari and I sat in the opening story.

Ibu Budi, preparing the family meal in her "kitchen."

Pak Budi and the youngest daughter in the dark, cramped house that sheltered eight. It had originally been built as a warehouse for storing the chairs their *priyayi* relations used at gatherings.

I am lost at night in the mountain forest with Sapto. We have both lost our shoes and are covered with mud. We took these photos specifically to see if the mischievous spirits or tigers that led us astray would appear in the pictures. Disappointingly, they did not. It was also immediately after this photo was taken that Sapto stepped out into the blackness and over the 6-foot-high terrace we had been sitting on.

I am with some close friends on the art school campus. That is Sapto with the eye patch, which somehow made its way to Java from a party I had attended in New York.

•••PART II

DEFINING NARRATIVES

• • • three

Dimensions of Oral Narrative

In the previous two chapters we have begun to investigate some of the social, cultural, and political pressures that shape the macro-level contexts of Javanese women's identity. We have explored the theories and expectations that heavily constrain how people speak in the Javanese language, and I have also discussed the ways in which society is stratified by the ideological forces of political control. In line with Mead's (1934) theories on the self and community, all of these social constructions are taken to be language-based, whether they are located in the speech levels; styles of interacting; or the slogans, speeches, and mass media that make up public, power-laden discourses. As we have seen in chapter 2, many of these pressures to conform and to acquiesce are even heavier for Javanese women. If upholding inequality by mastering the speech levels is locally defined as elegant, refined, and a sign of internal power, and if women who resign themselves to silence in the face of cruelty, domestic violence, and stark unfairness are locally seen as ideal women, where can we draw the line between "tradition" and abuse?

In this chapter we introduce the structural groundwork by which narratives are defined. From this foundation, we finally begin to hear Javanese women tell their own stories. We needed first to understand what these women consider a story to be. As mentioned, the majority of women whose voices appear on these pages are from several different communities even though they all live within the fortress walls of the palace. There are differences in the way they speak, and these differences are discussed as we examine the stories themselves.

I begin to define Javanese narratives by comparing standard structural and functional descriptions of narrative to the Javanese stories I have recorded. From here we see how and why they do or do not differ. While there are good sources of studies on literary and performance texts in Javanese, there is no previous body of work on Javanese conversational narratives, or conversational narratives in any other Southeast Asian language that I am familiar with. Where to even begin to look for these narratives in thousands of pages of transcripts became a rather daunting task, when they contained very little that even looked like a narrative.

What Is a Narrative?

While we all instinctively know what a story is and how to tell one, there is still no easy answer to the question, what is a narrative? The deeper into theoretical explanations we go, the more complicated it may become to answer. One of the reasons is that narratives have traditionally been one of the favorite domains for analysis in a wide variety of disciplines. Literary criticism, anthropology, history, psychology, sociology, and linguistics have all devoted a great deal of effort to understanding narratives, and all from rather different perspectives. My focus here is mainly on linguistics and discourse analysis in particular to assist in locating structural and functional aspects of storytelling. The influences of anthropology and social psychology are necessarily quite strong since my goal is to use the stories as an index of how these Javanese speakers construct and reflect social identity and their own culture of Javaneseness.

To begin with a working definition of narrative, I list the three main criteria for identifying a segment of discourse as a story in Western literature:

1. A story must relate a series of unique real or fictional events that can be specified according to place and time.
2. A story must be based on actions or events that contain an out-of-the-ordinary element that makes it reportable.
3. A story must contain the formal characteristics of narrative.

We will begin from point 3 since that is what the sociolinguistics literature stresses; that is, stories are mainly definable through their *structure*, with *function* taking somewhat of a back seat. Stories are temporally ordered clauses that make a point about the world that the speaker and recipient share (Labov, 1972; Labov and Waletsky, 1967; Linde, 1993; Polanyi, 1989; Schiffrin, 1984; Tannen, 1984). As a discourse unit, the story must have recognizable boundaries, as well as an internal structure. Labov and Waletsky recognize a segment of text as narrative if it consists of two adjacent clauses that describe a pair of events that are related either causally or temporally.

Since the pioneering studies on narrative structure by Labov, linguists have expanded his paradigm to focus on the ways in which stories are fitted into a conversation, the linguistic and social constraints on storytelling, and strategies for locating a story in the embedding talk (Labov, 1972; Labov and Waletsky, 1967; Linde, 1993; Polanyi, 1989; Schegloff, 1992; Schiffrin, 1984, 1994). Stories are introduced into talk when a speaker presents what is called "entrance talk," a transition discourse through which the storytelling intention is announced, its relevance to the current talk is explained, and the alteration of speaker roles is accepted by others (Jefferson, 1978; Polanyi, 1989; Schiffrin, 1984). But initiating a story is not an easy task because stories require an extended turn, something that is recognized in the literature as being in conflict with rights of participation (Sacks, Schegloff, and Jefferson, 1976):

> Of necessity, the teller focuses attention on himself in telling a story. Not only is he the center of attention while claiming the floor for the duration of the extended turn, but he also makes explicit his judgment of what he believes his recipients would find worthwhile enough to justify relinquishing their rights to the floor. (Polanyi, 1989:45)

Speakers' rights are of major significance in these studies, as is recognizing the transitions that lead from talk to storytelling sequences (Schegloff, 1992).

Reporting the story events is achieved through the complicating action clauses, which describe an event as a bounded occurrence in time, sequentially locked into its temporal progression. These utterances move the action forward and have what Polanyi (1989:16) defines as "an instantaneous rather than a durative or iterative character." This temporal juncture (Labov, 1972) is the very feature that creates the prototypical narrative (Tannen, 1984:97–100). Matching action clauses to real-world events helps explain the social and expressive purposes of narrative. This temporal ordering of storytelling transforms or reconstructs the past into a narrator's perspective through which speakers can share their privileged perspective with hearers, creating a vicarious involvement for listeners who are not expected to remain passive (Schiffrin, 1984).

In addition to the temporal criteria, stories have to have a point. The point is the part of a narrative that reveals the attitude of the speaker toward the story by emphasizing certain aspects of the story over others. The "point" must be shared and acceptable (Polanyi, 1989). Both a story and its point must be easily recognizable through their conventional structure and clarity. The form and function of the point always communicates information about the relationship that exists between interlocutors and also among speakers, their words, and their worlds.

At the other end, the response sequence (Schegloff, 1992), like Labov's (1972) coda, signals that the story is over and returns to the turn-taking norms of talk. For Polanyi (1989), the close of a story should be marked by "exit talk," in which recipients discuss the story's points and relevance and their interpretations of it. Cases in which recipients do not respond through exit talk are "a socially salient response indicating embarrassment, confusion, annoyance, lack of understanding, or low esteem for the teller" (Polanyi, 1989:49).

Functionally, narratives are a verbal technique for recapitulating experience within a temporal sequence that matches that of the events related.

This *linear sequencing of lived experience* is, by definition, considered to be the essential structuring component of narrative.

Narratives and Identity

The interdisciplinary application of social psychology, linguistics, and anthropology merges in analyses of narrative in the writings of Jerome Bruner (1987), Rom Harré (1984), Charlotte Linde (1989, 1993), Elinor Ochs (1993), Patricia O'Conner (1994), Donald Polkinghorne (1988), and others. In these writings, narratives as data are considered one of the most important social resources for the creation and maintenance of personal identity. They reflect the "individual" who decides to tell a story and his or her needs, choices, and social responsibility, and most significantly, they reveal a speaker's view of self with regard to the interlocutor. As Harré (1984; De Waele and Harré, 1979) states, the selected themes, structures, and contents of stories, in relation to explicitly or implicitly addressing the audience, provide direct access to the speaker's cognitive matrix. That is, they reveal an organized system for social knowledge and belief on which speakers act and account for actions, all of which are directly accessible to analysis through story language and content.

In light of storytelling as a selective, public process, selfhood as a social construction means that it is shaped from the outside and not just from the inside (Bruner, 1986, 1987; Harré, 1992; Polkinghorne, 1988; Vygotsky, 1986). Thus, descriptions of narrative as a type of theatrical performance in which speakers can guide and control the impressions they form (Goffman, 1984) are not sensitive enough to the "recipient design" (Polanyi, 1989; Sacks, Schegloff, and Jefferson, 1974) needs of social identity construction. For a story to be "reportable" or interesting enough to relate requires a great deal of shared intimacy, understanding, or purpose between the storyteller and others present. Enough shared knowledge must exist for the story to be "agreeable" in terms of its evaluation or for some form of verbal negotiation to take place (Polanyi, 1989). Thus by adding dimensions of social psychology and anthropology to our definitions, the narratives we tell can now be viewed more as the means through which we synthesize and integrate our experiences as a reflection of contextual needs, purposes, and relationships. It is through all of these factors that personal identity emerges, both constructed by and reflected in "narrative configuration" (Polkinghorne, 1988:150).

The stories we tell are more than simply bounded segments of discourse aimed at achieving some social feat. According to Bruner (1987), our stories are analogous to life—where "world-making" and stories are constructed in people's minds as continuous interpretations and reinterpretations of experience. One's life and one's stories are both selective achievements of memory recall; both are interpretive feats. The issue of verification, then, is irrelevant. In other words, the "problem" of indeterminacy or truthfulness of stories evaporates since interpretation is "highly susceptible to cultural, interpersonal, and linguistic influences" (Bruner 1987:14). In other words, what counts as "true" is shaped by prevailing power relations, which are negotiated by matching appropriate domains of discourse with expected rights, duties, and responsibilities (see Duranti, 1994, for a discussion of truth in Samoan discourse). Stories, and ways of telling them, will then reflect the dominant cultural theories about life and what it all means, making the stories people tell as "real" as life itself.

Cultures contain narrative models that they make available for describing the course of a life, through which culture itself can be characterized. On simpler levels, there is the stock of canonical life narratives available through myths, heroes, fables, and so on. But more relevant here, narratives are also indexes of culture because of the way they follow linguistic models in conjunction with the cognitive processes that shape local meaning, which all work together to guide members through narration of the events of their lives. The main argument for Bruner, then, is that cultural forces guide speakers through the process of narrating their lives. These forces have "the power to structure perceptual experience, to organize memory, to segment and purpose-build the very 'events' of a life" (Bruner, 1987:15). Yet, by returning the telling process to the historical, cultural, and linguistic frameworks that define it, Bruner concludes that it is the "*forms* of self-telling . . . rather than content that matters" (1987:16; my emphasis).

Charlotte Linde (1989, 1993) takes a similar stance to Bruner's on the significance of oral narratives as a reflection of cultural and linguistic forms. She also ties the storytelling act to its social context, viewing the narration as an act of negotiation in which storytellers must perceive their own rights, roles, and obligations. Negotiating the self presented in the story demands a reflexivity of self in relation to the belief systems that index membership into a given community and how these systems in turn affect narrative construction. As she shows, we need to locate first what type of a self is recognized as a self in this culture and then how we go about forming it (1993:98).

The first step, then, is to identify what properties of the self are reflected in and constitutive of narrative. These properties will serve as evidence for narrative as not just expressions of the self but also a means of assistance in creating our sense of self as a reflection of others and the values and beliefs of the communities we claim membership with. But as Bruner (1987:15) has noted, the cultural forces that guide speakers through the process of narrating their lives also have "the power to structure perceptual experience, to organize memory, to segment and purpose-build the very events of a life." Analyzing narratives, then, should not be done in isolation from these other influential factors.

The discussion that follows substantiates the role of Javanese narrative in structuring elements that reflect a different type of story, and thus self, than that already described. The main differences are found in what it means to be an agent. While we do have extensive literature on Javanese conceptions of self, much of this stems from a cultural and theoretical interpretation based on elite discourses. No studies have previously discussed Javanese conversational narratives or the types of Javanese identities that emerge through social interaction as practice. Literary and performance genres have been studied, but their relevance for working-class women seems too distant to deal with now.

Structuring the Analysis of Narratives

Structural analyses of narrative are highly valued for presenting categories and rules, and the stories of personal experience featured in Labov and Waletsky (1967) and Labov (1972) are the pioneering examples. Through these studies, oral narratives are shown to be bounded discourse units that can be segmented according to their informational function, that is, abstract, orientation, complication, evaluation, and coda. The abstract announces the intention to tell a story by summing up its relevance. In conversation, this occurs when a speaker signals a request for the floor for the extended turn that storytelling requires, for example, by asking, "Did I tell you what happened to me last week?"

The orientation follows an abstract to present the background information, such as time, setting, participants, and circumstances: "Well, that afternoon Sapto and I decided to go hike up that mountain just near Bandungan and spend the night in the tea plantation." This gives the audience enough information to interpret the story.

The complicating action is the main part of a story in which the events are described: "We walked up through the forest for about two hours before we realized we had completely lost the trail. As night fell, we found we were going in circles. Sapto kept insisting we should keep going."

Evaluation appears throughout the story and takes the form of the speaker's comments on the events: "And wouldn't you know it, the flashlight didn't work! Can you imagine? We were lost on the mountain in pitch dark!" The speaker's comments may contain several elements. One is emphasis: "I could literally see *nothing*! Between the humidity fogging up my glasses and the path being so slippery that we both had to go barefoot, and we still both kept falling on our butts, scratched by the brush and rocks, *and* there was this huge gaping, beckoning ravine just to our right that we could only hear by the echoing of the river far below!" Or breaks in action: "Finally we got out of the forest and reached the farmed areas. Ha, we thought the hard part was over! What we did not yet know was that the terraces, you know, the steplike levels cut into the mountain so they can farm on flat surfaces rather than on steep slopes?, well, these terraces were 6 feet high!" Or adjectives: "So after resting for a few minutes and wiping the buckets of sweat and mud from our faces, thinking we were home free now, we got up to walk straight on. Sapto took one step and *whiiipppppp* GONE! Silence. The gaping, beckoning ravine earned her sacrifice." Or reported speech: "I called out in a soft, cracking voice, 'Sapto?' No answer. I thought, 'Well, don't panic sister. You'd better just sit here and wait till morning. No sense giving that monster a second meal.'" As you can see, evaluation includes many features, all of which help the audience identify the story's point.

The coda is the mark of closure that resolves the story:

> And so let me tell you, we were thrilled and relieved to have made it pretty much in one piece to the village! We stopped by the mosque because a group of men was sitting there and asked for directions. These guys told us that even they never go up into that forest because it is seriously haunted and that the spirits twist the trail around on you! Everyone gets lost up there if they are foolish enough to be there after dark. They also said that of course the flashlight wouldn't work. Tigers absorb energy and the forest is full of tigers! One of the men took the flashlight from Sapto and turned it right on!

The coda also shifts the time frame from the story world's past to the storytelling present: "So that's how I learned to believe in Javanese magic forests!"

In comparing these structural features to Javanese narratives, several discrepancies will arise. These are mainly rooted in Labov's variationist view of narrative as "autonomous textual units whose internal parts stand in systematic relationships with one another" (as described by Schiffrin, 1994:285). The argument suggests that although many similarities with the Labovian framework do exist, narrative structures need to be interpreted in accordance with functional roles within a bounded context that includes relationships among participants in the storytelling event more than relationships among segmented parts of a text. My goal here is to propose a broader organizational structure tied to the dimensions of social function. The power element in the shaping of meaning will inevitably challenge expectations of constituent categories in the "well-formed" story.

The Javanese stories we examine, however, fall into several types, or genres, of which only those told by the high-ranking or elderly speakers show similarities to the structure of narrative previously mentioned. Participants who are not high-ranking, either through age or through achievement, as Ibu Asmoro is, or within the bounded context of interaction, that is, in comparison to their immediate speech partners, do not have the right to tell autobiographical stories. While the conversational narrative as a bounded speech event is always interactive, the differences here lie in cultural variations concerning the individual in society.

More than anything else, the Javanese stories reflect group harmony, sharedness, or a striving for unanimous understanding of events. When no elder is present, the stories tend to reflect the most common of human experiences, and they are also told jointly. Stories focus on highly accessible topics that recount shared events or events that are familiar and impersonal. The Javanese narratives in my corpus rarely evoke a "What happened?" response of interest about its reportability or unexpectedness. There are no minimum conditions concerning the quality of being out of the ordinary relative to general norms and to the expectations of the participants (Gülich and Quasthoff, 1985:171). In a society where being shocked (*kaget*) can make you ill and even kill (Wolf, 1996), and where "nothing ever happens" is a deliberate political strategy to eliminate dissent (Pemberton, 1989), the following discussion shows how these Javanese women focus on the relationships that exist between participants and not on specific events, opinions, or actions.

Structurally, the stories and their surrounding conversation display a fusion, so that the boundaries between them are not always clear. Speakers do not need to request the floor for an extended turn because the stories, much like conversation in appearance, are usually not found within extended individual turns. Instead, the stories are often constructed through active group involvement in the telling process. Gregory Bateson describes a similar group-inclusive process in Bali:[1]

> Even such continued speech as would, in most cultures, be used for the telling of stories does not occur in Bali. The narrator will, typically, pause after a sentence or two, and wait for some member of the audience to ask him a concrete question about some detail of the plot. He will then answer the question and so resume his narration. This procedure apparently breaks the cumulative tension by irrelevant interaction. ([1949] 1972:114)

I suggest that the Javanese speakers in my corpus, much as the speakers that Bateson describes, do not "wait" for someone to ask something but design their stories specifically to encourage participation. What Bateson refers to as "irrelevant interaction" is thus an important aspect of storytelling as a collectively organized, group-strengthening activity. What makes the observation so significant is that it is based on a social order that derives a type of localized meaning structured very differently from mainstream, English-based expectations.

The Structure of Narratives

The most influential narrative model is that of Labov and Waletsky (1967) and Labov (1972). In this model, oral narratives are shown to be bounded discourse units that can be segmented according to their informational function—abstract, orientation, complication, evaluation, and coda. This description of narratives begins with the structural models through which narratives are analyzed and includes the frameworks that define narrative as an interactive process. While these structural elements also play an important role in many Javanese narratives, the ways in which the story parts relate to their function as a whole are formally different. The following discussion expands on the surface structure model to show how it is related to the narrative text and how each unit contributes to the storytelling event itself.

The Abstract

The abstract is defined as the summary of a story. It serves to prepare a listener, to inform that a story will be told and what that story is about (Labov, 1972). Narratives require speakers to indicate their need for an extended turn (Jefferson, 1978; Schiffrin, 1984), so the abstract is an "entry device" into the changing distribution of speakers' turns.

Abstracts, however, are rarely found in any of the texts in my corpus, perhaps because of two important Javanese interactional rules. The first is that social hierarchies are clearly demarcated. Those that feel themselves to be in a superior position for reasons like age, gender, or occupation can tell all the stories they wish with no need for listeners' permission. I show elsewhere (Berman, 1992) that aged speakers frequently tell autobiographical narratives of epic proportions, which perform a caregiver function.

Second, in Javanese contexts an abstract seems to index exclusion to the storytelling floor. The younger generation of Javanese speakers that I focus on here tells stories more in groups than individually and, hence, require no exclusive right. My entire corpus of young women's stories reveals very few of them to involve personal experience. Instead, stories tend to be of general or mutual interest, and utterances require an uptake for the story to be continued. This means that a topic will be "posted" to give others the opportunity to respond in a story-round type of turn-taking pattern.[2] This storytelling strategy makes it difficult to distinguish a story from the embedding talk, as well as the interactional distribution of participants from those in conversation. The key, then, is to follow the development of the topic to see how or if it is expanded into a story.

In (1) below, Sari introduced a topic as she was browsing through the newspaper. She saw an article and photo of the *bekakak* festival, which was held recently near Yogyakarta. This festival involves a procession of a giant male and female pair of puppets, smaller puppets for "sacrifice," and lots of music. The topic and focus in this emerging story are determined through repetition, seen as Sari invites me to speak about the *bekakak* puppet festival. Endang, Sari's factory mate, tells her brief story in turns 190 and 194 after the time shift into the past is mutually accepted. No abstract is used.[3]

(1) *The Bekakak Story*

184. SARI: <u>Mbak Len</u> mau <u>nonton</u> <u>bekakak</u> tho?	Mbak Len did you watch the bekakak earlier?
Biasane kraton ki,	usually the kraton,
rombongan <u>nonton bekakak</u>.	a group watches the bekakak.

185. LAINE: Ow, nggih tho?   Oh, is that right?
186. SARI: <u>Mbak Len wis tau nonton</u>   Mbak Laine has already seen the
     kok.   bekakak y'know.
187. LAINE: Ia <u>wis tau nonton</u> taun   Ya [I] saw it last year
     kepungkur
188. ENDANG: Berarti neng kene   That means [you've] been here
     wis ånå <u>setahun</u> yo <u>Mbak Len</u>! for a year already then Mbak Len!
189. LAINE: <u>Setahun</u>   A year
→ 190. ENDANG: Aku mbiyen ki,   I once,
         <u>nonton bekakak</u> umur telung   watched the bekakak when I was
         taun   three years old
191. LAINE: Wah! kok . . . suwi! . . .   Wah! so long ago!
192. SARI: Isih <u>indil-indil</u>   [Then you were] still so tiny and cute
     saiki wis <u>ondol-ondol</u>   now [you're] gross and sloppy
→ 194. ENDANG: Gek ndilalah åpå kae,   So, suddenly what's that,
         nonton <u>ondel-ondel</u> sing gede   [I] saw those gigantic procession
         kae,   puppets,
         wedi aku.   I was terrified.

Endang's brief *bekakak* story (turns 190 and 194) illustrates several issues
relevant to Javanese stories. It shows how all speakers jointly construct
the topic's development (or orientation), as opposed to a single speaker
who requests the floor through an abstract. Sari initiates the topic from
the news photo by directing it to me through her request for information
(turn 184). Since I do not take it up, Sari tries again to gain interest for the
topic by repeating *Mbak Len* and *nonton* ("watch something") to show
that my experiences with the festival are centered information. I repeat
Sari's utterance in confirmation and add the past time, a year ago.[4] Endang
repeats the time reference to verify my length of time in Java and to confirm the past-time precedent into our conversation. The actual story is
brief, fitting naturally into the conversation. Its construction, as well as
the experience discussed, is shared by all present.

Example (1) illustrates how the topic is posted in turn 184, to be tossed
around among all the speakers through repetition of its key terms. This
invites all those present to take part in its construction as it determines
the mutual accessibility of the topic. While *aku mbiyen* ("I once"—190),
like *kepungkur* (a past-time referent—187), creates the past time frame,
and the pronoun indexes the experience to be told as belonging to the
speaker (Endang), the orienting style of topic development has shown
this topic to be shared. Endang further orients her story by adding her
age at the time of the event she describes. But this does not give Endang
exclusive rights to the floor, as seen when Sari signals her own involvement in turn 192. Sari knows that the large *bekakak* puppets are called
ondel-ondel, so her utterance plays on that term by presenting her own
orientation to the story. Sari offers her rhyming imagery of *ondel-ondel*

(procession puppets) by describing Endang when she was three years old as *indil-indil* (tiny and cute) and now as *ondol-ondol* (gross and sloppy). Yet, she does this before Endang ever mentioned *ondel-ondel*. It can then be argued that Sari, in fact, is prescribing Endang's next utterance, to which Endang obliges by maintaining the rhyming word play. Who, then, is the storyteller?

A coconstructed involvement is created by this sound and rhythm imagery in (1), where meaning and detail are based simultaneously on mutual participation and repetition in the cocreation of the scene (e.g., Tannen, 1989). The story might have been an exclusive description of Endang's childhood experience, but it was oriented to allow all the speakers equal rights in its telling. It is impossible to know if Endang had a particular story to tell at that time and if she dropped it to follow Sari's rhyming. Through the joint construction of the rhythmic imagery, stories and particular details are deferred for a group-oriented sense making, whereby anyone present is given a place in the story's construction.

What (1) does show, however, is a strong sense of listenership by all the speakers, which suggests the coconstruction of experience to be normal and even expected. This cooperation is developed through repetition and the fusion of conversation and story boundaries, which index all of those present and the intimacy of their relationships rather than a specific teller and her tale. The lack of an abstract maintains the conversation and story fusion because it never indexes a teller and her wish to tell a particular story. An abstract would have signaled the genre as being more formal, a structured personal experience with a goal. Example (1) had no abstract, and the story functioned to index the shared commonality of *bekakak* and a child's experience at seeing the puppets,[5] which, this suggests, is more important than Endang's presentation of a childhood memory that is purely her own.

Such cooperative discourse is common in descriptions of all-women talk as the characteristic feature in consolidating and affirming a group stance over individual ones (Coates, 1989; Coates and Cameron, 1989; Gilligan, 1982; Johnstone, 1991; Kalcik, 1975; Tannen, 1990). As Coates found in her study of the fortnightly meeting of a long-established group of friends, cooperation is marked by specific discursive features—slow and joint topic development, minimal responses, epistemic modal forms, and simultaneous speech—which are used frequently and sensitively to signal active listenership and to support the current speaker. Asking questions, making comments, and jointly producing text all function to promote cooperative talk among women friends in an informal context.

The Javanese stories also display a joint construction of meaning at all levels including the phonological level; see example (1). Furthermore, a speaker does not object if another intrudes into her story. Blum-Kulka and Snow (1992) and Ochs (1988, 1993) define such a tolerance for coconstruction as indicative of "family" discourse, whereas the Javanese speakers discursively collapse "family" boundaries to include a great many more people than intimates and neighbors. The following stories all illustrate degrees of joint production of a topic, which is kept of mutual relevance to all present. Accessibility to all participants is a key factor in joint production. The strategies by which speakers signal their situated sharedness, or request information through which such sharedness can be achieved, reveal a great deal about local perceptions of meaning at both the immediate, situated level and the broader, cultural level.

Story (2) is an example of how speakers are all permitted a role in developing a story, even those who were not there. This story describes the events of Christmas Day 1992, when eight of us took four motorbikes to visit Pak Budi's aunt at her rural home on a mountain. Most of her neighbors' homes and all the roads were destroyed by a volcanic eruption several years earlier, making the place even more isolated. Getting there and then getting out necessitated riding up and down narrow mountain tracks in a dense forest with no electricity to light the way. Just at sundown, as we were heading home through the forest, one of the motorbikes died. We all had to stop and attend to it as the sky grew darker and darker. We were stuck on the side of a steep, muddy slope on a pitch-dark night, trying to fix the bike by match-light. Naturally it started to rain hard. The two men in our group decided to push the bike back up the mountain to the aunt's house, and the remaining six women waited for them since none of us knew the way out of the forest. With thoughts of tigers, poisonous snakes, scorpions, and the like, we huddled in groups under our shared rain ponchos and laughed about the predicament.

The next day, at the Budi home with Atik, Sari (Pak Budi's two eldest daughters), and Surti (an old friend who works in the same office as Atik), we talked about our adventures. Only Atik and I had actually been there. The story emerges, however, because the others coax it out.

(2) *Christmas in Tempel, Sleman*

295. SARI: Medeni nek mbengi ya biyen   [Its] scary at night back then right
     Dek durung ånå listrik   Back before there was electricity
     medeni meneh kae   even scarier then
296. ATIK: Kait saiki durung ånå   Even now there is none
297. LAINE: Durung ånå durung ånå!   There is none there is none!
298. SURTI: Ha nek. nek bali bengi ngko   So then. when going home at night
     njuk peteng banget.   so it's very dark.
299. ATIK: Ha wis. Wingi peteng ya   Oh yea. Yesterday it was dark wasn't
     Mbak Len ya?   it Mbak Len?
300. LAINE: Oo: peteng. Hii: OH yea: [it was] dark [scary noise]
301. ATIK: Jam enem [hahaha] ben   Six o'clock [hahah] for the experience!
     pengalaman!
302. LAINE: Kok såyå mbengi, såyå wah: Don't you know, the later it got
     wedi aku!   the—wah: I was terrified!
     [hahaha]   [hahah]

303. ATIK: Ånå kunang barang hahaha   There were fireflies and all hahha
jare laler ånå genine [hahaha]   they say [these are] flies with fire
[haha]
304. SURTI: Ha njuk, le ndandani motor,   So then, fixing the motorbike,
njuk piye nek peteng,   so how [can it be done] in the dark,

In each case, as the story in the forest begins to unfurl, others tease out the events. In turn 295, Sari brings up the topic of darkness and no electricity in the past. But since she has not been to visit her aunt for a year, she did not know there is still no electricity. Sari opens the topic by asking Atik for confirmation on how scary the place is in the dark. This is what forms the "abstract." Here it functions as a posted topic and thus requires the uptake of others for it to continue, which it does. Then, in turn 298, Surti posts the expanded topic to include not just the dark and how scary it is, but the fact of going home through the forest in the dark:

298. SURTI: Ha nek. nek bali bengi ngko   So then, when going home at night
njuk peteng banget.   so it's very dark.

Thus, the story is actually oriented in turns 295 and 298 by others who make comments that require uptake by those who actually have the information. Following the topic postings of others, Atik, as the only person truly qualified to tell the story, simply affirms and requests my ratification, which I give:

299. ATIK: Ha wis. Wingi peteng ya   Oh yea. Yesterday it was dark wasn't
Mbak Len ya?   it Mbak Len?
300. LAINE: Oo: peteng. hii: OH yea: [it was] dark [scary noise:]

Atik and I both expand slightly by emphasizing the dark and the fear, but it is Surti who requests the event segments of the story when she mentions the broken motorbike:

304. SURTI: Ha njuk le ndandani motor,   So then fixing the motorbike,
njuk piye nek peteng,   so how [can it be done] in the dark,

It is only here, then, that Atik tells the story in brief, still coaxed by questions from Surti and additional supporting information from Sari and me. Thus, despite the fact that only Atik and I had the actual facts, the story only came out because of the way others posted the topic initially and continued to orient the lead into a story. Later, we see how stories actually develop. For now, it is important to see how others framed them and how those who were there never took on sole rights to the experience.

Examples (3) and (4) reveal storytelling situations that are different from (1) and (2). The stories are from the *kraton* corpus, so the speakers are *abdi-dalem* (servants of the royal court) and much older; thus their stories and styles of telling are also different. Group elders are privileged in the allocation of interactional space, as seen by their high frequency of autobiographical stories.

Of the two stories that follow, only the second has an abstract in the Labovian sense. While both stories display cooperation, Ibu Asmoro is much older and holds a higher rank as an abdi-dalem than Ibu Umaya and thus is allotted a prominent role in the determination of the story. While the discussion explores why one story has an abstract and another has not, it further investigates cooperation in the development of stories. Even though Ibu Asmoro has the right to the floor, Ibu Umaya is very active in assisting her elder interlocutor. Ibu Umaya uses minimal responses, frequent comments, and asks questions that display exactly where and what information is not accessible for her.

Both stories are about street crimes against women and both are introduced by Ibu Asmoro. The first emerges as a result of Ibu Umaya's invitation to Ibu Asmoro to visit her home. Ibu Asmoro declines with no direct reason, other than mentioning the distance. The sequence of stories, however, serves to inform Ibu Umaya that the true reason is fear of violence against women on the streets. The rejection is explained through a story about another *abdi-dalem*.

(3) *Attack on Sari Retno*

141. ASMORO: **Nggih**: yen mantuk **piyambak** anu tho **wonten** Gedung Kuning **menikå**	Y'know: it's that going home alone uhm at that Gedung Kuning (place name)
142. UMAYA: Wah: **mesakaken** ... tur **nggih merginipun**//	wah: that's such a shame. and y'know the reason//
→ 143. ASMORO: La mangkane tutke **nikå ingkang griyanipun** Piyungan, jam sepuluh esuk we, kalunge dipedot nguwong kog.	and so actually according to that whose house is in Piyungan, at ten in the morning, her necklace was snatched by some person, y'know.
144. UMAYA: Anu ... si ...?	whatsername?
145. ASMORO: Marsidah?	Marsidah?
146. UMAYA: **Mboten** ... **senes**. ...	no (repair) no.
→ 147. ASMORO: **Menikå** rak kalung**ipun pun**jambret.	Don't you know her necklace was snatched.
148. UMAYA: Sari Retno	Sari Retno (name)

This story begins with the change of focus marker *La* in turn 143. I classify it as a joint production because the introduction is the result of a collaboration about elderly women traveling and is not opened with an abstract. Ibu Asmoro minimally orients by simply mentioning a vague topic (going home alone) and where the event occurred (Gedung Kuning). Thus, despite no mention of the crime, Ibu Umaya already knows that the topic is Sari Retno's attack on the streets, to which she responds in turn 142.

Ibu Asmoro then gives the events of the crime in turn 143, verifying their mutual understanding despite no specific mention in the initial introduction. Whereas the abstract is meant to give a summary of the story to come, this story displays just the opposite: a vague hint at a possible topic. It is clear that Ibu Umaya also already knew about the attack as she responds and permits the subsequent continuation. Turns 144 through 146 show the women working together at recalling the name, which finally surfaces in turn 148.

The horror in the story lies in the fact that the victim has "already reached here," meaning she is "one of us," an *abdi-dalem*, which implies that she is also an old, impoverished woman who cannot defend herself. The violation is repeated with emphasis:

149. ASMORO: **Nggih** neng **ngriki pun** teken.	Yes, [she's] already reached here.
→**Dados** namung pedot rantai kiwå tengen **kalian** (?)	So the chain was just broken from left and right with (?)
150. UMAYA: Wow . . . tur sing **menikå** **nggih** bu,	Wow and so y'know bu,
yen **ngagem** kalung **menikå**,	when wearing necklaces,
gelang **menikå**,	bracelets,
yen siang **ngaten nggih** semelang.	if in the afternoon like that y'know [they] sparkle.

In turn 143, Ibu Asmoro identifies the victim, the time, the place, and the crime. But an important detail, the name, is missing, and the two participants cooperate in its recall. In turn 147, Ibu Asmoro repeats the central topic, the snatching. Once Ibu Umaya assists in the identification of the victim, Ibu Asmoro again repeats the central topic (turn 149), the grabbing of the necklace, now evaluated by describing what she imagines to be the brutal left-right yanking as the robber broke the chain off the old woman's neck.

Yet, the story of the theft is not so much told as it is alluded to. This does not lower its status as a story but rather strengthens its position as a reflection of the community and the information all its members share. The phrase that describes the victim is *Nggih neng ngriki pun teken* ("yes, [she's] already reached here [she's one of us, an *abdi-dalem*]"), which carries a great deal of shared knowledge that need not be spoken. It implies elite (through proximity to the sultan), in-group membership; advanced age; long-term friendship (or at least acquaintance); and for the most part, poverty. But most significant for this story, it implies an old woman's vulnerability to violence on the crowded streets. This is, after all, the reason that Ibu Asmoro will not visit Ibu Umaya.

Story (3)'s topic is easily recognizable because it is repeated the most often in the conversation. Focused on a theft, it is not about personal experience, but it does perform the social action of signaling community.

Story (3) is about the vulnerability of women, old, alone, and facing the dangers of the street in a time marked by a serious rise in crime. While vulnerability is never uttered, it is clearly a major topic of the story, as seen from the stream of conversation. Ibu Asmoro opens the story in response to an invitation to visit her interlocutor. Story (3) then functions as her rejection of that invitation. Ibu Umaya's turn 150 is a sensible response, offering advice on how to avoid falling prey to such a snatching.

Story (4), which followed (3), is a response to Ibu Umaya's preventive evaluation in turn 150. Ibu Asmoro's stories tend to focus on her independence and cunning, so she must respond to this storyline, which has positioned her as vulnerable and perhaps even feeble. In her next turn, Ibu Asmoro presents an abstract for her story because she alone wants to narrate her independence and bravery in facing robbers. She needs to show that she, too, can look after herself.

(4) *Outwitting Robbers*
→ 155. ASMORO: Haning **kulå nikå**,   As for me,
              nekat lo dek jaman begal.   [I was] very determined back in that era of robbers.
  156. UMAYA: Gali **nåpå** bu?   Street toughs are they bu?
  157. ASMORO: Jaman Landi rak begal   Dutch occupation don't you know lots of robbers
  158. UMAYA: Wow . . . **ngaten**   Wow like that was it

Turn 155 is an abstract that specifically intends to display the teller as able to deal with robbers and, hence, as sensible as her interlocutor (i.e., Ibu Umaya's turn 150) and far better able to take care of herself than Ibu Sari Retno was. The story itself is very long and full of orienting and involving imagery that all culminates in the speaker proving her own bravery in outwitting two robbers. But what is important here is the function the abstract serves and the type of story it introduces. Rather than index the interactive context, for example, people and shared knowledge, as (3) did, this story is meant to distinguish and praise its teller, showing how independent and brave she is. The existence of an abstract presents the story as complete, purposeful, and, most important, the property of the teller. Abstracts often index a narrative of personal experience.

However, this still does not mean that the teller has sole storytelling rights. Ibu Umaya will be actively involved in the shaping of the story. While she cannot jointly *tell* the story, she will be shown to actively construct its accessibility.

Up to this point, this analysis of storytelling in Javanese conversation has focused on the presence or absence of an abstract. The abstract is here defined as the "topic posting," which may be done by anyone present, not just those personally involved in the story's events. Posting a topic introduces the interactive cues that manage a story's topic and the ways in which participants are able to interact with it. A story opened with an abstract signals that the story is not thoroughly accessible and, hence, allows the speaker more exclusivity in the telling. A story without an abstract tends to invite other tellers into the telling as a joint effort whose contents are mutually shared. Most stories among younger speakers in my corpus contain no abstracts, whereas elder speakers do tend to take control of the storytelling context more often.

Orientation

The Labovian orientation identifies the time, place, persons, and situations, pinpointing the story world (the tale) as discrete from the current storytelling experience. As this section illustrates, there are two distinct functions for orientation, distinguished by group position and age. The older speakers, who have a clear hierarchical privilege to control meaning in the interactions, will tell autobiographical stories that index this right. The segmented parts of their narratives are quite similar to the Labovian model in both structure and function.

Younger speakers, however, have an almost exclusive tendency to tell stories that index their community and their sameness through cotellings. Yet, where relative positions in the social hierarchy are affirmed, this hierarchy becomes the salient controlling force in negotiating topic selection and directionality. This is where the orientation segment functions as a guarantee of the group ratification of the topic direction.

As I have already stressed, a great many of the stories seem to be based on given or shared information. The orientation, then, is required for the participants and not for the story, making it a very different type of action than that described by Labov. Most often the orientation looks no different than topic postings, and a simple noun phrase acts as an introduction for a topic. Once posted, it will then either be taken up, that is, repeated by another member of the group, or ignored and subsequently dropped by its initiator. Within the orientation segments, however, posted topics may be altered, expanded, or changed to suit the conversational needs of the group.

In studies of *wayang* and literary texts, Alton Becker (1984, 1988) looked at utterance coherence in Javanese discourse and showed how these texts require a reattunement from the coherence features of English. Zeroing (not mentioning a topic after its initial mention) and repetition, as the unmentioned and the mentioned again, are strategies for building topic chains. Since the conversational data are almost entirely jointly constructed narratives, topic chaining to focus in on meaning creates coherence in the building of the text and simultaneously among those that built it. The strategy of repeating the words of others, both within the immediate context (i.e., allo-repetition; Tannen, 1989) and from outside (i.e., the repetition of the words of those who were not present), anchors the speaker's utterances to their source and strengthens the iconic nature of repitition and allo-repetition as joint-idea construction (Ishikawa, 1991). Thus, while Becker (1984:434) shows how through repetition "A certain term becomes a center around which other terms take subordinate positions," we expand this statement to include contextual interactions. Here repetition signals not only coherence in topics but also intimacy and sharedness among participants.

Another coherence-building strategy described in Becker (1988) is "zeroing," in which the subject remains unnamed and thus needs to be identified through context or memory. The unnamed in Javanese texts can also be presented as a highly textured movement of an actor who is followed through sets of shifting roles. The direction of the movement and the relational effect are created by the density of repetition. Meanwhile, actors, as knowns or givens, are never named, creating a link of relational sharedness between narrators.

Cohesion in Javanese can be managed by leaving things unsaid, as well as by topic-chaining repetition. The chaining of topics performs highly specific functions in the location of directionality and alignment, rarely signaled today through affixation, as it was in older literary genres. Repetition, then, proves essential in the location of social identity since it displays those with whom a speaker aligns herself at the moment of speaking.

The following excerpt shows how a group consensus is carefully achieved or oriented before the story can develop. This reveals how group-focused an event storytelling is by showing how an orientation segment is negotiated *before* the telling of a story, allowing the group to collectively shape the emergent story within the social specifications of *cårå Jawa*; that is, the hierarchical coordinates of the social context will shape the stories. The speakers are Atik, Sari, Yanti, and Laine. Yanti and Laine had been discussing problems in teaching. Yanti has her privileged position as eldest and from her equally high-ranked experiences as a junior high school (SMP) teacher; Laine, from her experiences teaching Indonesian university students. Atik, as an SMP administrator, is also experienced in dealing with a school environment. But Sari has no such experience. Our topic of conversation has shifted to TPI (Indonesian Educational Television), a daytime TV station meant to be educational. Just prior to this excerpt, we had discussed how TPI mainly offers bad Indonesian movies rather than educational programs. Yanti has told us that TPI's programs cause her students to play hooky.

As has been mentioned, repetition is the most frequent strategy of Javanese women to signal their like-mindedness—or the appearance of it. In story (5), we see how a "group" orientation opens into a story. Since these stories are most frequently made up of shared information, it is the group position with regard to the information that is most salient. The group orientation is constructed through a round of uttered affirmations of their like-mindedness, what I term a "mutual ratification sequence."

(5) *TPI*

234. ATIK: <u>Pelajarane mung sithik</u>   There's very little education in TPI
     nggih TPI nggih.   right.
235. YANTI: <u>Pelajarane mung sithik,</u>   There's very little education,
     wis <u>dibolan-baleni</u>   everything is repeated
     sing saiki wis metu, suk ditokke   what comes out now, tomorrow is
     meneh   brought out again
236. ATIK: Nggih cenan. <u>Dibolan-baleni</u>   That's certainly right. Everything is
                                             repeated
237. LAINE: <u>Pelajarane sithik</u>, akeh ki   There's very little education, plenty
     filem.   of movies.

These examples of allo-repetition across participants (including the non-Javanese author[6]) represent the recognition of an idea, the destructive influence of Indonesian television, as well as the stance taken up by all about that idea; that is, TPI does not do what its name implies. The use of allo-repetition is then functioning as a direct discursive picture of the group's unanimity. In other words, the use of allo-repetition is an iconic representation of the group's stance about the proposition.

While Sari does not contribute to the iconic stance, she does support the group's position:

238. SARI: Mbok dikritik-kritik   It's criticized to no end anyway
     entek-entekanne bar wae.   y'know.
     Akeh sing dho ra setuju.   Many don't approve.

Not only is it our group that objects to TPI but also, as Sari informs us, many others hold the same opinion.

Yanti directly links TPI to her teaching problems, stating that the programs lead to playing hooky. Atik had raised the topic of *pembolosan* (playing hooky) in turn 230 but was interrupted. Now it is reintroduced by Yanti as a play on Atik's previous utterance, where she questions the accuracy of the *P* in TPI to mean *Pendidikan* (education):

240. YANTI: **Niku** jane <u>pembolosan</u>   That's actually skipping class.
     ngoten.
241. SARI: Pengangguran.   Unemployment.
242. ATIK: <u>Marahi pembolosan</u>.   It causes [them to] skip class
243. YANTI: Yen cah sekolah, <u>marahi</u>   In school children, it causes them to
     <u>mbolosan</u> dik.   skip out of class *dik*.

What I call a "mutual ratification sequence" is frequently voiced before a story. Consensus is a significant factor in the orientation of a group's stance, as well as the direction the conversation will take. In turn 241, Sari's contribution does not maintain the group's consensus, and she is gently corrected through repetition, which again performs a significant role in the determination of a topic's direction. Unemployment is not a topic appropriate for this group, in which no one but Sari is threatened by it.[7] Sari is urged to conform. Once the orientation as consensus is reached, Yanti begins the event segment of her story about television and playing hooky.

The "other repair" described above is an example of what Sacks, Schegloff, and Jefferson refer to as the "locally-managed, party-administered, and interactionally controlled means" through which turn size and turn order are brought under the jurisdiction of recipient design. Recipient design is the "multitude of respects in which the talk by a party in a conversation is constructed or designed in ways which display an orientation and sensitivity to the particular other(s) who are the co-participants" (1974:727).

The Javanese mutual ratification sequence suggests that the turn's content should also be added. But it has yet to be determined if recipient design, as described above and in the narrative literature (e.g., Polanyi, 1989), is the same as behavioral conformity. As Wolfowitz (1991:20) observes, "The strong Javanese preference for patterned interaction extends to a preference for predictable conversation topics." Keeler notes a similar predilection for repetition: "The Javanese habit of telling each other what they already know . . . is an important part of making everyone feel that they are in comfortable accord" (cited in Wolfowitz, 1991:19–20).

Despite familial and long-term intimacy and regardless of the group's knowledge of Sari's different perspective, she is encouraged to conform to those with superior status.[8] She will be especially careful not to make a mistake like that again, and she selects a safe position from which she can take her stance as faithfully allied with the rest of her cohorts. This is the purpose of the orientation segment as a hallmark of the hierarchical role in the negotiation of meaning.

Upon completion of Yanti's story, following the orientation sequence (5), the posted topic for the conversation has slightly shifted to Indonesian film, but the group's conformity must be regularly validated. We each present our stance concerning Indonesian film:

(6) *Indonesian Cinema*

274. SARI: Aku kok <u>ora seneng</u> ta film Indonesia.	I just don't like Indonesian films.
275. LAINE: Kurang ajar ki	They're ignorant
276. ATIK: Aku ya <u>ora seneng</u>	I too don't like them
277. YANTI: <u>Ora seneng</u> ning <u>kulå mboten</u> tau nonton he	[I] don't like them but I never watch either
278. SARI: <u>Kulå mboten</u> teng <u>seneng</u>.	I don't like them

The storytelling frame begins with yet another mutual affirmation sequence. Once all the positions are clear, Sari, always the chattiest and hence often the one to "make mistakes," begins to present her story event. But initially, she must repair a discrepancy. Yanti, as the senior member of the group, is speaking in a higher *madyå* style than the others. Despite previously uttering, *ora seneng* in *ngoko* in turn 277, she still follows it with a more formal level. It is possible to distinguish the two levels as serving different indexical functions. The *ora seneng* may be her repetition of Atik's turn and, hence, signals Yanti's affirmation of the group position. The level shift also shifts the speaker's voice since it now represents her own actions as indexed through the pronoun *kulå* (I). Sari acknowledges and repairs the discrepancy by repeating her initial utterance (274) in *båså*:

278. SARI: **Kulå mboten** teng <u>seneng</u>.   I don't like them.

Atik, perhaps also feeling that she must display some kind of respect, interrupts her sister to signal solidarity specifically to Mbak Yanti through her vocative (Wolfowitz, 1991):

279. ATIK: Elek e Mbak Yanti.   They're bad aren't they Mbak Yanti?

Sari follows through with her utterance, only breaking enough to avoid overlapping. She goes on to clarify, however, that she does watch these awful movies. Her story explains her style of watching, in passing only, and the reason, to accompany her mother:

278. SARI: Kulå mboten teng seneng.   I don't like them.
      Mbok ontenå niku   Even though they're there
      ming sak klebatan ngoten.   but just in passing.
      Dadi kulå//   So I//

Sari's story is not important here. What is important, however, is how the women negotiate the orientation of a story and the ways in which the orientation and the consensus it achieves shape the emergent stories. Relative status has a role in determining who has the most right to influence the style of orienting stories, revealing the multiple levels of hierarchy and coherence that are indexed through everyday uses of nonformal Javanese discourse. While each group member agrees on her dislike for Indonesian movies, Yanti speaks in a *madyå* to our *ngoko*. The inconsistency is amended by Sari in turn 278, where she repeats her utterance but in a raised *madyå* for the benefit of the senior member of the group.

While Yanti does have the highest position in the relative hierarchy, and her perspectives do carry the most interactive weight, she does not monopolize the floor. Others speak in similarly long turns, as well as tell stories, but the topics and the perspectives all follow Yanti's lead as will be seen again later.

Returning to the *kraton* corpus, we find that the hierarchical participation framework is more apparent in the ways in which the elder, Ibu

Asmoro, is given her rights of speaking and monopolizing the turn taking. Her story—the continuation of outwitting the robbers in story (4)[9]—is clearly one of personal experience and thus is not intended to emphasize the community, as has been argued so far. Yet, Ibu Umaya has her rights as an active participant in the joint construction of the stories Ibu Asmoro tells.

(4) *Outwitting Robbers Continued*

→ 159. ASMORO: Kulå nikå saking kitå ageng	I was coming from the big city
Jalan Harjono	Harjono Street
Mas Darto menikå	That Mas Darto
dho lungo golek wong wedok.	and the others had all gone in search of women.
160. UMAYA: Eee . . .	Eee
→ 161. ASMORO: Lha kulå saking Tegal Gendu	So I was coming from Tegal Gendu
mantuk piyambak.	going home alone.
162. UMAYA: Wah!	Wah!
→ 163. ASMORO: Jam kalih dalu	At 2:00 o'clock at night
164. UMAYA: Tindak?	Walking?
165. ASMORO: Nggih.	That's right.
Ning kulå kraos wonten tiang jaler kalih niku	But I sensed these two men were there
Kulå lajeng cincing mlayu, arahipun tebih kalian (?)	So then I reluctantly started to run it was far from (?)
Lajeng kulå menggok nggen damel kijing nikå	Then I turned into the place where they make headstones
166. UMAYA: Wonten Pakel?	Is that at Pakel?
→ 167. ASMORO: Enggih menikå sawek jam tigå	That's right, at around 3:00 o'clock
168. UMAYA: Wow . . .	Wow . . .

This segment shows how detailed the orientation has become. It includes names and streets, and the time is given twice to clarify how long the solo journey home had taken. The details are specific enough to allow Ibu Umaya to recognize the precise location. In turn 166 she makes a request for more information, which confirms her own recognition of the orienting details of the story. When the speaker has the position and the right to tell an exclusive autobiographical story, the structural segments follow closely the Labovian model's expectations. Yet, when the younger speakers are conversing, orientation takes the form of a group that is orienting toward a known story. The two groups construct a very different genre.

The orientation segment of the Javanese story performs several different functions, depending on the type of story being told. In the first segment, the story's function is to index community. There is no abstract, and all participants perform equally in a manner that stresses the appearance of unity. The orientation creates that unity through mutual ratification sequences, which build a foundation from which the story's events directly emerge. This use of orientation emphasizes the importance of the community and its harmony, which is the main purpose for storytelling among this cohort.

The second sequence from the *kraton* corpus displays quite a different scenario. The older women's narratives follow the Labovian format much more closely. Story (4) does contain an abstract, which signals it as a personal event, and thus has a specific teller with a socially sanctioned position that enables her to tell the tale. The orientation section contains all the details necessary to support an autobiographical story, that is not available for extensive coconstruction.

Complicating Action

The complicating action is the body of a story, in which the temporally related clauses describe the events in order of occurrence. The series of events, which makes some point about the world and culminates in a result, implies temporal ordering, that is, beginnings, middles, and ends to some kind of bounded action worthy of retelling to others. Yet, temporal ordering is not a feature of Javanese stories. What this section shows is that different story genres have different relational purposes in the telling, and it is this purpose that shapes the type and interactive roles of the event segment of the stories. In all genres, however, event clauses are those that represent the local framework of acceptable behaviors, norms, and values.

The Javanese corpus has thus far suggested two types of narrative genres. One, told by elderly sanctioned speakers, stresses autobiographical genres and follows a Labovian format. The stories told by younger women, in contrast, emphasize not the story's details but the group's unity, the sameness of perspective. Harmony and community are created and maintained through the act of cotelling stories. Event clauses, then, are the clauses that describe the meaningful features of the story, which among these groups of women represent the most shared and accessible norms and values. What is meaningful may have more to do with the community than with the story. Since maintaining relationships is the most important purpose of storytelling, the most meaningful event clauses may be those that display the most ellipsis. As Becker (1988) has shown, unnamed subjects are common ways to create involvement in Javanese.

Stories can index what is shared between participants through ellipsis. For example, story (9) is a family narrative among Atik, Sari, Laine, and Pak Budi. We are discussing my birthday party, held the previous evening. I had invited a very upper-class Australian, Andrew, to the party because he spoke Indonesian well but had never met or mixed with *rakyat*, the working classes. After the party, Andrew and I dropped a friend at the train station, a common gathering place for homeless children, transvestites, thieves, beggars, and *becak* drivers.[10] The station had mounted a TV set outside for the *becak* drivers, and I stopped to greet the group and watch a Javanese comedy (*kethoprak*, or traditional Javanese theater) after someone from the group summoned me by name. Atik and Sari, who already know of my friendships among the poor and homeless of Yogya, are still amazed by these connections but find my taking the very formal Andrew there even more amazing. They begin telling this story to Pak Budi. What is significant here is the group style for negotiating the meaning of an act the participants find shocking. The shocking background information is never mentioned directly, and the story is reframed to reflect acceptable norms.

(7) *Stasiun Tugu*

78. SARI: Ha.a. njuk ora kåyå wong londo Ora nggo perhatian	Yup [you're] not so odd [compared to other foreigners] [you] don't get the attention
79. LAINE: Iya tenan.	Is that right.
→ 80. ATIK: Anu. ningali <u>ketoprak</u> wonten <u>Stasiun</u> Tugu! <u>Stasiun</u> nggih!	Uhm, [they] watched ketoprak at Station Tugu! At the station y'know!
81. PAK BUDI: Wow!	Wow!
→ 82. ATIK: Ngantos jam kalih welas! [hohahah]	Up till 12 o'clock! [hohahah]
→ 83. SARI: <u>Kalih tukang becak</u> barang! [hahah]	With the becak drivers and all! [hahaha]
→ 84. LAINE: Ngguyu-ngguyu <u>kaliyan tukang mbecak</u> [haha]	Joking around with the becak drivers [haha]
→ 85. SARI: Anu "wonten ingkang ngastå wonten Sadhar mriki"	So uhm, "There's someone who lectures at Sadhar here"[11]
86. PAK BUDI: Wow. darani båså Inggris?	Wow. so [they] thought [you could only speak] English?
→ 87. SARI: Mboten! njuk niki rak <u>onten ketoprak</u>. la nonton <u>kalih tukang mbecak</u>, <u>tukang becak</u> niku! [hahaha]	No! and so this [Laine] don't you know there's ketoprak. and so [she] watches with the becak drivers, with those becak drivers! [hahahah]
→ 88. ATIK: ha.a rak Mas Andrew naming ngono! [hahaha]	that's right and don't you know Mas Andrew was there too! [hahaha]

Story (7) clarifies what types of information and values are shared by the participants and what actions and attitudes are considered strange. There is no abstract that recapitulates what I had told to Atik and Sari earlier, that is, that after dropping off Mbak Ning, Andrew and I watched the *ketoprak* with the street people. Aside from having no abstract, the story has very little uttered orientation. It need not mention *who* had stayed at the station until midnight because it is a given that neither of the Budi children or their Javanese acquaintances would ever do such a thing. The story opens directly with an event clause in turn 80 that presents the action (*ningali*, "watch") and repeats the location twice (the station). This is not an orientation but an evaluation. Repetition stresses the *where* because it is accepted among these local people that the station is not a place for good people to linger. Sari joins in the cotelling of the story by adding who I had watched television with. In turns 83 and 87, Sari repeats three times the words *tukang becak* (*becak* drivers), which adds her emphatic evaluation of the scene. Between the sisters, repetition of the location and the company I kept there reveal what they consider to be the central focus of the tale. Nothing more needs to be said as perspectives regarding both are already shared information. These event clauses encode the social norms and values of this family.

The Javanese are exceedingly class conscious (Guinness, 1986; John Sullivan, 1992). While the Budi family is quite poor, they would be civil, considerate, and even generous if need be, but they would not associate with those of lower status. They are tolerant of my digressions, however, as I found in this story. In turn 85, Sari utters an important Javanese event clause through reported speech, which, as is common in Javanese storytelling, indexes no overt speaker or frame shift.[12] She reconstructs what she interprets to be the words uttered by one of the *becak* drivers. Despite the strangeness of my choice of friends and locations for watching television, Sari's constructed dialogue reveals the respect she feels for me. She has these poor and unrefined people using respectful language when they speak to or of me. Line 85 is uttered in *kråmå* with the *kråmå inggil* honorific *ngastå* (to work).

→ 85. SARI: Anu "**wonten ingkang**   So uhm "There's someone who
    NGASTÅ wonten Sadhar **mriki**"   lectures at Sadhar here"

This is how Sari imagines I was invited to join the group watching television. This formal style would signal the speaker's (i.e., the *becak* driver's) acquaintance with me, as well as signal to the others present that I am someone to be treated with respect.

The storytelling serves several essential functions. It displays in-group attitudes among the tellers to confirm and enhance their in-group comprehension of events as normalizing and the harmony this leads to. This story shows how the family unit extends itself to accept the strange behaviors of its new member. By constructing stories about my behavior in comparison to another foreigner, Andrew, they can see that I am not really so odd after all. By creating scenes in which I am treated with great respect, situations that are beyond their comprehension, such as my associating with street people at the station, can be made understandable as acts of charity. Projecting deference into their discourse elevates these impoverished, often homeless, unwashed laborers and beggars as truly *Javanese* and, hence, not so crude after all. Coconstructing stories is a means through which the world can be made more harmonious.

Story (7), then, demonstrates a genre that is intended to coconstruct meaning. What specifies the genre is located by comparing what remains unsaid in relation to what is said. The juxtaposition of the unsaid character of the station in relation to the only details that are emphasized (i.e., *becak* drivers) and the *kråmå inggil* word *ngastå*, presents the new interpretation. What remains unsaid is a strong indicator of shared values that ring eloquently for these speakers,[13] and what is said re-creates a situation of abnormality into one of acceptance.

Looking again at the *kraton* corpus, we see that the older women have a very different type of storytelling genre. Ibu Asmoro's age and position are conducive to a rather more self-focused story since her position among the palace performers is that of sanctioned elder. In story (8), Ibu Umaya has just entered the servants' waiting area, where she greets Ibu Asmoro and me. Seeing the white bandage on Ibu Asmoro's bare foot, she asks her about the injury. It is Ibu Asmoro's habit to take a long walk each morning before sunrise, before the traffic, heat, dust, and chaos of the city begin. During one of those early walks, she had tripped and badly scraped her toe. Ibu Asmoro begins her autobiographical frame with event clauses that describe her injury as a sequence of actions. But it is Ibu Umaya who orients the story for Ibu Asmoro to tell by asking questions.

(8) *The Injured Toe*

63. UMAYA: Sugeng?		Are you well?
→ 64. ASMORO: Nggih, menikå <u>teksih</u>, anu . . . nåpå . . .		Yes, this is <u>still</u>, uhm . . .
<u>sawek</u> nggletek		<u>now</u> it's drying
globatipun <u>wingi</u> kulå (?) ngaten		the oozing <u>yesterday</u> I (?) like that
65. UMAYA: Wow . . .		Wow . . .
→ 66. ASMORO: Wong nutup to <u>lajeng</u> lingkep,		It was bandaged <u>so now</u> it's opened,
<u>Lajeng</u> kulå ngatenken.		<u>So then</u> that's [how I treat] it.

Ibu's tiny, bare foot is sporting a large white bandage which she has taken into her hand[14] as she describes the way she treats it—before actually telling what occurred. Each event clause is given a temporal marker to specify its sequencing (turns 64 and 66): *teksih* is glossed as, "still"; *saweg* is glossed as "progressive"; *lajeng* is glossed as "then." These temporals are necessary since the clauses are not uttered sequentially: "*now* it's drying [but] *yesterday* it was oozing and *so then* I did this."

Perhaps symbolic of her position of authority, Ibu Asmoro enters into her stories by assuming that all her listeners have a basis of shared information and, if not a heartfelt interest, at least a shared rule of showing deference to elders and those of superior status. Perhaps also she has simply permitted Ibu Umaya space to take a role in her story. Since Ibu Umaya has no shared knowledge of the events of the injury, she asks questions:

67. UMAYA: Wow. <u>kengeng</u> menåpå nikå ?	What happened?
→ 68. ASMORO: Dawah. <u>kengeng</u> aspal, kenging wedhi.rak <u>kenging</u> aspal ha ha . . .	[I] fell. struck the asphalt, from the sand. then hit the asphalt haha
69. UMAYA: Njih . . . njih, . . .	yes yes, . . .
→ 70. ASMORO: <u>Dados</u> menikå ketekuk, <u>dados</u> balungipun nikå, ingkang <u>ketekuk</u> ketingal	So then, this bent, so then the bone, the part that bent was visible
71. UMAYA: Eee . . . ,	Eee,
→ 72. ASMORO: Rahipun ndledek mawon	The blood just flowed

Ibu Asmoro's story is told succinctly and very matter-of-factly, with a minimum of evaluation. Ibu is trying to present her case as a truly serious injury but one that she is in full control of. Yet, the story emerged as a result of direct questioning from an interlocutor. In this respect, Ibu Asmoro does not completely control the topic development but is encouraged and even guided by a sympathetic other, whose every question and comment is carefully addressed:

73. UMAYA: Ee . . . <u>pun</u> bektå dateng Rumah Sakit Bu?	You've been taken to the hospital bu?
→ 74. ASMORO: Pun. Menikå kulå suntikken kaping kalih lajeng mboten patos sakit	Yes. I've been injected twice so it doesn't hurt so much
75. UMAYA: Nggih, nggih,	Right, right,
→ 76. ASMORO: Wah . . . karang buyer kulå menikå, Mlampah-mlampah jam sekawan, lajeng mubeng Kauman ngilen, Plengkung ngidul, lajeng ngetan, La kog <u>mak</u> yer ngaten. langsung <u>mak</u> buk	I've made a right mess of things, Walking at 4:00 A.M. then around the Kauman (place) to the west, Plengkung (the gate) to the south, then east, Then y'know [I] got dizzy, like so. then [I] collapsed.
77. UMAYA: Eh . . . semaput nggih bu ?	So you fainted right bu?
→ 78. ASMORO: E . . . Allah . . . isih kurang ngrekså to awakku? Dibanting	Ya: allah: I still don't look after myself do I? Slammed down,

> la ngriki njih,   and so [it was] here, right,
> jengking, jengking,   flipping over-flipping over,
> La ngriki ketekuk.   And so [it was] bent here.

Since arriving at the *kraton*, Ibu Umaya has maintained active involvement in Ibu Asmoro's stories by punctuating each utterance with her minimal responses. These responses serve to ratify, encourage, show interest, and request information to clarify portions of the story.

Through frequent back-channel responses (Tannen, 1984:69), that is, minimal responses (Coates, 1989:105–107) like short questions and evaluative comments—such as *eee, he, inggih-inggih, wow*, and so on—other participants can signal active listenership, involvement, and interest in another's story. Coates found that women use two different types of minimal responses. Interaction-focused discussions elicited more frequent responses than did narratives, which she terms information-focused. But this is not the case in these Javanese narratives, which seem to be equally informational and interactional and in which silence during another's narrative results in its sudden ending.[15] At most, Ibu Umaya punctuates each second idea unit with a minimal response, to signal respect for the elder and interest in her story. Even though Ibu Asmoro holds the floor, this senior position is actively ratified by another, who has the power to stop, develop, or change a topic through these minimal responses and questions. Ibu Asmoro uses the floor to tell her stories, but Ibu Umaya's questions are all given responses that can sway the main speaker from her storyline. The fact that all the questions are responded to, even those that are not in line with the story's current direction, shows that interactional deference is being expressed by both participants. This shows how important minimal responses are in signaling deferential involvement and topic maintenance, thus confirming their significant position in the *joint* construction of the narrative. Ibu Umaya is actively comanaging the topics, which is not at all a stance of submission.

Ibu Umaya interrupts to introduce the new topic of an *abdi-dalem* who had also had a fall. I term this a story because of the way it fits into the topic already set by repeating the word *dawah*, or "fall." In addition, the story has a past-tense adverbial in its orientation and two event clauses.

(9) *Romo Mardhi's Fall*
82. ASMORO: Wah: malah keleresan,   Wah: actually, [I] just woke up//
     lajeng tangi ki//
→ 83. UMAYA: //Kålå mben Råmå Mardi   //Day before yesterday Romo Mardi
     nggih   y'know
     sampun mboten wonten nggih   is no longer y'know (he
                                          died)

     Dawah . . . kålå wingi//   [He] fell. yesterday//
84. ASMORO: //Ow . . . nggih   //Ow right
     anggenipun nyarekke . . .   the funeral was held

Ibu Umaya's active role in the story's construction, shown by her various types of minimal responses, her active requests for clarification and further information, and her ability to interrupt, suggests that there may be a broad difference between showing *deference* to her more senior interlocutor and *deferring* to her (cf. John Sullivan, 1992:72). Ibu Umaya uses no *kråmå inggil* or *andhap* terms in this segment, but she frequently refers to her interlocutor as *ibu* or *bu*, an index of honored respect. She receives the polite *kråmå* but none of the indexes of respect from Ibu Asmoro, although Ibu Asmoro does use *kråmå inggil* to describe the funeral. The two women, despite major differences in status (signaled by the asymmetrical use of titles and varying access to the floor), are actively co-managing the story events, which is not at all a stance of submission or formality.

The autobiographical genre demonstrates the ways in which all participants are actively involved in the continuation of the story and in the shaping of its event clauses. Ibu Asmoro is the elder, with the position and right to control the topic. But the story should also suggest the prevalence of relationality in the framing of the event and how maintaining the discursive flow is more important than finishing the story.

In the following text, the story genre I call hierarchical harmonizing is demonstrated. The story type features lower-ranking participants taking the high-ranking member's perspective. This style of managing events illustrates how hierarchy shapes the norms associated with event clauses and, hence, the social meaning and identity of the speakers.

Sari, Atik, and Yanti are discussing their tastes in a type of fruit called *blimbing wuluh*, a species of starfruit noted for being very sour. We have all gone to a village just south of Yogya for our regular Sunday picnics out of the city. Sari and Atik had gone to the market and bought food just before we left Yogya. On seeing the starfruit, Yanti reminisces about it.

(10) *The Starfruit Tales*

130. YANTI: Nggo njangan åpå jenenge,　　　[It's] used for vegetable, what's it called,

jangan bening.　　　clear vegetables.
Aku mbiyen mangani ngono kuwi　　　I used to eat it like that
blimbing wuluh saking senenge　　　That starfruit because of the typhus
typus. he.e,　　　craving. right,
Saben ndinå mangani blimbing　　　Every day [I'd] eat star fruit.
wuluh.

131. SARI: He.e kebangeten [haha]　　　Right too much [haha]
Aku biyen cilikan ku yo　　　When I was little
seneng blimbing wuluh kog yo　　　I also liked starfruit isn't that right
Mbak Atik, hahaha.　　　Mbak Atik, hahah

132. YANTI: Ning durung madang　　　Before [I'd] eat y'know [I'd have] that
kog yo kuwi.　　　first.

133. SARI: Nggih Mbak Yanti, <u>seneng banget</u> åpå meneh nek lårå.

That's right Mbak Yanti, [it's] really good especially when [you're] sick.

134. YANTI: Rasane ki enak ngono.

it tastes real good like that [when you're sick].

135. SARI: Wetengku ki kepengin <u>kecut-kecut</u>.
dadi <u>kulå</u> pethiki,
njuk <u>kulå</u> kumbah,
njuk <u>kulå</u> pangan,
<u>Sakniki mboten</u> doyan.
<u>linu</u>.

My stomach craved real sour.
so I'd pick [them],
then I'd wash [them],
then I'd eat ['em],
But now [I] don't like [them].
[they give me] cramps.

136. YANTI: <u>Linu</u> to ketoke.

Cramps right it's obvious.

137. SARI: <u>Linu</u> jane.
Ning <u>kulå</u> kog,
<u>seneng banget</u> ngono lho.

Cramps actually.
But as for me,
I like them a lot y'know.

138. YANTI: <u>Aku mbiyen</u> enak
dadi mbok dikapok-kapokke.

I used to like [them]
but [I've] learned my lesson.

139. ATIK: Saiki nyobå nganggo iki,

Why don't you try these,

140. YANTI: Moh!

No way!

141. ATIK: Ya <u>kecut</u> banget.

Yes they're very sour.

142. YANTI: <u>Biyen</u> jan kuat banget aku.
kåyå <u>mangan</u> anggur ngono.

Once, actually, I was real strong,
[I could even] eat grapes.

143. ATIK: Padahal maem barang
aku sok nganggo <u>blimbing wuluh</u>,
segå nikå lho Mbak Yanti,
Angger mboten onten lawuh,
diiris <u>cilik-cilik</u>, hahaha
<u>Sak niki mboten sak niki</u>.

In fact, when eating,
I occasionally eat <u>starfruit</u>,
with rice y'know Mbak Yanti,
Providing there is no side dish,
[I] slice [them] real thin, hahah.
But not any longer now.

144. SARI: *<u>Sakniki mboten</u>.*

Not any longer

Story (10) contains three separate stories of supposed personal experience involving starfruit. Yanti, as the senior member of the group, initiates the topic through her reminiscence. When she was a child and had typhus, she craved the sour fruit. Now, as an adult, she can no longer eat it. The event clauses for Yanti's story are in 130 and 132:

130. YANTI: <u>Aku mbiyen mangani</u>
ngono kuwi
<u>blimbing wuluh</u> saking senenge
typus. he,e,
saben ndino <u>mangani blimbing wuluh</u>.

I used to eat it like that

That starfruit, because of the typhus craving. right,
Every day [I'd] eat star fruit.

132. YANTI: Ning durung madang <u>kog yo</u> kuwi.

Before [I'd] eat y'know [I'd have] that first.

Yanti's story is very simple and implies no action even though it is oriented in a relationally past time (*aku mbiyen*, "I used to") and offers a completed idea in relation to the present time. What specifically marks it as a story is the fact that its event clauses are taken up by others as a story. Its relevance in the construction of group harmony for the other participants clarifies the act of negotiating positions in accordance with the higher-ranking Yanti. Sari immediately takes Yanti's perspective in what signals the informational crux of the emerging story round,[16] as well as the underlying repositioning of the power relations demand. Yanti has politely made known that the sight of starfruit now makes her sick. Sari catches this and displays her full agreement with Yanti in renegotiating a group stance toward starfruit:

131. SARI: He.e kebangeten [haha]	Right, too much! [haha]
Aku biyen cilikan ku yo	When I was little
seneng blimbing wuluh kog yo	[I] also liked starfruit, isn't that right
Mbak Atik, hahaha.	Mbak Atik, hahah

She, too, loved to eat starfruit, signaling a past-time frame and repeating exactly the same adverbial markers that Yanti used: *aku mbiyen* (I once). Sari also invites Atik into the conversation and seeks her affirmation of the statement. Sari's next utterance points back to Yanti's initial comment, having typhus and craving starfruit:

133. SARI: Nggih Mbak Yanti, seneng banget,	That's right Mbak Yanti, [it's] really good
åpå meneh nek lårå.	especially when [you're] sick.
134. YANTI: Rasane ki enak ngono.	It tastes real good like that [when you're sick].

Sari has achieved her full orientation toward Yanti, who confirms the coconstruction by affirming and repeating Sari's offering, in a sense completing the circle. As mentioned above, these circular "mutual affirmation sequences" achieve a local style of orientation as interalignment, an intersubjective sense making through negotiation and consensus but predesigned by hierarchical positioning. Yet, in the event segments described here, the mutual affirmation sequence continues the orientation segment into the event section. This manages narrative as an interactive event through which a socially shared norm is being currently negotiated. But stories are often considered to be informational (see Coates, 1988:105–107, and above). Sari is now free to offer her story about starfruit, which began with turn 131 and the repetition of Yanti's topic-marking terms:

131. SARI: He.e kebangeten [haha]	Right. too much [haha]
→ Aku biyen cilikan ku yo	When I was little
→ seneng blimbing wuluh kog yo	[I] also liked starfruit, isn't that right
Mbak Atik, hahaha.	Mbak Atik, hahah

→ 135. SARI: Wetengku ki kepengin   My stomach craved real sour.
        <u>kecut-kecut</u>.
        dadi <u>kulå</u> pethiki,   so I'd pick [them],
        <u>njuk kulå</u> kumbah,   then I'd wash [them],
        <u>njuk kulå</u> pangan,   then I'd eat ['em],
        <u>Sakniki mboten</u> doyan. <u>linu</u>.   But now [I] don't like [them]. [they
                                              give me] cramps.

Sari aligns herself discursively to Yanti by mirroring Yanti's past cravings for starfruit. This mutual ratification permits her to elaborate on these cravings. A harmony now exists between the two women, leaving Atik to tell her tale. Yet what is perhaps particularly Javanese about this conversation is that both Sari and Atik *do* like to eat starfruit. We have just come from the market, where they had, in fact, bought some for lunch. Why do the Budi women both go to such an extent to mirror the perspective of Yanti even though they both like the fruit?

Sari's low status in this group may play a role in her eagerness to please others. She quickly jumps in to repeat the topic markers in Yanti's clauses, which through her uptake gives those clauses event status. Her uptake additionally transforms Yanti's event clauses into a story round, which re-creates meaning for the Budi sisters in line with the higher-ranked member. Sari's frequent vocatives also suggest that she is very conscious of her lower status in this group. Atik, as closer in age and rank to Yanti, is more hesitant to conform. She initially attempts to persuade Yanti to eat starfruit. But when this fails, Atik also conforms to the group's position:

139. ATIK: Saiki nyobå nganggå iki,   Why don't you try these,
140. YANTI: Moh!   No way!
141. ATIK: Ya <u>kecut banget</u>.   Yes, they're very sour.
142. YANTI: <u>Biyen</u> jan kuat <u>banget</u> aku.   Once, actually, I was real strong,
        kåyå mangan anggur ngono.   [I could even] eat grapes.
143. ATIK: Padahal maem barang   In fact, when eating,
        aku sok nganggo <u>blimbing wuluh</u>,   I occasionally eat starfruit,
        segå nikå lho Mbak Yanti,   with rice y'know, Mbak Yanti.
        Angger mboten onten lawuh,   Providing there is no side dish,
        diiris <u>cilik-cilik</u>, hahaha   [I] slice [them] real thin, hahah.
        Sak <u>niki mboten sak niki</u>.   But not any longer now.

Atik cannot beat them (turn 139), so she joins the story round by constructing her view on eating starfruit. Her event clauses, like Sari's and Yanti's, describe the uneventful preparation and eating of starfruit. There is, in Atik's story, however, no adverbial opening in the tale to index a past era, as seen in the previous two. Yet, this does appear in the final idea unit in turn 143; Atik says, "But not any longer now," to which Sari allo-repeats in confirmation:

144. SARI: <u>Sakniki mboten</u>.   Not any longer.

These three women are negotiating a basic similarity of experience and taste in a trivial, uninteresting, extremely mundane detail. Action is not a part of the story events, but it is a significant part of the telling process. Events are based less on the speakers' experiences of reality than on their active sense of duty to the well-defined and highly constraining creation of group harmony, which has been noted elsewhere in Javanese studies (Keeler, 1984; Siegal, 1986; Wolfowitz, 1991). The similarities of detailed but insignificant experiences, the *sharedness*, is of primary importance to the speakers: "Java is . . . full of small talk, and polite conversation draws on a large store of stereotypical remarks. To use them is not thought stultifying, as some Westerners may find, but rather gracious, comfortable, indicative of the desire to make every encounter smooth and effortless for all concerned" (Keeler, 1984:xvii).

Event clauses in stories are those that represent the underlying norms and values of the group as they are being negotiated. As seen in stories (7), (8), (9), and (10), events can take a variety of forms, depending on the group function they are meant to serve. In the first situation, story (7), the events are constructed to negotiate a more acceptable position vis-à-vis a well-defined and shared meaning, that is, the family position on my association with members of the lower classes. This family genre displays the salience of unmentioned information in event clauses, which strongly indicates what is shared and what is shocking, both remaining unmentioned among the group. In story (8), in which an old woman is telling an autobiographical tale, we see how the participants are actively involved in its shaping through questions, comments, and other minimal responses. Thus, despite clear hierarchical differences among the participants, all of these minimal responses have the ability to shape the events according to group terms. The lower-status participant was even able to tell her own story (9) as a natural response to the previous story's events. The last situation, story (10), shows how three young women actively construct harmony by conforming to the position taken by their higher-status interlocutor, re-creating events in alliance with her. The differences between the negotiation of meaning based on event clauses in situations (7) and (10) is that in the Stasiun Tugu story, the change transcends the situational boundaries, whereas in the Starfruit Tales, the new events will change again when the situated relational hierarchy changes, that is, when Yanti goes home.

In all of the story types, the events are jointly produced, and the action of negotiating relative in-group positions, perspectives, and ultimate harmony is the purpose of the interaction. Events are not based on truth but on mood, and they represent the coconstructed values of the immediate context.

Evaluation

The evaluation elements of the story are those that mark its significance and thus are the basic, essential features of storytelling. Evaluation is defined as that part of the narrative that reveals the speaker's attitude or purpose in telling the story by emphasizing the relative importance of certain events. It stresses the importance of some events over others by language modification of or deviation from the typical clause sequence.

In Javanese, evaluation also serves to index various levels of relational information about the story in relationship to speakers and those spoken about. In this respect, evaluation plays a significant part in the deciphering of participation frameworks, both internal and external to the story. Inward evaluation focuses on the story and takes the forms of repetition, adjectives, reduplication, intensification, and reported speech; outward evaluation indexes the social context and takes the forms of allo-repetition, vocatives, and maintenance of the storyline.

Consistent with what we have seen thus far of Javanese stories, evaluation is likely to be anything that ties one speaker's utterances to another's. For example, since repetition is a main device for indexing topic and alignment, it is also a major type of evaluation. Repetition signals the willingness to interact and to support, communicating a great deal of information about the relationship being constructed (Bateson, 1972; Gumperz, 1982; Tannen, 1989).

Looking back at story (10) for evaluation, Sari and Yanti display adjectives and intensifiers in support of the emerging group position on starfruit:

133. SARI: Nggih Mbak Yanti, <u>seneng</u>   That's right, Mbak Yanti. [it's] really
     <u>banget</u>,   good,
     <u>åpå meneh</u> nek lårå.   especially when [you're] sick.

Sari repeats the adjective *seneng* plus the intensifier *banget* (really good) and the intensifying adverbial phrase *åpå meneh* (especially) to emphasize her view of the fruit. Her second phrase, *åpå meneh*, not only intensifies her pleasure as particularly high when she is ill but also doubly ties her cravings to those claimed by Yanti. This example of evaluation in Javanese serves a double indexing purpose: it points to an element of the story, and it points to an element of the context.

Yanti takes up Sari's position by confirming her affirmation. Thus a mutual affirmation sequence serves to construct the foundation needed for harmonious storytelling. Yanti's utterance is a repetition of her earlier stance, and as such, it not only evaluates her craving for the sourness of starfruit when she had typhus but also signals her like-mindedness with Sari. It is, then, an evaluation of their relationship:

134. YANTI: rasane ki enak <u>ngono</u>.   It tastes real good like that [when
                                                  you're sick].

Yanti uses *ngono*, an anaphoric demonstrative that means "like that," to link her utterance to Sari's. Their harmony is now fully ratified, allowing Atik to show her position.

Sari's evaluation appears in the form of the reduplication of *kecut* ("sour") as *kecut-kecut* (the general quality of sourness) and the repetition of her actions as an agent through rhythmic activity, all of which intensify the action (Labov, 1972, 1984; Tannen, 1989):

→ 135. SARI: Wetengku ki kepengin | My stomach craved real sour.
kecut-kecut. |
dadi <u>kulå</u> pethiki, | so I'd pick [them],
njuk <u>kulå</u> kumbah, | then I'd wash [them],
njuk <u>kulå</u> pangan, | then I'd eat ['em],
Sakniki mboten doyan. linu. | But now [I] don't like [them]. [they give me] cramps.

Atik's evaluation is in the reduplication, which intensifies the act of slicing the fruit (*cilik-cilik*, "very small"), while it doubly links her utterance with Sari's reduplicated *kecut-kecut*:

143. ATIK: Padahal maem barang | In fact, when eating,
aku sok nganggo <u>blimbing wuluh,</u> | I occasionally eat starfruit,
sego nikå lho Mbak Yanti, | with rice y'know, Mbak Yanti.
Angger mboten onten lawuh, | Providing there is no side dish,
diiris <u>cilik-cilik</u>, hahaha [.] | [I] slice [them] real thin, hahah.
Sak niki mboten sak niki. | But not any longer now.

Atik's story also demonstrates evaluation by maintaining the theme of starfruit within a short story, illustrating how she and Sari both need to index their respect and conformity to Yanti. Evaluation is implicit in the coercion to conform as speakers evaluate their position in relation to others. In this case, both Sari's and Atik's stories explicitly follow the temporal framework they have repeated from Yanti. Thus, evaluation as an index of an inner story point serves what purpose? As Bruner (1987) suggests, these stories reflect cultural theories about life and what it all means, making them as "real" as life itself . Whether or not the propositions are truthful is irrelevant. The fact that the stories emerged signals the speakers' alignment to Yanti. It is their relationship that is evaluated, and *that* is the point of the story.

Further evidenced by Atik's, Sari's, and Ibu Umaya's frequent vocatives, which are directed toward the high-status member, story clauses are often punctuated in ways that break out of the story frame. These vocatives reveal a fragmented directionality, threatening internal evaluation and the heightened involvement that it is said to create (Labov, 1972; Tannen, 1989). In the following example, Sari is beginning her story, but she requests her elder sister's ratification first:

131. SARI: He.e kebangeten [haha] | Right, too much! [haha]
Aku biyen cilikan ku yo | When I was little,
seneng blimbing wuluh <u>kog yo</u> | I also liked starfruit, isn't that right
<u>Mbak Atik</u>, hahaha. | Mbak Atik? hahah

As the segment suggests, Javanese evaluation may be focused both inward toward the story and outward toward the significant contextual relationships that require attending to. In the case of starfruit, we have reason to believe that Atik and Sari shape their stories to create harmony with Yanti, who they perceive as requiring respect.

The following sequence occurred between Yanti and Atik while they were discussing the recent and very serious problems of a mutual friend, Mbak Surti, who has already appeared as one of the tellers of story (2). Mbak Sur is Atik's workmate in the office of the same junior high school (SMP) where Yanti teaches. Surti visits the Budi home regularly, dropping Atik off from work, and thus is well known by all the family members and guests. Sur's father is extremely ill, which has caused serious problems for Sur also. The stories, in response to Yanti's request, describe Pak Surti's past and present health problems.

(11) *Pak Surti's Illness*

50. ATIK: Riyin niku mpun tau nåpå.	In the past the problem was what.
nggon saluran kencing niku onten batune,	in the urinary tract there was a stone,
nate operasi nek mbiyen.	it had been operated on.
Ning saiki, malah ginjele sing kenå.	But now, it's the kidney that's affected.
51. YANTI: Lårå.	Painful
52. ATIK: Låråne	It's painful
Mung sakniki nganu kok Mbak Yanti.	But now, [what can I say] Mbak Yanti.
mlakune mboten iså dadi anu	[he] can't even walk any more
nåpå ngewel gemeter ngaten lho.	[he] trembles and shakes so.
Mboten kuwat ngangkat awak.	[He's] not even strong enough to lift his body.

Atik's explanation of Pak Surti's problems is extremely terse. Turn 50 succinctly states that the past problem (*riyin* and *mbiyen* mark past time, as does *nate,* glossed as "once") was in his bladder while the current problem (*saiki* means "now") lies in his kidneys. It is exactly the detail Yanti had requested. In a story genre structured by "other" interaction, it makes sense that neither abstract nor orientation would be part of the story frame.[17] This also shows that the linear nature of the story is a meaningful part of its structure.

But in turn 51, Yanti offers a sympathetic "painful," which Atik takes up and allo-repeats. She then follows Yanti's affective stance to present her evaluative description of the sad state of the man's health. The evaluation clauses do not present Atik's personal involvement but her attempts at drawing out Yanti's sympathy. Atik does not reify her own emotions, but she signals a frame shift to the present, *mung sakniki* (but now), followed by a discourse marker of avoidance, *nganu, anune,* or *anu,* very frequently used in Javanese to index an unmentionable or a forgotten of whatever type.[18] Atik's emotional state is then indexed by her *nganu kok*, where the *kok* actually serves to emphasize that which she cannot put into words:

52. ATIK: Låråne.	Its painful.
Mung sakniki <u>nganu kok</u> Mbak Yanti	But now [what can I say] Mbak Yanti

But by punctuating the utterance with the vocative *Mbak Yanti,* the speaker is redirecting focus from herself and her unmentioned feelings to her interlocutor as a way of forcing Yanti's emotional involvement in the story.

After this description of Pak Surti's current physical state, Yanti requests that Atik present her synopsis of the ailments:

53. YANTI: Lha inggih soale?	So then y'know the problem is?
54. ATIK: Soale nggih pripun.	The problem is what.
tenagane mboten onten.	his energy is gone.

Yanti has specifically requested information that only Atik has access to. Yanti fully ratifies and even directs Atik's meaningful event turns, as well as triggers her evaluational stance. The lost energy topic immediately leads to the topic of how Surti's vigil beside her father is affecting her own health. Atik alone shifts back to Surti's condition in her story, returning to her main concern, her friend Surti.

(11') *Pak Surti's Illness and Mbak Surti*

54. ATIK: Mbak Sur tambah kuru nikå lho.	Mbak Surti has gotten much thinner y'know.
Kok <u>gumunku</u>	I'm real shocked
"lho kok mung kowe tho sing mikir?"	"How is it that it's only you who thinks [about your father]?!"
<u>Gumun kulå</u> kalih wong siji nikå.	I'm shocked at that person.
Wong atase nduwe kangmas	[She] has an older brother
nduwe Mbakyu nggih kathah.	[she] has elder sisters y'know plenty.

Atik's story here shows her personal involvement and concern for Surti's predicament through markers of expressive sympathy based on positive support. While her position is indexed to herself—"*I* am shocked"[19]—to the point of repeating the sensation, she is maintaining a distance by omitting a great deal of highly personal information that would strengthen her sympathetic stance. This excerpt is discussed more fully in terms of gender roles in chapter 7. For now, it is sufficient to state that Atik perceives the need to present a nongossipy and untroubled self to Yanti.

Atik's personal, self-indexing stance, what she wishes to portray as her own words to her friend, occurs only with respect to Surti. With respect

to Pak Surti, Atik's evaluation is demonstrated through adjectives, intensifiers, and a nonpersonal sympathy, indexing a broad difference in the
ways in which she responds to the two individuals, as well as her own
position in relation to each situation. Atik directly communicates with Sur
on a daily basis at work, conversation obviously being the key channel.
Her story displays the position Atik feels herself to have the right and
obligation to take: *Kok gumunku* "*Iho kok mung kowe to sing mikir?*" (I'm
real shocked. "How is it that it's only you who thinks [about your father]?!")
The utterance reveals to Yanti the directness, intimacy, and concern that
Atik has shown to Surti in the face of her problem.

Yet, Atik is powerless to help the sick man, with whom her relationship must be one of distant deference. She evaluates his situation to mirror her position of external powerlessness:

52. ATIK: Mung sakniki nganu kok   But now, [what can I say] Mbak
    Mbak Yanti.   Yanti.
    mlakune mboten isa dadi anu.   [he] can't even walk any more.
    nåpå ngewel gemeter ngaten lho.   [he] trembles and shakes so.
    Mboten kuwat ngangkat awak   [He's] not even strong enough to lift
                                          his body

Evaluation here is formed by restating each facet of illness. "[He] can't walk"
and "[he's] not strong enough to lift his body" are repetitive in that the latter entails the former while it is also an enhancement of the former. Both
clauses are framed as negatives, which achieve a heightened expectation
of mobility and strength as a norm and thus intensify their loss (Tannen,
1989). "Trembles" and "shakes" are difficult translations; *ngewel* indicates
shaking through to the feet, and *gemeter* indicates a more localized shaking. Together they strengthen the picture of illness and helplessness. The
varying ways in which Atik frames her evaluation reflect a difference in
positioning with regard to who she is speaking about and, hence, locates
that relative position within the underlying framework of participation.

In sum, this section has illustrated the various levels of relational information indexed through evaluation. Not only does evaluation achieve
involvement and recognition of the story's purpose, but also it doubly
serves to index relationships between speakers and those spoken about.
Evaluation plays a very significant part in the deciphering of participation frameworks, both internal and external to the story. Inward evaluation
as used above takes the form of repetition, adjectives, reduplication, intensification, and reported speech; outward evaluation can include allo-
repetition, vocatives, and maintenance of the storyline.

Coda

The Labovian coda signals the end of a story by resolving its action statements and bringing it back to the present time. With not much action to

resolve here, we see how the conclusion of a story is often marked by a deictic shift from distal to proximal, where *this* is what happened moves back to *that* was it. In Javanese stories, the coda has a similar function to the Labovian description, when there is one. Stories are rarely completed since their functions are usually so different.

In story (10), the coda is clearly marked, and each speaker firmly ties a liking of starfruit to a long-past era but not to the present:

135. SARI: <u>Sakniki mboten</u> doyan.   But now [I] don't like [them].
     linu.   [they give me] cramps.

Yanti also carries the past up to the present in turn 138, where she states how she *used to* like what she can no longer eat today:

138. YANTI: Aku mbiyen enak dadi   I used to like [them] but [I've] learned
       mbok dikapok-kapokke   my lesson

Atik also closes her story by carrying action up to the present:

143. ATIK: <u>Sakniki mboten sakniki.</u>   But not any longer now.

The only time referent in Atik's story is the concluding utterance, "But not any longer," to which Sari adds her repetitive confirmation, strengthening the importance of the link to the "now":

144. SARI: <u>Sakniki mboten.</u> [.]   Not any longer.

Yet, while the starfruit story round had a coda, the other stories we have seen thus far do not. Ibu Asmoro's robber tale was interrupted, as stories of individual experience often are. If time is not the structuring factor in the story, it is not likely to require such temporal closure. Because of the interactive, rather than informational, nature of the stories, speakers often have no place in the telling sequence for endings.

Conclusion

This chapter has used the segmenting facets of the Labovian model to investigate how this text-based structuring framework can be directly related to the hierarchically based structuring framework that shapes Javanese narrative contexts. Working from a known, surface-structure orientation for narratives, the chapter describes how such micro-level features are shaped by the macro-structure orientation of the participants. While the conversational narrative as a bounded speech event is always interactive, the differences here lie in cultural variations regarding the individual in society. As found in Hill and Zepeda (1993), analysis of this corpus of narratives leads to a conception of individuality as something other than the locus of egocentric responsibility and agency.

Thus far, I have demonstrated that narratives are produced interactively and jointly and that discursive choices reflect where one stands in a continuum of personal to impersonal reference through multivocalic, sociocentric story worlds. The stories all illustrate degrees of joint production of topic and the ways in which it is kept mutually relevant to all present. Accessibility to all participants is a key factor in joint production and in the strategies by which speakers signal their situated sharedness— or request information through which such sharedness can be achieved. These strategies reveal a great deal about local perceptions of meaning at both the immediate, situated level and at the broader, cultural level.

The next chapter will define the essential structuring elements of informal Javanese oral narratives. These structural elements are indexicals of both a story frame and the outer interactional frames that reflect the contextual coordinates of speakers' relative roles, rights, and obligations. Understanding what these structural elements mean within their natural contexts will help us interpret the storytelling context, the stories, and the participants as they are all perceived by the tellers themselves.

•••four

Locating Javanese Oral Narratives

In the previous chapter I compared the Labovian *structural* paradigm to the Javanese *social* structure of relative rights and obligations as a foundation from which to illustrate the constraints the social order imposed on story design. This chapter advances the social focus by defining the structural features particular to Javanese narrative and showing how and where they appear in actual stories. The following stories are examples of what I suggest are four Javanese indexes of a narrative: (1) past-time adverbials, (2) reported speech, (3) shifting speech levels, and (4) text boundary indexicals.

These features are significant in our exploration of language and identity because they all seem to contain doubly indexical properties. That is, they index both the existence of a story in a stream of conversation and the position of the speaker in a social order of rights and obligations. The analytical significance of double indexicality is its natural tendency to index the position of a speaker in relation to her text, her context of others, and the macro-level contexts of community and culture. Thus, through these doubly indexical terms we should be able to see exactly how firmly these women tie their own sense of self to the social contexts they are currently a part of.

The story that illustrates the role of these four indexes emerged among three speakers who are all *abdi-dalem* in the section of the palace called *Kridå Mardåwå* as *wiyågå* (predominantly male musicians in the *gamelan*) or as *pesindhen* (female singers). This is the same division of the palace that I became a member of through Ibu Asmoro, the senior member and overseer (*pengirit*) of the group of women singers. Ibu Asmoro has taken me to the home of Romo Riyo[1] for my singing lesson. Bu Harto, whom we also know from the *kraton*, is another *pesindhen*. She lives close by and has dropped in, knowing my lesson was to take place. Within the social hierarchy of rights and obligations, it is important to know that Ibu Asmoro is 78 years old, Romo Riyo is 70, and Ibu Harto is about 65. Ibu

Asmoro and Romo Riyo seem to compete regularly for the floor, with gender and social position perhaps giving Romo an edge over Ibu. Ibu Harto, however, is clearly of a much lower position and her deference to the others is obvious.

Romo's home is very modest (e.g., there is no indoor plumbing), but it is not a poor home. Even though there is some furniture, we are all sitting cross-legged on a woven bamboo mat on the floor, the position of Javanese musicians and singers (*silå*). To Romo's left is his *gender*, an instrument from the *gamelan*, with which he helps me find the right notes. We have all been offered glasses of sweet, warm tea.

The stories in (14) illustrate how speakers both construct and reflect their self-other-community relationship as they doubly index their stories.

(12) *Ibu Asmoro and the Prince*

→ 461.	ASMORO: Aku wis ora sinden kok.	I don't sing any more y'know.
462.	HARTO: Ning **mboten wonten**	But when you aren't there
	IBU nikå	
	sami gelå lo Bu.	everyone is so disappointed mum.
	NUWUN SEWU menikå	please excuse me
→ 463.	ASMORO: Ning wong **GUSTI**	But it was the prince
	menikå	
	mboten PARENG kulå,	who won't allow me [to sing],
464.	HARTO: Ning **IBU njih** . . .	But yes ma'am.
465.	ROMO: Ha **enggih** . . .	That's right.
466.	ASMORO: Wong dieman kok **nggih?**	[He] takes pity [on me] isn't that right?
467.	ROMO: Ha **inggih**,	That's right
	rak **namung** ngemong **ngaten** . . .	just for training and such,
	mawon,	
→ 468.	ASMORO: **Njih pokokipun**	Right the point is
	"**namung PIRSÅ lare-lare**	"just watch over the children
	ingkang mboten keleresan	[those] who are not correct are to be
	pun NGENDIKANI."	told."
470.	HARTO: La **injih**, **milå IBU**	That's right, that's why mum
	namung NDALEM PUNTEN	I graciously beg your forgiveness
	SEWU menikå	
	IBU menikå ajeng nglatih	mother when we are rehearsing
	DALEM SEWU DAWUHi	I sincerely beg for the honor of your
	sambut ngleres IBU esti,	corrections mother,
→ 472.	ASMORO: Ha **enggih**, **kålå** minggu	That's right, that last week,
	menikå,	
	kulå mboten SOWAN,	I didn't visit [the palace],
	njuk digrundak **nikå**.	then [everyone] was angry [with me].
473.	HARTO: **Injih injih la injih** . . ,	right right that's right . . . ,

→ 474. ASMORO: "Bu kok **mboten**   "Mum why didn't you come [to the
      SOWAN to?"   palace]?"
      "Ha kesel" he.   "Oh [I was] tired" he.

Ibu Asmoro opens the topic by reminding me, as she has already told me on a number of occasions, that she no longer sings in the *kraton*. What I discuss here is how the structuring of this story creates its potency as a story, and how this is verified interactively.

This is a story Ibu Asmoro tells over and over again in all the speech situations I have either recorded or witnessed. The story frame is opened with 461, "I don't sing anymore, y'know," which marks a relational rather than specific past time. For a woman to have lost her exquisite singing voice is grounds for shame among most of the singers, where competition, back-stabbing, and even black magic are fierce. For Ibu Asmoro, however, the result is quite the contrary. These stories are told with great pride because they create and enforce her power over those that hear it. But first, the story must be recognized as a story and extracted from its embedded interaction.

The main complications in recognizing utterances as a story are that stories rarely emerge in an extended turn with no interruption or turns from other participants; no abstract, that is, no specific discursive marker, signals that a story is to come; time references are not specific; and actors are rarely named. In turn 461, for example, Ibu Asmoro posts her topic, not singing anymore:

→ 461. ASMORO: Aku wis ora sinden kok.   I don't sing any more y'know.

Ibu Harto immediately comes forth with an offer of praise for the older and higher-ranking Ibu Asmoro:

462. HARTO: Ning **mboten wonten**   But when you aren't there,
      IBU nikå
      sami gelå lo Bu.   everyone is so disappointed mum.
      NUWUN SEWU menikå.   please excuse me

After complimenting Ibu on how well liked she is by the other singers, Ibu Harto humbles herself by begging forgiveness. This indexes her acknowledgment of their relative status; lower-ranked participants must humble themselves to their betters.

Ibu Asmoro continues her topic by introducing the other character, Prince Yudhoningrat, who is the director of Kridå Mardåwå:[2]

→ 463. ASMORO: Ning wong **GUSTI**   But it was the prince
      menikå
      mboten PARENG kulå,   who won't allow me [to sing],

Ibu does not bother to tell her listeners what *Gusti* (lord) it was, nor does she give the details in this telling. Everyone already knows. Maintaining her topic hints at the emergence of a story, enhanced by the relational indexes, which add a great deal of evaluative information that expands indexical meaning well beyond the limitations of the brief clause. Introducing the prince as the actor who caused the speaker to stop singing becomes the story's event clause because of the evaluative indexes of relative status and the extreme pride inherent in gaining the prince's attention to a humble servant. The words *Gusti* ("lord," "the Almighty," or "an aristocrat") and the very polite *pareng* (permit) both index the source of the command, in this case the prince, as someone relationally much higher in status and as someone Ibu Asmoro has great deference for. In addition, Ibu Asmoro knows that her listeners also have a deferential awe for the royal family.

Further signaling a story is the uptake the turn receives from others. Both Ibu Harto and Romo Riyo affirm listenership and respect by showing their agreement:

464. HARTO: Ning **IBU njih** . . .   But yes ma'am.
465. ROMO: Ha **enggih** . . .   That's right.

Ibu Asmoro, then, externally evaluates her potentially devastating predicament with the prince, that is, his command to stop singing, with her very positive interpretation. He has not insulted her by robbing her of her great pride, her singing, but rather he has shown his concern for her well-being. She actively requests confirmation of this interpretation through the final-position tag question:

466. ASMORO: Wong dieman kok   [He] takes pity [on me] isn't that
       nggih?   right?

The prince rarely converses with the singers, so Ibu interprets his command as interest in her and especially respect for her age and vast experience, she being 45 years his senior. She wants the others to be envious of her "intimacy" with the prince. Romo takes up her request and confirms this interpretation:

467. ROMO: Ha **inggih**   That's right,
       rak **namung** ngemong **ngaten**   just for training and such,
       . . . **mawon,**

Ibu's knowledge and expertise are still proclaimed and appreciated as she is designated the one to maintain standards of presentation and performance within the ancient and highly ritualistic environs of the *kraton*. Not many take the traditions this seriously any more, but Ibu certainly does. Not only has she devoted a lifetime to the courtly rituals, but she was also one of the most famous and loved of the court singers (in her own stories). It is the prince who confirms this when she quotes his royal command:

→ 468. ASMORO: **Njih pokokipun**   Right the point is
         "**namung PIRSÅ lare-lare**   "just watch over the children
         ingkang mboten keleresan   [those] who are not correct are to be
         pun NGENDIKANI."   told."

While the prince is taking away her permission to sing, he replaces her pride by giving her power over all the other singers. The repetition of the royal quotation is the cue that Ibu's utterances are indeed a story because of the vast amount of shared knowledge they immediately evoke. Ibu frequently repeats this royal quote because it proclaims her to be the one who knows best, entrusted with maintaining the quality of 50 other singers' performance and appearance.

Structurally, turn 468 exhibits an essential, particularly Javanese, storytelling strategy. While there are no markers of reported speech—no "he said," no "and so the prince said," this is unmistakably a quotation of another's discourse because of the speech levels used. The words *pirså* (watch), and *ngendikani* (to be told), are *kråmå inggil* terms and never used in reference to oneself. In this very brief story, then, Ibu is also informing us that the prince himself speaks to her with highly respectful, honorific language. This one turn, whether or not a faithful rendition of the prince's actual words, will certainly preserve and even strengthen Ibu's dignity within the palace gossip circles. This is indeed a very powerful utterance, and the story, fully supported by the prince's words, appears frequently in Ibu's repertoire, as it must.

Ibu Harto affirms her position in reference to Ibu Asmoro's honored status by begging for the latter's critical recognition. Perhaps it was because of the previous turn, but Ibu Harto now uses the other-exalting, self-humbling style of courtly speech. This is explicit proof of the powerful effect of Ibu Asmoro's previous turn:

470. HARTO: La **injih**, **milå IBU**   That's right, that's why mum
         namung
         NDLEM PUNTEN SEWU menikå   I graciously beg your forgiveness
         IBU menikå ajeng nglatih   mother when we are rehearsing
         DALEM SEWN DAWUHi sambut   I sincerely beg for the honor of your
         ngleres IBU esti,   corrections mother,

Ndalem is *kråmå andhap* for the first-person pronoun, glossed as the English "your humble servant," and *ndalem punten sewu* is strictly court discourse. Ibu Harto is displaying extreme deference and respect here. Ibu Asmoro enjoys the prestige she is awarded and she is also venerable enough to say so by relating another brief story about how much she is missed if she does not make an appearance at the palace:

→ 472. ASMORO: **Ha enggih kålå** minggu   That's right that last week,
         menikå,
         kulå mboten SOWAN   I didn't visit [the palace],
         njuk digrundak **nikå**.   then [everyone] was angry [with me].
   473. HARTO: **Injih injih** la **injih** .., Right, right, that's right,
→ 474. ASMORO: "Bu kok **mboten**   "Mum why didn't you come [to the
         SOWAN to?"   palace]?"
         "Ha kesel" he.   "Oh, [I was] tired" he.

While turn 472 contains a past adverbial (*kålå minggu*) to signal the
potential storytelling frame, its style of telling in conjunction to the progression of topics affirms a general state of affairs.[3] "Last week" might
just as easily be substituted by a hypothetical "if I were to not *sowan.*"
The adverbial marks this utterance, however, as part of a story, as confirmed by Ibu Asmoro's next turn, 474, the reported speech and all the
shared information it evokes:

→ 474. ASMORO: "Bu kok **mboten**   "Mum why didn't you come [to the
         SOWAN to?"   palace]?"
         "Ha kesel" he.   "Oh [I was] tired" he.

Without reported speech indexes, listeners must rely on shared knowledge of situations and personal stance in these topics to follow the storyline.
Participants all know that it has been her routine for 64 years to come to
the palace each Sunday, Monday, and Wednesday, plus special performances. If she does not appear, the *abdi-dalem* will most certainly in-
quire. When she does appear again, her absence will be a major topic of
discussion, as Ibu herself illustrates in turn 474. Ibu takes on both roles,
as those who ask and as herself in response. No signal of speaker shift is
uttered beyond speech style. Others *mbåså* to her; she uses *ngoko* in return.
    What needs to be noted here is that, just as in the *bekakak* story (1)
and the starfruit story (10), Ibu Asmoro's two stories are not complete,
discrete, one-speaker units. They are part of a continuing progression of
utterances that are affirmed, amended, and anticipated by other participants. None of the texts displays a solitary speaker who is telling a story.
Instead, they show how others are welcome, expected, and invited, participants in the telling process.
    Ibu Asmoro's two stories display the features that I claim are impor-
tant in the structuring of Javanese stories because they all perform indexical
functions that link the story to aspects of sociocentric relevance in the
self-other to the I/we-community relationship. The features of Javanese
narrative are past-time adverbials:

   461. ASMORO: Aku <u>wis</u> ora sinden kok.   I don't sing any more y'know.
   472. ASMORO: Ha enggih <u>kålå minggu</u>   That's right. that last week,
         menikå,

reported speech:

468. ASMORO: Njih pokokipun   Right, the point is
     "namung pirså lare-lare   "just watch over the children
     ingkang mboten keleresan pun   [those] who are not correct are to be
     ngendikani"   told."
474. ASMORO: "Bu kok mboten   "Mum why didn't you come [to the
     sowan to?"   palace]?"
     "Ha kesel" he.   "Oh [I was] tired" he.

shifting speech levels:

468. ASMORO: njih pokokipun   Right, the point is
     "namung pirså lare-lare   "just watch over the children
     ingkang mboten keleresan pun   [those] who are not correct are to be
     ngendikani"   told."
474. ASMORO: "Bu kok mboten   "Mum why didn't you come [to the
     sowan to?"   palace]?"
     "Ha kesel" he.   "Oh [I was] tired" he.

and text boundary indexicals:

470. HARTO: Ndalem punten sewu   I graciously beg your forgiveness,
     menikå
     Ibu menikå ajeng nglatih   mother when we are rehearsing
472. ASMORO: Ha enggih kålå minggu   That's right that last week,
     menikå,
     njuk digrundak nikå.   then [everyone] was angry [with me].

Past-Time Adverbials

Specific time is rarely indicated in any of the stories. Many of the adverbial time indexes signal a general, or relational, time. Temporality, according to Suharno (1982:70–71), is marked by terms that occur sentence-initially in relation to other sentences that convey the reference of time. For example, *biyen* (once)—which appeared in the *bekakak* puppet story, (1); the starfruit story, (10); and the Pak Surti illness story, (11)—marks a time that is relationally past in reference either to the present or to another time indexed in an adjacent clause. Terms like *dhisik* mark something as having occurred "prior to" something else, but if the time gap is an hour or a year does not seem to be important. If more orientation is needed to enhance accessibility, it will most certainly be requested.[4]

We look again at the *bekakak* story below to see examples of relational time and the complexities of translating temporality:

→ 190. ENDANG: Aku <u>mbiyen</u> ki
nonton bekakak <u>umur telung
taun</u>

I once
watched the *bekakak* [when I was]
three years old

191. LAINE: Wah! kok . . . .<u>suwi</u> . . .

Wah! so long ago!

192. SARI: <u>Isih</u> indil-indil,
<u>saiki wis</u> ondol-ondol.

[Then, you were] still so tiny and cute,
now [you're] already gross and
sloppy.

→ 194. ENDANG: Gek, ndilalah åpå <u>kae</u>,
nonton ondel-ondel sing gede
<u>kae</u>,
Wedi aku.

So, suddenly what's that,
[I] saw those gigantic procession
puppets,
I was terrified.

In turn 190, Endang opens the story frame with the word *biyen*, which immediately signals that a past event is about to come. She further orients this event by stating that it occurred when she was three years old, although, she later told me, in fact, she could not remember how old she was but had only wished to signal the distant past. Sari's comments in turn 192 contain three adverbials: *isih* (still), *sakiki* (now), and *wis* (already, done), which describe, albeit humorously, the physical changes from child to adult. Sari uses "still" to index the distant-past comment, and "now" and "already" for the current time. Since "still" does not usually signal the past, Sari's comment shows how she is shifting her own diectic perspective, along with the temporal value of the adverbial, in a way that matches Endang's time reference. In the English translation, we are required to add the past tense "were" for the utterance to make sense.

Endang's event clauses in turn 194—*gek, ndilalah åpå kae*—cannot be translated in a way that does justice to the temporal meaning either. What seems to be an involvement-catching term, *gek ndilalah* (so suddenly), is punctuated by a demonstrative of a kind I call text boundary indexicals. These terms represent the relationship that exists between spatial and temporal deictics, of which the word *kae* is the third of three possible inflections. *Kae* can mean "over there," far from the speaker and hearer in a spatial sense, and it can also mean a "distant time." There is, then, an interesting conflict between the internal evaluation, "so suddenly," and the reminder of distant past that punctuates these idea units.

In his descriptions of old Javanese literary or performance texts, Becker (1979, 1988) has suggested that time is not iconic in Javanese, meaning that clause order does not presuppose the order of actual occurrence. This underlying difference in verb function affects text-building strategies, especially with regard to coherence (Becker, 1979). Most of the texts here, however, follow a temporally sequential ordering of clauses, but as Becker has pointed out, temporality is not the way in which the texts are organized.

Other examples of temporal orientation show the recognition and acceptance of nonspecific time, as well as the active requests for more specificity sometimes issued by others. The following examples are excerpted from the robber tales from Ibu Asmoro and Ibu Umaya (texts 3 and 4). Ibu Asmoro is building up to her second robber tale. She orients it by presenting her general good sense in avoiding trouble when going out.

(3) *Sari Retno's Attack*

151. ASMORO: Yen kesah tebih-tebih	When going far,
barang-barang nikå	I wrap up all my things [jewelry]
kulå buntel kulå gembol	I hide them in my cloth
152. UMAYA: Njih,	Yes,
153. ASMORO: Mongko le nganggo	Instead [they] can be worn
yen wis arep nyambut gawe	when ready to work [haha]
[haha]	
154. UMAYA: Mongko yen <u>sakmenikå</u>	Actually, now is the same, [as then]
dhå sami wah::	awful

Turn 154 shows that Ibu Umaya fully understands the temporal placement of Ibu Asmoro's turns 151 and 153. Even though there are no temporal markers in these turns, Ibu Umaya knows the statements to be past actions when she says "<u>now</u> is the same." Her inclusion of *dhå sami* (<u>both</u> same) assures us that she did fully understand the temporal gap in Ibu Asmoro's story. This recognition of an unsaid temporal reference shows how speakers expect and quite normally assume that participants will actively infer information that is not specifically mentioned.

In her next turn, Ibu Asmoro presents an abstract for her story, about her independence and bravery in facing robbers.

(4) *Outwitting Robbers Continued*

155. ASMORO: Haning kulå nikå	As for me
nekat lo <u>dek jaman begal</u>	I was very determined back in that era of robbers.
156. UMAYA: <u>Gali</u> nåpå Bu?	Street toughs are they Bu?
157. ASMORO: <u>Jaman Landi</u> rak begal	[During] the Dutch era don't you know lots of robbers
158. UMAYA: Wow. ngaten,	wow, like that,

The story itself is about a specific event that occurred when the speaker was leaving a performance at 2:00 A.M. and walking home alone. Ibu Asmoro's story is placed in "the era of robbers." Ibu Umaya is unsure when that was, so she asks if the robbers were *gali*. Older Javanese will identify the word from *gali-gali*, meaning "street gangs," a relatively new term that originated for the murderous gangs that killed for vengeance during the so-called anti-Communist uprisings in 1965–1966. But this was not the case, and Ibu Asmoro places her story in the Dutch era. Since this covers a 350-year span, the listener must infer from previous conversations and shared knowledge that Ibu Amora's unspecified time referent was before Independence, 1945, more than 50 years ago.

Romo Riyo also uses similar temporal markers. What seems to be important, for elderly speakers at least, are the eras in which an event occurred. For these *abdi-dalem*, the significant measure of time is the reigning sultan. Romo has already finished his story of the murder of his friend Tomo when he tells us that before Tomo died, Tomo was summoned by the sultan.

(13) *Dhik Tomo*

464. ROMO: <u>Saweg kles menikå</u>.	[This was] during the Clash
Dados ingkang nimbali njih	So [Dhi Tomo] was summoned y'know
ngerså dalem piyambak	by Sri Sultan himself
<u>kaping sångå</u>	the ninth [sultan]
465. ASMORO: <u>Ping sångå</u>	The ninth
466. ROMO: Ha menikå,	And so,
dumugi menikå	[they] arrived
sareng sampun tilar aman-aman ngaten,	[and] all together [they] left [the palace] safely,
sareng <u>sampun Merdikå</u> menikå	[and] together [they] made it to Independence.

Following his long, detailed story of the life and brutal murder of Tomo, Romo concludes by placing the story in Indonesian history. The *Kles* (Clash) refers to the period of war just after Independence in 1945. The ninth sultan reigned from 1940 to 1988. Since Tomo was murdered after Independence, Romo uses turn 464 to give Tomo a great deal of prestige. The ninth sultan is undeniably the favorite among *abdi-dalem*, with many myths and legends attesting to his benevolence and spiritual powers. For the sultan himself to summon Tomo would indeed be an honor.

As the two elderly *abdi-dalem* compare notes on their lives and introductions to *gamelan*[5] and court life, they focus on themselves and their ages. Ibu is not sure of her own age and her exact date of birth, but she does tell us that she began studying at the age of 12. Romo began when "still young," although, again, many Indonesians do not know details of their birth. It may well be this fact alone that prevents these speakers from being more specific.

(14) *Comparing Introductions to the* Gamelan

88. ASMORO: Wong kulå,	As for me,
magang <u>taksih umur rolas taun</u>,	[I began my] apprenticeship at the age of 12,
89. ROMO: Injih:	Yes
90. ASMORO: Dados <u>sak priki menikå</u>,	So up to now,
<u>swidak tigang taun</u> nek	that's 63 years then=
91. ROMO: Hainjih:	That's right
92. ASMORO: meh <u>sewidak sekawan</u>,	=Almost 64

Wong kulå <u>Januari menikå</u>,   As for me this January,
<u>pitung wolu</u>.   78.

93. ROMO: Ning kulå menikå anu,   As for me uhm,
    <u>awit alit</u> gadah bakat injih   early on [I] had talent y'know
    Wonten seni menikå.   There was art.

What is specific for them is the reigning sultan and particular events:

99. ROMO: Niku saget adan-adanan   [I] could [play] the call to the mosque
    menikå saget.   already.
    <u>Rumiyen</u> bade,   Back then [it was] going on,
    mbok menawi <u>bade jumenengan</u>   perhaps the eighth sultan [was] about
    <u>kaping wolu</u>.   to take the throne.
100. ASMORO: O: <u>kaping wolu</u>   Oh, the eighth

Ibu Asmoro presents her comparative time frame:

106. ASMORO: Dados kulå menikå,   As for me,
     <u>bakdå suro dalem ping pitu</u>.   just after suro (Javanese month) of
                                          the seventh sultan.
107. ROMO: He:ee injih: Uh huh yes:
108. ASMORO: (?) Kulå anu ajar sinden   (?) I uhm [began to] study singing

Anxious to figure out what years they were talking about, I asked when
the seventh sultan reigned. My question was answered, although not as I
had hoped.[6]

118. LAINE: Aduh! kaping pitu menikå,   Wow! The seventh [sultan],
     pinten taun kepengker?   how many years ago was that?
119. ASMORO: O: ha ping pitu menikå,   Oh: the seventh,
     anu <u>sak derengipun ping wolu</u>: uhm before the eighth [sultan]:
120. LAINE: Hi ya: ha ha ha wuih!   Oh yea: hahah wuih!

    Yet, while the evidence so far is leaning toward a concept of story
time as intertextually relational, the following extract challenges that view.
Yanti is orienting a story for Atik about an awful, stressful two days she
had had when she was teaching high school in the morning and helping
her friend prepare for a huge religious feast all afternoon and evening. At
night she was unable to sleep because of her father's sudden illness. With
no introductory abstract, Yanti launches immediately into the orientation.

(15) *Yanti's Stress*
59. Kulå <u>dhek setu</u> wingi awan terus   Last Saturday afternoon, I went to the
    ngulon,   west,
    <u>setu tanggal selawe</u>,   Saturday, the twenty-fifth,
    <u>selawe</u> kan, teksih onten   the twenty-fifth right, school was still

sekolahan,	open,
selawe karo nem likur.	the twenty-fifth and twenty-sixth.
Pokoke dinå setu niku.	The point is on Saturday.
Kulå niku masak kan ting nggene kåncå kulå.	I cooked, right, at my friends' house.
Masakke lonthong opor niku lho. . . .	[we] cooked *lonthong opor*.

Yanti's story begins a highly specific, repetitive time orientation, which later in the story will be found to be wrong: Atik states that the twenty-fifth was, in fact, a Friday. Why Yanti is so specific in her time orientation is unclear. Yet, the entire story follows this extreme style of emphatic detail, coming rather close to what the Javanese refer to as *setress*, a type of insanity.[7] Yanti's long and detailed story of her two days from hell evokes the frantic pain, frustration, and exhaustion of the actual events. It may be that the rhythmic patterns of the tale, and hence the specific time, are as exceptional in narrative as the actual experience was in her life. Yanti's story is about how she was trapped in a rigid temporal framework of experiences that causes her great suffering. She frequently breaks out of the story sequence to evaluate externally her inability to get out because of her responsibility to others—her students, her friends, her family, her father—and to the religious holiday and feast they are preparing. Her agent's stance represents not an egocentric, personal control or responsibility but a sociocentric responsibility. It is a reflexive awareness of herself being acted upon by uncontrollable forces, one of which is time.

In summary, we have seen how time has an important role to play as an index of story frames. Although a major aspect in the recognition of stories because of the frame shifting it signals, time in Javanese does not function like the past tense does in English stories. Time in Javanese narratives coordinates the emerging pattern of experiential relationships, in which events and evaluations act, are acted upon, and re-act. Oral narratives are not made coherent through temporal sequencing but rather through the subtle shifting of various levels of relational movements (e.g., Becker, 1979, 1988), of which time is only one.

Reported Speech

In his study of indexicality in face-to-face interaction, Hanks (1990) states that it is a "default assumption" of interactants to regard speakers as the source of the proposition, the selector of the words, and the one responsible for those words. In Goffman's (1981) terms,[8] this means that the author, animator, and principal are one and the same. Through these "production formats" (further discussed in chapter 5) we can differentiate the various footings speakers may take as they speak, which can help clarify the finer distinctions of responsibility in talk. The Javanese proclivity for using reported speech, however, is symbolic of their prefer-ence for creating decentered frames, in which the author, figure, princi-pal, and even animator may all be dispersed throughout a broad commu-nity of indexed voices.

We see here how reported speech indexes relational information about speakers (animators), others (figures and authors), and the communities (as principal), through which ideas about local knowledge, responsibil-ity, and authority can be revealed. This decenteredness is created through a multitude of voices that represents a complex world of social differen-tiation and interactional space across which "the locus of face, knowl-edge, and responsibility is not an atomic individuality, but a diffuse and highly socialized construction" (Hill and Zepeda, 1993:222).

The direct quotation of past conversations has been recognized else-where as a very common, although easily confusing, Javanese norm (Keeler, 1984:260). Indirect quotations such as "she said that . . ." are not rare in my data, as others have reported. Yet, reporting speech without directly naming who the words belong to is by far one of the most com-monly used strategies for reenacting a past event, making it a significant part of the storytelling process. The strategy is so widespread that I sug-gest (after Tannen, 1989) that the occurrence of reported speech entails a story.

"Constructed dialogue," as Tannen (1989:101) refers to the phenom-ena, "is as much a creative act as is the creation of dialogue in fiction" because of its (re)creation of particular times, places, speaking charac-ters, and instances. It is storytelling in a holistic manner, requiring active interpretation of a real or created past, brought alive again for whatever purposes a speaker selects. As Besnier (1993) suggests, it can carry infor-mational value, pass judgments, express varying degrees of affect or re-sponsibility, and can be made to represent specific traits of invoked speakers. Becker is talking about literary Javanese when he describes a rather different aspect of the phenomenon. He calls reported speech "a supremely social act: by appropriating each other's utterances, speakers are bound together in a community of words" (quoted in Tannen, 1989: 133). Reported speech is Javanese storytelling par excellence because it allows tapping into that vast community, sharing its pool of verbal wealth and experience, and most of all, it verifies membership.

The two following stories emerged as both Romo Riyo and Ibu Asmoro were narrating their introductions to the *gamelan* and ultimately their life of dedication to the palace. Ibu Asmoro begins the autobiographic story round by orienting the time scales we are dealing with here. Romo then begins his story.

(14) *Comparing Introductions to the* Gamelan

88. ASMORO:	Wong kulå,	As for me,
	magang taksih umur rolas taun,	[I began my] apprenticeship at the age of 12,

89. ROMO: Injih: Yes

90. ASMORO: Dados sak priki menikå   So up to now,
    swidak tigang taun, nek //   that's 63 years, then

91. ROMO: Hainjih: that's right

92. ASMORO: //Meh sewidak skawan   //Almost 64 (years as an *abdi-dalem*)
    wong kulå Januari menikå,   as for me this January,
    pitung wolu   78 (her age)[9]

93. ROMO: Ning kulå menikå anu   As for me uhm
    awit alit gadah bakat injih   early on [I] had talent y'know
    wonten seni menikå,   there was art,
    Menikå pun gandeng bapak   Already hand in hand [with my]
    menikå,   father
    → "Yo melu nang kono,   "Hey come along over there,
    → nang pendåpå kono nang   to that *pendopo* to the west there
    kulån kono
    → nggone Pak Bei Kartowiryono"   the home of Pak Bei (name)"

94. ASMORO: He:e   He:e

95. ROMO: Injih wonten kilen rumiyen   That's right back then to the west
    Sami kangge gladi ajar ndalang   Altogether practicing studying
    menåpå menikå,   puppetry or whatever,
    Menikå kulå injih kemutan mawon   That's how I remember it
    teksih alit menikå   [I was] still young
    pun gandeng båpå kulå menikå: hand in hand with my father
    → "Pak! nek ngene ki åpå pak?"   "Pak! What is this here pak?"
    → "Neng ning neng neng nong,"   "Neng ning neng (the sound of the
                                                      gamelan)
    Menikå saget kagem adanan   This was the call to the mosque
    menikå

96. ASMORO: Injih: Yes:

97. ROMO: → "Ki åpå pak nek ngene   "What is all this here dad"
    iki pak"
    → "Oh: kuwi: "oh that:
    → ki dhå nangsak"   that's together (?)"
    → "Yo nek ngono: no ni nong no   "Its like this, *no ni nong* (sound of
    ni nok no: . . ."   *gamelan*)
    Menikå saget mawon: kuwi geges   [You] can [do] it. That [is what]
    kuthå: [aroused(?)] the city.

98. ASMORO: Wow: ha   Wow: ha

As we can see in turn 93, Romo is orienting his story in line with the
parameters already set by Ibu Asmoro, that is, beginning to show interest
in the *gamelan* at a young age. Romo's story events actually begin when
he slips back into his own past to tell us how he had first held his dad's
hand (*gandeng Bapak*) while walking toward the intriguing sounds of
the *gamelan*. In those days, before loudspeakers, the *gamelan* was used
as a call to prayer by the mosques and to meetings in the *kampungs*. This

is what Romo first learned to play. He recalls his father's first invitation to come to the open *pendopo*, where the instruments are kept:

93. ROMO: Ning kulå menikå anu   As for me uhm
    awit alit gadah bakat injih   early on [I] had talent y'know
    wonten seni menikå,   there was art
    → Menikå pun gandeng bapak   → Already hand in hand [with my]
    menikå,   father
    "Yo melu nang kono,   "Hey come along over there,
    nang pendåpå kono   to that pendopo
    nang kulon kono   to the west there
    nggone Pak Bei Kartowiryono"   the home of Pak Bei (name)

In turn 95, Romo returns to the storytelling context to explain the location[10] and what occurred there. He repeats the significant topic information here, that is, age, to stress the relative time factors involved. Age is further enforced by the graphic memory of his first trip: holding his father's hand and revealing his naive interest by asking for an explanation:

95. ROMO: Injih wonten kilen rumiyen   That's right, back then to the west
    Sami kangge gladi ajar ndalang   Altogether practicing studying
    menåpå menikå,   puppetry or whatever
    Menikå kulå injih kemutan mawon   That's how I remember it
    teksih alit menikå   [I was] still young
    pun gandeng båpå kulå menikå: hand in hand with my father
    "Pak! nek ngene ki åpå pak?"   "Pak! What is this here pak?"
    "Neng ning neng neng nong,"   "neng ning neng (the sound of the gamelan)

    Menikå saget kagem adanan   This was the call to the mosque
    menikå

Romo presents the three speaking parts that make up his story: his father's first invitation to approach the *pendopo*, his own inquiry, and the sound of the music itself. There are no lexical indexes to cue the different speaking parts, although intonation and context do reveal the changes. We are also told how his father began to teach him to play:

97. ROMO: → "Ki åpå pak nek ngene   "what is all this here dad"
    iki pak"
    → "oh: kuwi: "oh that:
    → ki dhå nangsak"   that's together [?]"
    → "Yo nek ngono: no ni nong   ("its like this, no ni nong (sound of
    no ni nok no: . . ."   gamelan)
    menikå saget mawon: kuwi geges   It can [be done]. That [is what]
    kuthå: [aroused(?)] the city.

Thus through repetition of constructed dialogue, we can see how a whole scenario is being created. A little boy and his father are sharing a very special moment with a clear emotional impact, all of which we interpret through inference. From this story we also learn of the social significance of the *gamelan* at that time, that is, its role in calling the people to prayer or meeting. This was the first music Romo learned to play, and we can easily imagine through his narration how significant a moment it was for him. It literally directed the rest of his life.

Ibu Asmoro also uses constructed dialogue to create her autobiography in story (21). Her stories are quite different from Romo's because she always creates a self that is very independent, headstrong, and rebellious:

121. ASMORO: Ning kulå menikå teksih alit
surut ning sampun

As for me [I was] still young
but already a member

122. ROMO: Ha injih,
Sampun kemutan ngoten koq

That's right,
that's how [we] remember it

123. ASMORO: Injih:
Nah menikå surut dalem ping pitu
dereng magang
Lajeng bakdo jumenengan ping wolu menikå
kulå kepingin ajar: ngantos pun sibratken koq.
Kulå kalian Bapak.

Yes:
So [I] came in during the seventh [sultan]
not yet apprenticed
So after the seventh's rise

I wanted to study to the point of being thrown out even.
Me and my father

124. ROMO: O: inggih.

oh: yes.

→ 125. ASMORO: "Wis kelang-kelangan ndhog siji"

"[I] already lost one egg" (daughter)

126. ROMO: Rumiyen mboten angsal tå nggian?

[You] didn't have permission then, right?

127. ASMORO: Mboten angsal
wong mbah kulå santri kolot,
kakung kulå kaum,
pak de kulå kaum,
Wis pokoke,
wis ben mbokne ilang-ilangan ndog siji,
Nggih pak!
Nek ndoke wok-an,
nek ndoke wreden wantun kulå menikå injih.
Kadang mboten mantuk ajar wonten Wirogunan
Pun wuruki Den Jatikumoro,
Nek kulå ajar teng Wirogunan

[I] wasn't permitted
my father was conservative Muslim,
my brother was Muslim,
my uncle was Muslim,
So the point is,
that's that [my] parents lost one egg,

That's right Pak!
as a girl (?)
As a girl (?) I was very bold y'know.

Sometimes [I] didn't go home [from] studying at Wirogunan
[I] was taught by Den Jatikumoro,
as for me studying at Wirogunan for

sek kalih taun	two years
rung payu	not yet right
Kono gending gede,	[They played] the big *gending* (style of music) there
→ "Ha nek ajar teng pundi Den?"	→ "So if [I want to] study where Den?"
→ "Neng Sindunangunan."	→ "At Sindunangunan."
→ "Sesuk sore malem Jumuah tekå" ha ha ha	→ "Tomorrow afternoon Thursday evening come" hahaha
dateng lajeng //	[I] went, then//
128. LAINE: He: he	He: he

In turn 125, Ibu Asmoro repeats the words her father said to her:

→ 125. ASMORO: "Wis kelang-kelangan ndhok siji"   "[I] already lost one egg" (daughter)

as a sign of their conflict. Ibu Asmoro presents herself as extremely eager to study singing even though everyone else in her family forbade it. She was alone in her decision, as she emphasizes by naming all the (male) members of her immediate family as old-fashioned, religious Muslims. In other contexts, she has elaborated on this story by clarifying the violent extent of the encounter with her father. Here with Romo, however, it is enough to focus on the young age and the resolve to follow her own wishes despite the conflicts. Her father's firm rejection is emphasized by his acceptance of the loss of his daughter, which Ibu Asmoro repeats as constructed dialogue.

In her next turn, she constructs her own image as independent and strong-willed when she emphasizes again her firm decision to study. After informing us who she studied with and for how long, she reconstructs her initial inquiry:

127. ASMORO: "Ha nek ajar teng pundi Den?"	→ "So if [I want to] study, where Den?"
→ "Neng Sindunangunan"	→ "At Sindunangunan"
→ "Sesuk sore malem Jumuah tekå" ha ha ha	→ "Tomorrow afternoon Thursday evening come" hahaha

Thus, following Romo's story frame and reconstruction of his introduction to the *gamelan*, Ibu Asmoro returns to the same frame and shows us how she, too, first made her inquiries. She also gives us details, such as where the lessons took place, even adding on what night. What is important here is that despite the differences in Romo's and Ibu Asmoro's purposes in telling the stories—Ibu Asmoro's stories always emphasize her moral strength and independence—they both use reported speech to invoke a particular image of themselves in relation to and, in fact, through another figure in the story. In both cases, too, the reported speech gives the sense of formulaicity, in Romo's case because of the immediate repetition. In Ibu Asmoro's case, she has told almost the identical story to me several times under different circumstances. Her father's words are repeated almost exactly, whereas the conversation with Den Jatikumoro seems to be more of a construction to orient her story with Romo's.

As elderly Javanese, especially as individuals of rank and prestige in the *kraton abdi-dalem* circles, they are socially able and expected to tell autobiographical stories. This is absolutely not the case for community members who are not of such an age and with least relative prestige within the immediate context of speaking.

For the next story, we examine a different community. The following excerpt comes from data collected among a group of middle-aged *Ibu-Ibu* (women, mothers) from the Bausasran area in the center of Yogya and northeast of the palace. I had lived briefly in their *kampung*,[11] but after moving, I continued to visit several times a week to play in their *gamelan*. The women are discussing the problems that result when members of their *gamelan* group do not show up for rehearsal. Ibu Harjo's story reenacts the conversation she had had with Pak Joyo, the wealthy owner of the musical instruments, who lives on the street-side fringe of the *kampung*.[12] It is here that the women hold their *gamelan* rehearsals.

(16) *The Usual Chaos*

84. HARJO :	**Enggih: kulå** anu:	Yes: I uhm:
	"Pak **pripun, ngriki** sek kisruh"	"Pak what's going on this is all chaotic"
	"La kisruh **kepripun** tho?"	"Chaotic in what way?"
	"**Hinggih** biasa tho Pak wong **niki**"	"But isn't it usual Pak"
	"**Mengkeh** ngenteni **ajeng** rapat sik"	"Wait first for those who will meet"
	"**Nggih** malah beneran."	"Yes, that's quite right."

The introduction of the topic of chaos (*kisruh*) is elusive in that no explanation, no incident, no detail is referenced. The story is made up of reported speech alone, with no abstract, no orientation, no events in its boundaries. It is a symbolic reenactment of a dialogue that fulfills a social need, or one must assume it would never have been said. The "chaos" is referenced externally, as the same problem currently occurring in the speech situation; that is, the players have not shown up for rehearsal. The advice Pak Joyo gives is to wait, to ultimately have faith that the right thing will "happen" in the end. This is important advice and offers a good understanding of Javanese agency.

The use of reported speech is not just a way of deferring responsibility, as so many of the scholarly works claim (e.g., Besnier, 1993; Duranti,

1993; Graham, 1993; Shuman, 1993). Here it is also a way of sharing the decision-making processes with others, that is, those being invoked, as well as those listening. Creating a polyphonic frame in storytelling is a strategy for focusing on the collectivity, not the individual. It does not defer responsibility from an individual but rather stresses one's responsibility to the community. Story (16) shows how Ibu Harjo evokes a scene in which all the participants are sharing in the negotiation process by not dominating it. Talk—and reported speech is a prime example— is a way of understanding and mediating social relations (cf. Duranti, 1993).

Such a discursive style may also be described as diffusing personal responsibility by evading questions through indirect answers: "Chaotic in what way?" Pak Joyo asks. "But isn't it usual, Pak," Bu Harjo responds. The "usual" is left for the audience to define, as is so much more. The story's format invokes a past situation, a complicating action—in this case a problem—and a way of dealing with it that does not have to depend on any specific action but, rather, *in*action; nor must it be presented within the confines of the textual boundaries. The invocation of a past dialogue evokes all the shared knowledge that constructs, reflects, and strengthens the boundaries of the community. It is, then, a prime display of exactly what it is that makes the participants a unified community by revealing what is that they share.

Reported speech exposes the dynamic interrelationships existing between participants by showing what their expectations are with regard to the immediate context. Javanese speakers may also take highly creative liberties in the framing of reported speech. For example, I had gone to the Budi house to meet Atik, Sari, and a few other friends to wait for Yanti. I opened the topic.

(17) *Yanti's Wedding*

92. LAINE: Mbak Yanti kandhane arep mantenan	Mbak Yanti [I] hear is going to get married
93. ATIK: Mbuh kae!	[I] don't know anything about that!
Mbak Yanti le kåndhå arep mantenan	Mbak Yanti it's said is going to get married
Mbak Lena muni ngono.	Mbak Lena said so.
"Aku tak jagong	"I want to attend
mumpung isih ning kene," ngono.	while [I am] still here to do so," she said.
"Selak aku mbali Amerika." ngono.	"I am about to go back to America." she said.

Story (17) shows how Javanese speakers use reported speech for creative and cooperative means. What I did say is clearly available for all to hear (turn 92). Yet, Atik adds a great deal of information that she attributes to me, to the extent of using an agentic *I*. The word *ngono*, used to punctuate each information unit, marks the turn as something she heard me say. In this case, it is something I could have said but obviously did not. For the benefit of the rest of the group (all of whom were good friends and knew all about my plans, which incidentally did not include my imminent departure), Atik feels perfectly comfortable in constructing my words as an example of my underlying thoughts about what it was that I had actually said.

In turn 93, the words attributed to me and the surrounding discourse are in the same speech style. Reported speech is often, but need not be, punctuated by text indexes that specifically mark the frame shift. Phrases such as *aku ngono* ("that's what I said") or just *ngono* ("like that") function as reflexive, anaphoric indexes, which need not be overtly egocentric. The existence of *ngono* helps the listener recognize that these words are reported speech, either spoken by some other individual, as in (17), or by the current speaker, as in (18). Yet what these texts invoke is a great deal of contextualized information that gives it storytelling status. Atik's reported speech re-creates a past (albeit recent) and also tells a story about me as she takes the liberty of constructing my feelings about our friend's upcoming marriage.[13] It invokes many of our past conversations, upon which Atik is able to re-create my thoughts with some degree of accuracy. Since Javanese storytelling does not have to be confined only by the *said*, the *unsaid* that these texts evoke, in addition to the creative inferencing that constructs them, allows them story status.

(18) To Len's Hotel

15. OTONG : mau arep tak ampiri ndono he.	Earlier I was going to stop in over there y'know.
ke hotelnya sana he!	to your hotel there y'know.
"Mbak Lena *ada*?" aku ngono.	"Is Mbak Lena there?" I said like that.

In story (18), Otong, Atik's younger brother, is telling me what he almost did but did not. He goes so far as to directly quote the words he would have used had he gone to my place of residence and needed to ask for me. These words were never spoken, but the style of relating these non-occurring events is identical to Atik's direct quote of what I did not say in (17). The use of *aku ngono* ("I said that") or *ngono* ("like that") is a frequent anaphoric marker of reported speech.

Uses of reported speech like these are prime indicators of a storytelling frame. Reported speech is symbolic of action, action that does not have to involve any past physical accomplishment but rather an interactive or thoroughly imagined one. Specific speakers need not be indicated since information, if necessary, is accessible from the context. Reported speech further indicates relational information about speakers; about others; and about the communities through which ideas about local knowledge, responsibility, and authority can be revealed.

Shifting Speech Levels

Speech-level shifts function as a type of deictic—such as pronouns, demonstratives, and time and place adverbials—which anchor an utterance to its context by encoding specific aspects of the context in the utterance itself. These social deictics, or speech levels, create an additional dimension of hierarchical coordinates through respect, age, or clarification of some other valued or devalued trait. They are one of the keys or cues through which evaluational interpretations of speaker-other-community relationships are clarified, and as such they are an integral part of the storytelling process.

Shifting speech levels are an important feature in Javanese because of the wide variation in choices available and the highly evaluative meaning they expose. As an index of stories, this feature is far more apparent in older speakers' discourse than in texts from the younger speakers. Otong (text 18) shifts into Indonesian rather than different levels of Javanese, a change typical of the younger generation of Javanese speakers no longer able or willing to master the complexities of *kråmå*.[14] Yet, the shifting of speech levels, more than any other feature in Ibu Asmoro's stories, is the contextualization cue that reveals how a story is to be interpreted. As a structuring element in storytelling, it not only places speakers (i.e., those being spoken about in the story) within a hierarchical social order of rights and obligations but also helps the participants interpret such events by specifying these social positions.

But this, as Erving Goffman notes, is also the realm of theater. Speakers perform the multiple roles of director, writer, and costars in ways that are best described in Goffman's terms. Central to frame analysis is the *key*, "the set of conventions by which a given activity, one already meaningful in terms of some primary framework, is transformed into something patterned on this activity but seen by the participants to be something quite else" (1974:43–44). Shifting speech levels seems to me to be a perfect example of one such key.

Just as in the theater, Javanese speakers stage shifts in speech levels and styles (or in speakers through reported speech) that define the relational activity so essential to interpretation within the broader framework of community. Note again Ibu Asmoro's quotation of the prince's words, using honorifics, followed by Ibu Harto's marked change of speech levels.

(12) *Ibu Asmoro and the Prince*

468. ASMORO: **Njih pokokipun**	Right, the point is
"**namung PIRSÅ lare-lare**	just "watch over the children
Ingkang mboten keleresan	[Those] who are not correct are to be
pun NGENDIKANI."	told."
470. HARTO: **La injih milo IBU**	That's right, that's why mum,
namung,	
NDALEM PUNTEN SEWU	I graciously beg your forgiveness

menikå
Ibu menikå ajeng nglatih,   mother when we are rehearsing,
DALEM SEWU DAWUHi sambut   I sincerely beg for the honor of your
ngleres Ibu esti   corrections mother

In terms of how and why a story is told, the use of speech style variants
and the reported speech that assists in style shifting encode many types
of internal evaluation. Ibu Asmoro's brief turn (468) makes use of these
flexible possibilities as cues to influence the behavior of others. She is
allowed to modestly mark herself as an *authorized recipient* of deference.
Since the conditions for this deference do in fact exist, the desired deference is offered in turn 470.

Speech levels also mark inferred and preferred social boundaries. Actors
in a story world are manipulated into a Javanese hierarchical life-play, in
which speakers may allow themselves—or detract from others—a preferred place in the social order. Recall the Stasiun Tugu story, (7), in which
the Budi family is coming to terms with my odd behavior by coconstructing
a narrative that re-creates my personal experiences. The point of the story,
or the successful resolution of its dilemma,[15] appears in Sari's reported
speech. Her constructed dialogue has the poor, unrefined people of the
station using the *kråmå inggil* honorific *ngastå* (to work) when they speak
to or of me, signaling my safety both physically and in status:

→ 85.   SARI: Anu "**wonten ingkang**   So uhm, "there's someone who
        NGASTÅ wonten Sadhar **mriki**"   lectures at Sadhar here"

Speech-level variations, then, in addition to being *keys* (Goffman, 1974)
and discourse markers (Schiffrin, 1987), are also pragmatic indexicals, the
class of words Levinson (1983) calls social deixis. Yet, in the story and
social context, the shifting of one word into an honorific has the social
force to reframe successfully my deviant behavior into something more
recognizable and, hence, acceptable.

Recall Romo Riyo's introduction to the *gamelan* story (14). Here, too,
we saw how Romo signaled his change of frame through speech levels:

95. ROMO: **Injih wonten kilen**   That's right back then to the west
        rumiyen
        Sami kangge gladi ajar ndalang   Altogether practicing studying
        menåpå menikå,   puppetry or whatever,
        menikå kulå injih kemutan   That's how I remember it
        mawon
        Teksih alit menikå   [I was] still young
        pun gandeng båpå **kulå menikå:** hand in hand with my father:
        "pak! nek ngene ki åpå pak?"   "Pak! What is this here pak?"
        "Neng ning neng neng nong,"   "Neng ning neng," (the sound of the
                                              gamelan)

Menikå saget kagem adanan   This was the call to the mosque
menikå

We can clearly see that as Romo moves from the storytelling context, that is, as he orients his story for his listeners, he maintains his discourse in full *kråmå*. The move to reported speech is further signaled by a move to *ngoko*. Romo has fully entered the past time of the story world, and he reproduces his and his father's voices and the music as we can imagine they had sounded. The speech-level shift gives the words authenticity as reported speech and helps create a story as a snapshot from a life that participants are permitted the honor of watching. The change in focus, or frame, through the speech level and style in Romo's story is also a change in the organization of his interaction. This shows a double change in the way he is defining and sustaining the situation as a personal experience. Not only do the shifts signal changes within the story, but also they signal differences in the recognition of the audience. The orientation is clearly for the listeners' benefit, while the events are presented as something far more private and privileged. The use of frame shifts such as reported speech and speech levels are stylistic assets through which participants are aided in the interpretation of an utterance.

In another dramatic example, Ibu Asmoro, at the *kraton* with Ibu Umaya, shifts speech levels to present iconically her various positions in relation to the various levels of information she presents. This story describes her experiences as a singer (*pesindhen*) in the early days of Indonesian national radio (Radio Republik Indonesia or RRI):

(19) *RRI Violence*

106. ASMORO: **Menikå** kuping di   Our ears were boxed.
     templeki,
     Wong sinden kok kåyå kirik   The singers were stepped on like
     kepidak   puppies
     Ha **nikå nåpå-nåpå** nyerik**ken** to,   It was all so painful y'know,
     Kulå kendel**ken mawon** . . .   I just got tough.
     Harjonopawoho **nggih**, wow . . .   Harjonopawoho (name) y'know,
                                        wow.

     Wong sinden kog kåyå tai   [He treated] the singers like shit
     Dados sami nggodå **menikå**,   While at the same time tempting,
     Lajeng kulå manggihi *kepala*   So I met with the head of RRI
     RRI
     NYUWUN medal.   [and] asked to be released.
107. UMAYA: Wow . . .   Wow
108. ASMORO: Bayar**ipun menikå,**   The pay [I got was the] same as Bu
     kalian Bu Larasati **mawon**   Larasati.
     "**Kathah PANJENENGAN**   "There is a lot that you desire.
     sampun KERSAnipun . . .
     artå nikå **pundi-pundi wonten**   Where will you get the kind of

timbang **kulå** . . ."	money I give you"
Nekan . . . nekan mangkel	It was frustrating

In this story, Ibu Asmoro is explaining why she chose to leave her coveted singing job at RRI.[16] This story is part of her morality repertoire, where she displays her actions as motivated by integrity rather than greed, which is bolstered by her independence and bravery in dealing with a (usually gender-related) problem. It was tempting financially, but she had a firm set of principles that did not allow abuse. Her use of varying speech styles serves to index and distinguish various levels of self-positioning. The abusive descriptions appear in *ngoko*:

106. Wong sinden kok kåyå kirik	The singers were stepped on like
kepidak	puppies

Her nonagentic feelings as external evaluation are presented in *madyå*:

106. **Ha nikå nåpå-nåpå** nyerikken to	It was all so painful y'know

And her own agentic actions are described in *kråmå*:

106. **Lajeng kulå manggihi** kepala	So I met with the head of RRI
RRI	
NYUWUN medal.	[and] asked to be released.

The reported speech she presents as being the words spoken to her from the director of RRI are presented with *kråmå inggil* honorifics:

108. "**Kathah PANJENENGAN**	"There is a lot that you desire."
sampun KERSAnipun . . ."	

to distinguish her as highly respected in an environment that habitually abuses women.

For her, and within the boundaries of this story, the speech levels coordinate specific activities and feelings within a hierarchical grid of self-positioned values. Coherence in this story is created by an episodic movement in relational consequences. From an egocentric locus, these events are displayed as evaluational reactions through symbolic style shifts. Abusive behavior is marked as crude and base through low Javanese. Nonagentic feelings that describe the awful experiences are in *madyå*, which in this case is signaling her external evaluation as a movement closer to the speaker, but not too close. Her agentic actions, depicting her highly principled yet difficult decisions, are in full *kråmå*, and her rendition of the words she had spoken, **NYUWUN medal**, are in *kråmå andhap*, signaling the formal respect she displayed despite the injustice. These speech-level variations index at an iconic level the dignity and high Javanese honor she maintained in spite of the cruelty inflicted on her. Those in power at RRI treated her badly, but she still addressed them in formal, and humbling, honorifics. Yet she further restores her dignity to those who hear the story by presenting the RRI director's words in *kråmå inggil*. He, like the prince in story (12), is showing how worthy of respect she is.

To repeat, speech-level shifts function as a type of deictic key and—to anchor an utterance to its context by encoding specific aspects of the context into the utterance itself. Speech levels are social deictics, which orient a story through dimensions of social ranking such as respect, age, or clarification of some other valued or devalued trait. But they also act as indexes of frame shifts within a story, and thus affect the ways in which participants should interpret events.

Text Boundary Indexicals

Text boundary indexes, because of their frequency and their location, most directly signal the organization and interpretation of Javanese spoken texts. They include the words **menikå**, **nikå**, and *ki*; *iku/kuwi* and *kae*; **mekaten**, **ngaten**, and *ngono*; and even **njih**, *lho*, and *tho*, as well as other demonstratives and classes of discourse markers that appear in the same clause-final position. Their significance for us in the interpretation of stories is as markers of perspective and emphasis that structure the development of idea units as natural chunks of discourse (Chafe, 1986). As markers of interpretation, these words will be shown to switch focus from an informational to an interpersonal frame. They touch on the outer, sociorelational frames of the story as they allow speakers to display interpersonal involvement and respect for an interlocutor and signal a speaker's distance from, or the extent of, her involvement in the story frame. Furthermore, I suggest that these edge markers are an index of turn-transition relevance points, which can function as a direct invitation to others to take part.

As a standard structural aspect of informal interactions, these text indexes are extremely frequent. Yet, they seem to have no semantic meaning; nor are they translatable in English. As an index of coherence, however, they seem to locate, inform, and define both structural and interactive aspects of an utterance. In many respects they seem to perform a task similar to that described by Scollon and Scollon for Athabascan: "Words that were once treated as repetitious and tiresome such as might be translated with 'and' or 'and then' are now known to be crucial to the narrative organization" (1981:106). Following such a lead, I suggest that these indexes create a natural verse structure through their patterns of repetition (Tannen, 1989:72). They serve extremely well as indicators of intonational or semantic closure (Chafe, 1986), punctuating text into the meaningful units that demarcate the discourse structure as interaction (cf. Scollon and Scollon, 1981).

In past research, however, such words are identified only as Javanese demonstrative pronouns. They are distinguished according to changes from front to back vowels, which allude directly to speaker-hearer positions, spatially, cognitively and temporally on a three-way plane. *Iki* refers to the here and now, objects, people, times, places, and ideas close to those in the immediate situation; *iku*, or *kuwi*, refer to the addressee, things, times, places, and so on, not linked directly to the speaker. It may also function in generic use or as an anaphoric text indexical. *Kae* is external to the speech event and independent of participants. It refers to distant places, times, people, objects, and ideas. All these demonstratives have *madyå* forms, one standard *kråmå* form, and two nonstandard *kråmå* forms.

	ngoko	madyå	kråmå, standard	kråmå, nonstandard
proximal	iki/ki	niki	menikå	meniki
distal	kuwi	niku	menikå	meniku
external	kae	nikå[17]	menikå	

What has not been noted in past research about these words is their boundary functions. Their frequent occurrence strongly supports theories of spoken language units, or chunks, as an organizational method of presenting information. Each of these chunks is a focus of consciousness (Chafe, 1986); and in Javanese, these chunks, or idea units, are often punctuated by edge markers that index various types of contextual information, that is, as keys of relative distance, time, and/or status. It is also possible that their function may be tied to their location, that is, on the boundaries or the edges of both the utterance and the interpretational frame. They may function as indexes of attention to the listeners, as signals that ease interpretational burdens.

Boundaries of story frames in Javanese discourse seem to be highly significant for social and interactional reasons. Highlighting these boundaries serves to invite others into the interactional space, signaling that the story is in public domain rather than a speaker's personal property. Whereas Sacks et al. (1974) are greatly concerned with problems of turn allocation and ways of coordinating turn-transition relevance points in a stream of conversation, Javanese has text boundary indexicals that display these precise points. Look at (12) again, with the edge markers highlighted.[18]

(12) *Ibu Asmoro and the Prince*

461. ASMORO: Aku wis ora sinden <u>kok</u>   I don't sing any more y'know.
462. HARTO: Ning mboten wonten Ibu   But when you aren't there,
     <u>nikå</u>
     sami gelo <u>lo bu</u>,   everyone is so disappointed, mum,
     nuwun sewu <u>menikå</u>.   please excuse me
463. ASMORO: Ning wong Gusti <u>menikå</u>   But it was the prince
     mboten pareng kulå,   [who] won't allow me [to sing]

464. HARTO: Ning Ibu njih..	But yes ma'am.
465. ROMO : Ha enggih..	That's right.
466. ASMORO: Wong dieman kok nggih?	[He] takes pity [on me] isn't that right?
467. ROMO : Ha inggih	That's right.
rak namung ngemong ngaten	just for training
. . . mawon	and such.
468. ASMORO: Njih pokokipun	Right, the point is
"namung pirso lare-lare	"just watch over the children
ingkang mboten keleresan pun	[those] who are not correct are to be
ngendikani"	told".
470. HARTO: La injih . . .	That's right,
milo Ibu namung	that's why mum,
ndalem punten sewu menikå,	I graciously beg your forgiveness,
Ibu menikå ajeng nglatih	mother when we are rehearsing,
dalem sewu dawuhi sambut	I sincerely beg for the honor of your
ngleres Ibu esti.	corrections, mother.
472. ASMORO: Ha enggih,	That's right,
Kålå minggu menikå	That last week,
kulå mboten sowan	I didn't visit [the palace],
njuk digrundak nikå	then [everyone] was angry [with me].
473. HARTO: Injih . . . injih la injih..	Right, right, that's right.
474. ASMORO: "Bu kok mboten sowan	"Mum, you didn't come to the
tho?"	palace?"
"Ha kesel" he	"Oh, [I was] tired," he

Before I discuss some of these Javanese edge markers, I review what has been written about them elsewhere. Uhlenbeck ([1949] 1978) labels *iki* and its various forms as exclamatory pronouns whose function is to direct attention toward elements of the situation. But the examples he offers show that he does not include these text boundary examples but rather the utterance initial words, which do function purely as demonstratives, for example, *iki lho!* (look here!), and the text-final anaphoric uses, for example, *layange unine kåyå iki* (the letter's contents are like this). Uhlenbeck shows that the function of *iki* is that of a proximal deictic. He does not include the interactive uses. Errington does not mention the *menikå* words, but he does refer to the full class as "psycho-ostensive particles" that "detract from the refinedness of speech"[19] (Joseph Errington, 1988:221), which suggests the items to be negatively evaluated. Kaswanti Purwo and Keeler claim *ki* and its variant styles, *niki, nikå, niku, menikå*, function "as a boundary marker between topic and comment" (Kaswanti Purwo, 1976:147). While Kaswanti Purwo and Keeler (1984) are correct in their interpretations, they are correct only for perhaps half of the occurrences in natural speech.

John Lyons (1982:121), in accordance with most of the scholarship on linguistics and philosophy, describes the function of deixis "to relate the entities and situation to which reference is made in language to the spatio-temporal zero-point, the here and now, of the context of utterance. Admittedly, this zero-point is ego-centric, as everyone who ever talks about deixis would agree." As Hanks (1990) suggests, however, the grounding of indexical reference is linked to the conceptual structure of a certain kind of thought, not the semiotic constitution of a certain kind of communicative practice. This investigation of text boundary indexicals attempts to tie the items to patterns of sociocentric thought.

Since fewer than half of the occurrences in my corpus actually fit into Kaswanti Purwo's (1976) description of topic and comment, in which "topic" refers to the topic within a clause (which is not necessarily the same as the topic of a story), the remaining edge markers need to be accounted for. Turns 462, 470, and 472 each contain two instances of *menikå* but only one in each fits Kaswanti Purwo's description as a topic-comment boundary. Turns 462 and 470 are glossed below:

462. a. "but when you aren't there

Ning	mboten	wonten	Ibu	nikå
but	*neg.*	*exist*	*mother*	*t/c boundary*

b. everyone is so disappointed, mum,

sami	gelå	lho	bu[20]
all	*disappointed*	*excl.*	*mother*

c. please excuse me"

nuwun	sewu	menikå
beg	*1,000*	*?*

470. d. "I graciously beg your forgiveness"

ndalem	punten	sewu	menikå
I	*forgiveness*	*1,000*	*?*

e. mother when we are rehearsing

Ibu	menikå	ajeng	nglatih
mother	*t/c boundary*	*about to*	*rehearse*

The occurrence of the demonstrative in lines a and e are, as Kaswanti Purwo (1976) describes, a topic-comment boundary. The subject *Ibu* ("Mother," but can also be translated as "you") in both cases is punctuated by the marker (*me*)*nikå*, which is then followed by the comment. The demonstrative is a boundary marker between the subject *Ibu* and the predicate. In both cases, however, it can be argued that the word indexes and stresses the topic.[21]

The second occurrences of *menikå* in lines c and d are impossible to translate semantically:

472. f. "That last week,

kålå   minggu   menikå
last   *week*   *that*

g. I didn't visit [the palace]

kulå   mboten   sowan
I   *did not*   *visit*

h. then everyone was angry with me."

njuk   digrundak   nikå
then   *psv + angry*   *?*

In f, Ibu Asmoro is using *menikå* as a demonstrative that generalizes a past, unspecified time. For the previous several weeks she did in fact *sowan* because I had met her in the palace. Thus I am able to verify that the demonstrative is not indexing proximity or specificity. It is functioning as something quite different from Ibu Harto's uses in 470a, where the *menikå* forms a proximal service as index to the immediate context. Bu Harto begs forgiveness from her interlocutor within the current physical, temporal, spatial, and hierarchical context. But 472h is quite different again in its position, that is, following an object focus verb (with no object). Perhaps *nikå* is no more than a marker of "missing information," where neither subject nor object is specified. More data are clearly needed to locate a pattern.

Romo's autobiographical story (14) also demonstrates the same type of phenomenon, in which many of the idea units signal their completion through a text boundary indexical:

a. 93. romo : Ning kulå menikå anu,   As for me [*menikå*] uhm,
b. awit alit gadah bakat injih   early on [I] had talent, y'know
c. wonten seni menikå,   there was art [*menikå*]
d. Menikå pun gandeng bapak   Already hand in hand [with my]
    menikå,   father [*menikå*]
e. "Yo melu nang kono,   "Hey come along over there,
f. nang pendåpå kono   to that pendopo there
g. nang kulon kono   to the west there
h. nggone Pak Bei Kartowiryono"   the home of Pak Bei (name)
i. 95. romo: Injih wonten kilen   That's right back then to the west
    rumiyen
j. Sami kangge gladi ajar ndalang   Altogether practicing studying
    menåpå menikå,   puppetry or whatever
k. Menikå njih kemutan mawon   That's how I remember it
l. Teksih alit menikå   [I was] still young [*menikå*]
m. pun gandeng båpå kulå menikå: hand in hand with my father
                                               [*menikå*]

n. "Pak! Nek ngene ki åpå pak?"	"Pak! What is this here pak?"
o. "Neng ning neng neng nong,"	"*Neng ning neng* (the sound of the *gamelan*)
p. Menikå saget kagem adanan *menikå*	This was the call to the mosque [*menikå*]

As can be seen, there are various types of boundary indexes, all serving various functions in the text. Within the limits of turn 93, only (a) functions as a topic-comment marker, whereas c. and d. have the unspecified function I refer to above. Lines (e), (f), and (g) all signal their ideational closure through the distal demonstrative *kono* (over there) and as third in a series ranging from *kene* (here), *kånå* (there, distal), and *kono* (there, external). Not only is *kono* patterned by repetition throughout each idea unit in the reported speech, it is also an index of external location. Romo's father would have been speaking about a place fairly close to their home in relational understanding, if not location, and more likely to be indexed as *kånå* rather than the external *kono*. The question I am concerned with, then, is if the choice of *kono* is an index of temporal distance to the immediate context of speaking. If it is, these words, as text boundary indexes, specifically link the story world to the immediate context as markers of the interpretational frame rather than as indexes of specific information in the story world.

Line (j) seems to function in conjunction with *menåpå* to expand its meaning as a general term for whatever was there to be studied. Line (l) also contains a vague meaning, perhaps referring to the unmentioned speaker himself since it is common in Javanese and Indonesian to refer to specific or unspecific people by demonstratives. Perhaps, too, it is an anaphoric index of the story's topic since being young and introduced to *gamelan* is the global topic around which the stories emerged. Line (m) has no clear meaning:

j. Sami kangge gladi ajar ndalang menåpå <u>menikå</u>,	Altogether practicing studying puppetry or whatever [*menikå*]
k. Menikå njih kemutan <u>mawon</u>	That's how I remember it
l. teksih alit <u>menikå</u>	[I was] still young [*menikå*]
m. pun gandeng båpå kulå *menikå*	hand in hand with my father [*menikå*]

Whether or not there is a determinable reference in the text is not really the main issue here. In the case of (k), where *mawon* has a specific meaning of its own (just, only), it still marks closure in the line as an information unit, as does *injih* in line (b), which I gloss as "y'know." In this respect, many of these words can be understood to index meaning both in the story and externally to index the interpretational frame. As a mark of meaningful boundaries, these words also help allow turn-taking locations.

To show that these boundary markers are not limited to formal or elderly speakers' styles of interaction, the following story is another from the Atik and Yanti corpus. This story continues from Pak Surti's illness story, in which Atik is answering Yanti's questions about Surti's father's (Pak Surti, or "father of Surti") very serious health problems. At this time, he has been hospitalized, but we were all concerned that the care he was receiving was not adequate. Yanti has questioned the history of the treatment so far, and Atik is explaining (turn 128).

(11) *Pak Surti's Illness (Continued)*

a.	Nggih. awale kan tibå <u>niku</u>.	Early on, right, [he] fell <u>niku</u>.
b.	teng nåpå, teng kamar mandi ning nggih mpun gerah	at uhm, at the bathroom but y'know [he] was already ill
c.	wong mpun dipresakke <u>ki</u>	So [he'd] been examined <u>ki</u>
d.	njuk <u>ki</u> ginjal.	and [they found a] kidney [ailment]
e.	nang nggon doktere muni gejala ngeten <u>niku</u>.	and so the doctor told about the symptoms and all that niku
f.	Njuk kon mondhok mboten purun <u>tho Mbak</u>.	So [he's] ordered to the hospital but refused tho Mbak
g.	"Isa nggih (?) keki obat jalan?"	"Can't [I] be given out-patient care?"
h.	Pokoke dijangka waktu lima hari obate <u>niku</u>	The point is, [they] were given medicine for five days niku.
i.	nek obate entek kemajuane mboten onten, opname.	If there's no improvement, [he's] back in the hospital.
j.	Dereng ngantek entek obate <u>niku</u>,	But before the medicine was finished niku,
k.	Bapake dhawah <u>niku</u>.	her father fell niku.
l.	Mbak Ning wis //	Mbak Ning already, (false start)
m.	pokoke mlebu rumah sakit.	the point is, [he had] to enter the hospital.
n.	Pertama <u>niku</u>	At first niku
o.	mung diinfus <u>nikå</u>	[he] was just given an intravenous drip niku
p.	Dadi seger ben langsung biasa <u>ngoten lho</u>.	So [he seemed] refreshed and directly usual ngoten lho
q.	normal	normal.
r.	Dikira mpun mari	it was thought [he] had healed
s.	Jebule durung diobati <u>tho</u>	But it turns out [they] hadn't yet treated it tho.
t.	ginjele <u>niku</u>.	the kidneys niku.

Although the proximal or distal indexing qualities of the demonstratives need to be inferred from the context in *kråmå* speech because of the single form *menikå*, the *madyå* indexes do distinguish relative space as proximal or distal. Almost all of the forms here take the distal *niku*. Through the patterning of the repetition, the words show their role as indexing situational chunks. They are extremely useful in translating from Javanese as they mark out the units of organization occurring in a speaker's mind (e.g., Chafe, 1986) and as she actually tells her tale. The edge markers maintain the chunks as units of meaning in a text by marking its end.

As has been mentioned earlier, *ki*, *niku*, and *menikå*, are recognized as structural markers of the topic-comment boundary. Yet, of the eight occurrences here, plus one *ki* as the *ngoko* form, only three have a related function: (a) indexes the boundary between the act "fell" and its location, (j) indexes the juncture between a main clause and its subordinate clause, and (n) separates a sequential adverb from the action it describes. The remaining six occurrences do not mark any boundary beyond that of closing the idea unit.

Defining the terms *ki*, *niki*, and *menikå* and its variants as a topic-comment boundary is difficult to defend since the story's topic and the topic of the majority of the clauses—that is, Pak Surti—is mentioned only once (and indirectly as Bapake in line (k) in 30 lines of a chunked text. Topic-comment is not an underlying structural format here. The subject is not named, although the text evolves around his movements, experiences, fears, setbacks, and respites. Precisely as Becker (1988:xiv–xv) describes in a translation of an early nineteenth-century Javanese text, a pattern emerges from the repetition of experiential movement, "like following the trace of an invisible actor through shifting roles." Unnamed does not mean out of focus or forgotten.

Presenting the story as "chunked" highlights additional markers, which also occur at the edges of ideas, indexing closure and relational status. Line (f) includes a respectful vocative, and line (p) is also a demonstrative in *madyå*. Atik's use of *kråmå madyå* in all these words gives them a double indexical function, in which speech level signals hierarchical space on a social plane; it shows her respect for Mbak Yanti.

The text indexes in the clause-final positions switch focus from an informational to an interpersonal frame. They touch on the outer, sociorelational frames of the story as they allow speakers to display interpersonal involvement and respect for an interlocutor. The *nikå*, *niku*, and *ngoten* are demonstratives not just of egocentric footings; they can nevertheless signal a speaker's distance from, or the extent of, her involvement in the story frame. In the preceding story, Atik uses mainly distal markers, mainly to signal respect for her interlocutor. But perhaps they also show us her marginal involvement with her topic and how different it is from her central involvement with Surti (see chapter 3 on evaluation and chapter 7 on gender oppression). Structurally the words punctuate nearly every idea unit to simplify the identification of each idea. As indexes of turn-transition relevance points, they can function as a direct invitation to others to take part. The words have no semantic meaning within the story and can easily be removed with no information loss.

In sum, the recognition of text boundary indexes greatly assists in the identification of stories by highlighting the separate idea units that make up a stream of discourse. They help display the rhythmic development of a text by distinguishing the events or ideas that are represented through the chunks, which aid in comprehension. They may further function as indexes of relative social positions by allowing a speaker to frequently mark her respect to others. Although further study is needed, the ways in which a text is constructed have evaluative functions (e.g., Tannen, 1989), even more so when the edge marker takes on a style-shift value.

Conclusions

I have shown here how four elements of Javanese discourse in informal situations are strategically used by Javanese speakers in organizing their stories and as cues for indexing various levels of meaning. These features are (1) adverbial time markers, (2) reported speech, (3) speech-level shifts, and (4) text boundary indexicals. By investigating how these structuring elements function in interactive story contexts, I have shown how each reflects meaning within a Javanese framework of interpretation. I have also illustrated how each of the four elements supports the role of oral narrative as a significant indicator of self-other-community relationships.

A notion of relationality is central to storytelling. Participants display their interpretation of the essential aspects of their relationship to others in the immediate context and to those that are referenced in the speech. Relative status is the most obvious of these relational qualities, traditionally assumed to be indexed through speech-level shifts. In informal interactions, relative status is also displayed through styles of uptake and the ratification of a posted topic. The oral narrative, as I have suggested, is a way for speakers both to construct and to reflect their self-other-community relationships. By tying the discourse firmly to social contexts, I have tried to show how the fusion of a story into a conversation may be a symbolic representation of how the speakers view themselves as fused into the community within the immediate context and within the wider culture. Thus, control of topic, style, autobiography, uptake, and speech all directly index relational status within the immediate context. Each of the four structural elements of Javanese stories, as well as the stories themselves, perform an essential function in displaying aspects of that relationality.

What we still need to clarify is how variations in a story's referential and social meaning change, depending on the socio-spatio-temporal context of the story. The chapters to follow will cover such issues as symmetry and asymmetry to explore how these relational stances assist in the construction of stories of real experiences and their discursive styles.

•••PART III

PARTICIPATION IN
SOCIAL CONTEXTS

five

Empowering the Powerless

The Coconstruction of Experience

This chapter and the two following explore different facets of participation and the related issue of responsibility as they give structure and meaning to three situated sequences of narratives. Sari, the second daughter in the Budi family, was the central speaker in each of the three situations. But each of the storytelling contexts involved different participants who interpreted and hence performed their roles in the speech event in accordance with that interpretation. I have argued that meaning is strongly tied to social context and it is through these stories that we begin to see how aspects of meaning are actively shaped. We specifically learn to recognize how participation in a conversation is synonymous with being responsible for it. Responsibility here has a wide range. Initially, we need to keep in mind that there is no freedom of speech in this society and that disagreement or conflict of whatever kind tends to be avoided. Furthermore, it is my intention to show that these Javanese speakers do not reflexively see their "tradition" as oppressive but rather actively participate in sustaining it as a high cultural ideal. With a tradition of refinement and elegance in all social interactions as the backdrop, these Javanese speakers are acutely aware that words released into the public sphere carry consequences. These situations illustrate the extent to which the story is linked to a sociocentric framework that begins with the participants and extends into the broader domain of community membership and the elements of hierarchy that shape it.

The stories, with Sari as the consistent speaker, revolve around the negotiation of a social dilemma. In a society that rewards equanimity as a sign of personal power and spiritual strength, we examine how Sari, her friends, and indirectly tens of thousands like her handle their personal experiences of abuse. Sari and her cohort, a group of young, female factory workers, were forced to endure fear, blatant inequality, and violence. For these politically naive women, however, this factory experience is the first in which they were personally confronted by actions in stark conflict with the "natural" order, which both feeds and is maintained by Javanese refinement. Those that own the factory are not Javanese and thus have no skills in legitimizing inequality from "natural" perspectives.[1]

I have documented the story Sari tells over the next three chapters over the course of several weeks and through three different situations to illustrate the drastic transformation it undergoes in each telling. The ways in which the story is altered is directly attributed to changes in relational positions and how speakers perceive their rights, roles, and obligations to their sense of self-other-community. We see how this attachment to participation and responsibility is stronger than the right to denounce the clearly illegal acts of Sari's factory managers. While all the tellings take place in the same shabby sitting room described at the beginning of this book, participants change and thus the story also changes.

In the first telling, Sari and two of her fellow factory coworkers are describing their experiences in a style that I refer to as empowering. Their attempt at resistance, however, will be interpreted in conjunction with the dominant ideologies that dictate its inevitable failure. Their particularly Javanese style of protest demanded that they erase all indexes of hierarchy within their own immediate contexts of self and other. Yet, the broader contexts of others and community rejected such a "bold" stance, and the fear of challenging the social order prevented wider support. The second telling in chapter 6 highlights the familial relationships that preserve the women's disempowerment. In this situation, Sari explains the motivations of the protest to a cohort's father while Pak Budi is also present. Here we see how power is negotiable, depending on such issues as access to information, age, gender, and participation. Sari's role as narrator and defender of the cause is presented as a "collective" self. Never given from the position of an agent, Sari's narrative suggests a conception of agency that rejects spatiotemporal anchoring, while it firmly—and naively—accepts the responsibility of resistance as a collective. The final telling in chapter 7, places Sari in a relationally disempowered position to her elder sister Atik and their friend Yanti. Although the protest is quickly crushed and the women are all blacklisted as criminals, Sari still reframes her story in accordance with the shared norms and expectations of her immediate superiors. What these chapters show is the explicit effects of community on the construction of experience vis-à-vis the stories, and of identity vis-à-vis the storytellers.

Participation as Responsibility

The women's narratives in this corpus and the mainly informal speech situations in which they evolve are all jointly produced speech events in which sequences of relational events (i.e., events as representative of social norms and expectations) unfold. These stories are shaped primarily by the relationships that exist between participants and the communities that define these relationships. Conceptions of participation in Javanese inter-actions are inevitably linked to hierarchy, which means that standard dis-cursive practices strategically order relational positions into a local brand of harmony. Thus, the speech situations illustrate how the experiential and cognitive selves they construct are the products of a speaker's respon-sibility to the community's sense of order. The stories presented expose the conflict that arises when the social order and its unconditional legiti-macy and domination interact with the abuse of power and the expecta-tions of silent acquiescence.

Responsible agency, in a Javanese cultural matrix, explicitly highlights the refined performance elements of publicly spoken words, ensuring that the consequences of talk do not disrupt the harmony of the speech situa-tion or the wider community. Cooperative participation and interactive relationships are social strategies for sharing responsibility in the construc-tion of meaning, which further ensures that meaning or members never offend or threaten the status quo. Since we have already seen how these Javanese speakers create multivocalic frames in storytelling, we can begin to see this as a means of focusing on the collectivity, not the individual. Collective storytelling does not take responsibility away from an individual speaker but rather reveals the speaker's responsibility to the community, which includes the shaping of publicly appropriate identities.

The strategies of participation that speakers take up reveal how the needs of social interaction at the immediate and broader levels of con-textual knowledge shape identity. Thus, responsible agency is a matter of choice, demonstrated by the degree to which a speaker participates in a conversation and, hence, takes up its positions as her own. Agency, then, is synonymous with participation in these texts, and it can be mea-sured as an index of a speaker's choice in being responsible to the group-constructed conception of meaning and harmony. But as the following chapters reveal, in a society that rejects conflict, criticism, and disagree-ment as inappropriate and even illegal, participation is a thoroughly po-liticized act.

The linking of participation to responsibility has its precedent in Hill and Irvine (1993). In their introduction, they describe responsibility as a communicative event in which decisions about agency are played out. Responsible agency in these terms can be "claims and disclaimers of authorship or spokesmanship, decision-making about a course of action" (1993:4). Agency, then, need not be the subjective agent we expect from so much of Western-based literature, that is, the intentioned speaker cen-tral to models of communication.

As Duranti (1993) has shown in Samoa, another non-Western society, talk and interpretation are activities for the assignment of responsibility, not intentions. Just as I have argued from these Javanese data, words do not represent private meanings but rather are interpreted as a way of understanding and controlling social relationships. Utterances are often assessed through their consequences rather than their original circumstances in a way that negates the force of the speaker's intentions. With such normative constraints as these, the social order is protected and members are locked into their hierarchical order of rights and obligations. Yet in the politically oppressive Indonesian context, these hierarchical means for achieving harmony are defined as elegant and refined, and acquiescence as a way of life for those who submit is glorified and locally interpreted as a sign of personal power. Harsh media censorship, laws that prohibit criticism of the government or any of its representatives, and the evocation of national enemies such as communism whenever those at the bottom of the social ladder attempt to speak, ensure that coercive means buttress the cooperative means of eliminating alternative positions from public discourse.

As the following chapters illustrate, participants have a collective right to determine the force of their speech actions and, subsequently, the consequences of those actions. If participation is the collective assignment of responsibility to the immediate, and to varying degrees the broader, community, participation in the narratives implies involvement not just in the speech event but also in the social consequences reflected in the participants' words and positions. Silence, or a lack of participation, becomes a highly meaningful act of rebellion or rejection.

The following chapters illustrate the roles of the participants as they appropriate the identities and discourses required for the situation. This act of appropriation is apparent in the shaping of the stories that emerge as a direct consequence of the public performance of a series of oral narratives, which describes personal experience. Responsibility to others in a complex world of social differentiation and interactional space underlies cooperative participation in the construction of meaning and the relevance of stories (Hill and Irvine, 1993).

Introduction to the Data

By the time I recorded the 45-minute conversation in Javanese and Indonesian that I have reproduced in part here, I had already been recording talk in the Budi family home for over a year and a half. I was a well-established part of their daily life. Sari was aged 26 at this time. As the conversation opens, Sari and Sigah are discussing their friends' love prospects. Endang will arrive about 15 minutes into the conversation. Sari, Sigah, and Endang are coworkers in a local garment factory. All are unmarried and roughly the same age, but Sari is the oldest and the host, allotting her the position of power within this context.

These three women had recently met when Sari was hired by the Taman Tirto garment factory. Several weeks into the job, however, factory policy toward the workers suddenly changed. Salaries were cut drastically below minimum wage or withheld altogether, and the women were required to work more than 12 hours per day, 7 days a week. Quitting was not an option as unemployment in Indonesia is high and legitimate job opportunities are scarce, especially for those not financially able to pay exorbitant bribes. So this small group of young women decided to fight for their rights.

The factory's treatment of the female workers is without doubt illegal, but Indonesia rarely enforces the laws that defend workers' rights and minimum salary requirements. That the salaries of female factory workers are 40–60% lower than men's is not locally evaluated as inequality or unfairness. This method for Indonesia to attract investors by guaranteeing the lowest wages in Asia (actually, second only to Bangladesh) is defined as a necessary act of support to aid in the development of the state. Falsely assuming that women do not support families, but are supported, and that women are not main wage earners, but support earners, the authorities claim that there is no need for wage and gender equality.[2] Newspaper articles, slogans, and community organizations constantly praise women for their sacrifices in the name of harmony and national development. For this tiny band of women to be meeting in an attempt to build a united stand against abuse was as exceptional as it was dangerous. Those at the bottom of the social hierarchy are expected to accept their fates (*nrimo*), which is what most of the factory women had indeed done.

Yet, the hierarchical values that effortlessly silence and ultimately abuse these young women in their factories are similar to those that silence them in their own homes. The elaborate hierarchical systems that mediate Javanese social interaction and the cultural values it represents help maintain the social order and guarantee the appearance of calm elegance and orderliness. Even though this small group of working-class women did recognize illegal oppression and abuse in the factory, they could not conquer the social-interactional traditions in their fight for their rights. How they manage to launch a battle and yet remain within the cultural constraints that demand acquiescence gives us a rare and intimate perspective on Javanese forms of resistance. The analysis of this story reveals how the cohort empowered themselves to take up the fight despite these cultural constraints.

The fight began when Sari and the others visited the government-run Department of Labor (Departemen Tenaga Kerja, abbreviated as Depnaker), initially to collect pamphlets. They read over the rules and regulations for the employment of women to decide exactly what laws were being broken and how to advance their case. They followed the specific and clearly defined rules presented in the pamphlets, which involved registering an official complaint with the department, holding meetings with its representatives, and then allowing the department's spokespersons to negotiate with the factory owners.[3] The women also campaigned for other workers to join the cause by holding meetings and creating a support group lottery for those needing time off or transportation home late at night.

While the protest was short-lived and the outcome was inevitable failure, it poignantly demonstrates the potential for oppression inscribed into the daily norms of speech practices in Java. Through the creation of a protest discourse, the women were able to resist the commands of authority. But it was only among their cohort, far from the horrors of the factory, that their voices could be substantiated as a voice of resistance, albeit one that was barely heard. The following texts illustrate how participation aligns with responsibility in the framing of women's narratives. Ultimately, we see how this linkage of participation to responsibility is turned around to disastrous effects.

Positioning the Disempowered

We examine participation and responsibility by investigating the ways in which Sari, Sigah, and Endang used repetition in their conversation as a device for creating the appearance of a consolidated community in protest. Repetition served two essential functions in the talk. It confirmed the cohorts' solidarity by verifying their like-mindedness in undertaking this dangerous act of protest and by distinguishing them from the immoral and unjust authority. Since we are dealing with two levels of repetition, that is, repetition of nonpresent voices and repetition of those present, I follow the cohorts' style of distinguishing presence from nonpresence by using different terms: repetition and allo-repetition (Ishikawa, 1991; Tannen, 1989). Repeating the (nonpresent) voice of authority empowered the women by verifying the morality and correctness of their own fight, while allo-repeating one another's words unified the group's assurance of support and strength in this brave endeavor.

While descriptions of the Javanese language have previously focused on its highly complex system of speech levels, the following speech situation displays none of the hierarchical elements associated with even the minimal norms of daily Javanese social interaction. These minimal forms include vocative kinship terms (Wolfowitz 1991:39), which appeared prior to the protest and again after it was over as markers of relative age: *mbak* for elder sister and *dhi* for younger sibling. This avoidance of indexicals of relative social place was symbolic of the creation of a protest discourse.

The conversation began as I entered the Budi home and switched on the recorder. Sari and Sigah were talking about others at the factory. In response, I asked Sari how her meetings with Depnaker were going. As an observer of the initial steps, the collection and review of pamphlets, and as a close family friend, I had good reason to ask out of friendly concern and as an easy topic for small talk. Turns 38 through 41 show my negotiation for specific information around Sari's posted orientation topic. Sigah, the Taman Tirto coworker whom I had not met before, seemed a bit reserved at first but that quickly disintegrated as she got caught up in the social action of storytelling.[4]

The factory management had imposed overtime on their workers.[5] When this command was issued, management claimed that any worker with a signed letter from a parent, stating his or her objection to over-time, would be released. In her story (turn 42), Sari claims that she had not intended her letter as a test of the factory's policy. But as she approached with the letter, she found that the release policy was untrue.

(20) *"I Don't Want to Know"*

37. LAINE: La piye to Mbak nek Depnaker ki.	So how's it going then, Mbak at that Depnaker.
38. SARI: Sesok selåså	Next Tuesday
39. LAINE: Sesok selåså rep åpå?	Next Tuesday [you] plan what?
40. SARI: Arep maju protes kuwi.	[We] plan to advance the protest.
41. LAINE: La piye to Mbak.	So what's that about then Mbak.
42. SARI: *Kan. nek. anu ki.*	It's like. if. whatsit.
kon *tandatangan pulang pagi* ngono[6]	this order to get a signature to go home early
Yo *kan, kebetulan* sing maju ki aku.	So y'know, coincidentally the one who stepped forward was me.
"Pokoknya saya tak mau tahu!"	"The point is I don't want to know about it."
"Lho pak *ini kan, ada* *tandatangan dari Bapak!"*	"But sir here right there's a signature from my father!"
"Pokoknya saya tidak mau tahu,"	"The point is I don't want to know about it."
Nganti sakiki <u>ora dibayar tho</u> . . .	Up to now [salaries] haven't been paid.
45. LAINE: <u>Ora dibayar tho?</u>	[You mean salaries] haven't been paid?
46. SARI: Okeh . . . sik ånå sik kurang slawe ewu	Lots. from before there's a debt of [rp]25,000,[7]
47. LAINE: Wow	Wow
48. SARI: Kurang rongpuluh ewu, *padahal* kuwi wong kurang wong telungatus	A loss of 20,000, but the thing is this loss is for 300 people
49. LAINE: lho. kok iså,	Oh. How can they do that,
50. SARI: Mulane dhå metu <u>kabeh!</u>	So that's why everyone will strike!

In story (20), Sari is describing how the management in her factory prevents interaction with the workers. It thoroughly disempowers Sari and her coworkers by disallowing any communication: *pokoknya, saya tidak mau tahu* ("The point is, I don't want to know about it."). This speech act succeeds in its purpose as a powerful performative by effectively silencing the workers. I call this utterance a performative because it does not simply describe a state of affairs but also actively creates that state (Levinson, 1983:228). In this case, the achieved state is one in which the factory workers are effectively robbed of any dialogue with management.

Despite having created the rule itself, Sari shows that the voice of authority is the voice of lies. She repeats the words that silenced her twice: *pokoknya, saya tidak mau tahu* in Indonesian, the language used by management. She displays her own surprise at discovering the duplicity of the rule, explicitly indexed through *Lho* as she re-creates her own response in Indonesian as reported speech:

42. SARI: *"pokoknya saya tak mau tahu!"*	"The point is I don't want to know about it!"
→ "Lho pak *ini kan, ada tandatangan dari Bapak!"*	→ "But sir here right there's a signature from my father!"
"Pokoknya saya tidak mau tahu."	"The point is I don't want to know about it."

Sari is reconstructing the voice of authority as surrounding and stifling her own voice. She can follow the authority's own rules and still be rejected. Her evaluation of these experiences to the cohort is uttered in Javanese, creating a discursive boundary that separates what will emerge into good and evil. By presenting herself as fully respecting the rule and completely naive about its deceit, Sari is highly effective in displaying the underhanded way in which that authority silences her. She repeats that utterance frequently throughout her narrative to identify the boundaries of the power play she is fighting, a boundary made more salient by code switching.

In addition to explaining that salaries have also been withheld, Sari has presented the reasons for the workers' grievances against management: overtime with no recourse to exemption. This is why, she tells me in turn 50, all the workers will go out on strike. Within Javanese storytelling processes, Sari's story is told forcefully and effectively. Yet, she offers no directly incriminating details about the overtime. The order to get a signature for overtime release is directly translated as "go home [*pulang*] in the morning [*pagi*] which is apparently a repeated, or formulaic, phrase since it is uttered in Indonesian." Words like *pagi* (morning) or *siang* (midday), *sore* (late afternoon), and *malam* (evening) index particular times of day, but they also clarify relational time (see chapter 4). *Pulang pagi* can mean to go home in the morning or it can mean to go home earlier than another specified or implied time. We are left to infer all of these essential facts from the few lines of constructed dialogue:

42. SARI: *Kan.* nek. anu ki.	It's like. if. whatsit.
→ kon *tandatangan* pulang pagi ngono	→ this order to get a signature to go home early
Yo *kan, kebetulan,*	So y'know, coincidentally,
sing maju ki aku.	the one who stepped forward was me.
"pokoknya saya tak mau tahu!"	"The point is I don't want to know about it!"

"Lho pak *ini kan ada <u>tandatangan</u> dari Bapak!*"	"But sir here right there's a signature from my father!"
"<u>*Pokoknya saya tidak mau tahu.*</u>"	"The point is I don't want to know about it."
Nganti sakiki <u>ora dibayar tho</u> . . .	Up to now, [salaries] haven't been paid.

In the acceptably hierarchical and paternal relations that exist between manager and (female) worker, the conditions for such an authoritarian stance are conventional in Java. Sari and the other workers remain silenced, as good Javanese daughters would. Their stories display this disempowerment as an absolute manifestation of silence as a norm of politeness vis-à-vis social hierarchy (e.g., Wolf, 1996). Since the women have no voice with which to resist publicly, they resort to clandestine resistance, or the "hidden transcript" (see Scott, 1990).

The use of reported speech for Bakhtin ([1934]1981) was a crucial sign of the heteroglossic nature of all social discourse. He has shown how the multiple voices writers give to speakers in their texts index how others are to interpret the meaning or significance of that text. In the women's oral narratives, they repeat the words that oppress them to create a formulaic rallying cry through which the ugliness of their own suffering is brought to life in a way they are able to control or, at least, denounce within their own contexts. Through reported speech, Sari has discursively created a dichotomous arena in which this power play will be fought fairly.

Sari's story, then, takes on a different significance. Unfamiliar with the discourses of protest, as those low in the social hierarchy must be, the women create their own by invoking what they assume are the locally appropriate ways and means of talking resistance. In such a discourse, external evaluations of anger or threats are never uttered. Instead, the cohort use internal evaluation as they repeat the words of the factory managers. By repeating the authority's words, its positions of power are displayed as unjust and immoral. In comparison, the workers present themselves as a unified band of silenced but morally right victims. Thus, as their decision to protest solidifies, their styles of interacting as a group also solidify.

The participation strategies that emerge through narrative in this section are an iconic reflection of what the women interpret to be the discourses of protest. The key features of such a discourse are first, the joint production of narratives through "rounds," for example, the repetition and allo-repetition of stylistic features and positions from all members;[8] and second, the avoidance of any status-marking or individuating indexes, that is, speech levels, vocatives, and personal pronouns.

In the protest discourse in (20), Sari stresses her unity to her cohorts by underplaying her role. "By coincidence only" (*Yo kan kebetulan*), she was the one who came forward and spoke. Within Goffman's (1974) participation framework, Sari is an animator; she downplays her role as figure, even though it was she who stepped forward with the letter. She does not present herself as principal either—or not sole principal. To reject the discourses that disempower them, the workers must create a new one. The discourses of empowerment to this small band of young Javanese women are based on moral correctness and a fully shared commitment to the consequences of their words in a world where words are as dangerous as actions. Membership depends on equal participation, and equal participation implies an equal responsibility for the consequences of that involvement.

Empowerment through Unity

Sari stresses group participation over any individual roles in turn 50, where she states that *all* the workers will strike:

50. sari: Mulane <u>dhå metu kabeh</u>!   So that's why everyone will strike!

This is not accurate, as she and Sigah will later explain. Most of the workers would rather tolerate abysmal conditions for poor pay than face the confrontation and possible loss of jobs and wages.[9] But for the unity discourse to prevail, Sigah is required to participate in the story. She enters the story's frame by supporting Sari's reference to all the workers who are going on strike. She defends the moral position,

54. sigah: <u>Sing lawas</u> dicatut <u>kabeh</u>   The old [workers have] <u>all</u> been
                                                          cheated

which shows the significance of the way in which Sigah matched Sari's related statement in referring to "all" the workers (*kabeh*).

The discursive encoding of unity is an empowerment strategy that requires the participants to jointly produce the protest narratives. Unity enhances the narrative as a speech act by creating an iconic sharedness among words, deeds, and the responsibility for them. In the following text, Sigah joins Sari to conarrate their factory experiences.

(21) *Everybody's Scared*

71. sari: Angger entuk akeh <u>ngono ki</u>   As long as [they] get all they can
          rådå ora percåyå!   [they] just can't be trusted!
          Dikurangi sedinå meneh ki.   [We've] just had another pay cut.
          telung atus, patang atus,   300 [to] 400
72. sigah: *Tapi* <u>nek</u> kon protes <u>ngono</u>   But if ordered to protest Mbak,
          <u>ki</u> Mbak,
          <u>Dhå wedi</u>   everybody's scared.
73. yati: Wow   Wow

74. SARI: <u>Nek</u> wong Jåwå <u>ngono ki</u> *kan*,	The Javanese people are like that y'know,
<u>wedi</u> di *PHK*!	always afraid of being fired!
75. YATI: Karyawanipun nggeh katah nggeh?[10]	There are a lot of workers aren't there?
76. SIGAH: Telung ngatus	Three hundred
77. LAINE: Telung ngatus?!	Three hundred?!
78. SARI: Dadi <u>sek lawas</u> ki <u>dhå metu</u> Mbak,	So the old workers have all gone Mbak,
<u>ganti</u> sing anyar.	exchanged for new ones.
mengko sewulan, rongwulan <u>metu</u>.	later after a month, two months out.
<u>ganti</u> meneh!	changed again!
79. LAINE: He//	He//
80. SIGAH: <u>Nek</u> carane ngono,	It's their style,
gajine ora di undak-undaki.	so no salary is ever raised.
81. LAINE: Nang kene ånå undang-undang lho!	But there are laws here!
82. SARI: Ånå ning wis "*nggak mau tahu*.."	There are [some] who just "don't want to know."
"*Pokoknya*" . . . piye wingi kae jawabane,	"The point is" how'd that go yesterday, that response,
"*peraturan itu dapat diubah*?"	"The regulations can always be changed"?
Ånå *peraturan* anyar yo ora dikeki <u>ngerti</u>,	There are new regulations but they are not regarded,
ngko <u>ngerti- ngerti</u> wis <u>ganti</u> . . .	[so we think we] understand [they] change again.
83. SIGAH: *Mana yang* diemut *kalau peraturan-peraturan diubah-ubah*!	What can be done if the regulations are repeatedly changed!
84. LAINE: He . . . e	Right

Since the function of the joint production is to share responsibility for the construction and consequences of the narratives and the protest, as well as the narratives *as* protest, the more voices that enter the discourse, the more animated and informative the women become. When voices were individual, as in (20) and (21), the speakers discursively stated that "all" workers will strike and "all" have been cheated. The joint construction also corrects for a lack of support from the other workers:

72. SIGAH: *Tapi* <u>nek</u> kon protes <u>ngono</u> ki Mbak,	But if ordered to protest Mbak,
<u>dhå wedi</u>	everybody's scared
73. YATI: WOW	wow

74. SARI: <u>Nek</u> wong Jåwå <u>ngono ki</u>   The Javanese people are like that
    kan,   y'know,
    <u>wedi</u> di *PHK*   always afraid of being fired

This excerpt (turns 72–74) informs us of the fears involved in protest. It is
not *all* the workers that join the protest. It is, in fact, no more than roughly
25 out of more than 300 women. While many of the others are very sympathetic, the rest would rather tolerate the exploitation than risk conflict
or job loss. Yet, the protesters define the unmentioned lack of support as
fear, in effect, positioning themselves as care-givers, while at the same
time not distinguishing themselves from the others. They speak as if they
act in unity for the betterment of all. Sigah says, *dhå wedi* (<u>everyone</u> [is]
afraid), and Sari informs us that it is *wong Jawa* (the Javanese people)
who are afraid of being fired. The inclusive stance highlights the workers
as united in fear, but it specifically avoids presenting them as divided.

This unity is built on the tightly organized, interactively complex
speaking round as a process of achieving thematic and stylistic cohesion (cf. Tannen, 1984). Both speakers focus their turns on similar points,
allo-repeating key words and their evaluations of them. Both women
explain the fear as all-inclusive, while they both avoid any of the distinguishing facets of the events described. One frequent method to make
the conarration stance explicit is to link the utterances directly to, or as
a continuation or completion of, the previous one by using discourse
markers:

71. SARI: Angger entuk akeh <u>ngono ki</u>   As long as [they] get all they can
    rådå ora percåyå.   [they] just can't be trusted.
    Dikurangi sedinå meneh ki   [We've] just had another pay cut
    telung atus, patang atus,   300 [to] 400
72. SIGAH: *Tapi* <u>nek</u> kon protes <u>ngono</u>   but if ordered to protest Mbak,
    <u>ki</u> Mbak,
    dhå wedi   everybody's scared
73. YATI: Wow   Wow
74. SARI: <u>Nek</u> wong Jåwå <u>ngono ki</u>   The Javanese people are like that,
    kan   y'know,
    wedi di *PHK*   always afraid of being fired.

Sigah's use of *tapi* (but) in turn 72 shows that her turn is a continuation
of Sari's preceding turn through which Sigah presents additional information that evaluates Sari's event clause. *Tapi,* as the English "but," has a
comparative function in that it brackets a unit of talk as a contrast to the
preceding argument, which Sari has just presented. Sigah's utterance con-
trasts Sari's statement that the workers have been subjected to another
pay cut by adding how such a situation is counter to expectations of fair
play. Yet despite such blatant infringements on their rights, the workers
are still afraid to protest. While the ideas themselves are contrastive, the

occurrence of the discourse marker, "but," links them as a continuous idea (Schiffrin, 1987).

The utterance initial use of *nek* (a conditional, or "if" clause marker) in turn 74 explains in further detail the contents of Sigah's turn. Sari's *wong Jawa ngono ki* (the Javanese are like that) contains the text deictic (Levinson, 1983) *ngono*, which points to, and ties its topic to, Sigah's utterance. The word *nek* cannot be translated into English as a conditional in these contexts but may be better understood as meaning "with regard to." In turn 80, *nek* also clearly marks the utterance as the continuation of a preceding one:

78. SARI: <u>Dadi</u> sek lawas ki dho metu Mbak,	So the old workers have all gone Mbak,
Ganti sing anyar.	Exchanged for new ones.
Mengko sewulan rongwulan metu.	Later after a month two months out.
Ganti meneh!	Changed again!
79. LAINE: He//	He//
80. SIGAH: <u>Nek</u> carane <u>ngono</u>,	It's their style,
gajine ora di undak-undaki.	so no salary is ever raised.

In both turn 74 and turn 80, *nek* precedes an idea unit with a final demonstrative *ngono*. Both utterances cannot stand alone but explicitly mark their topics as located in a previous turn and, hence, dependent on that turn for its meaningful coherence. Sari's turn-initial *dadi* (turn 78) marks her idea unit as an inferenced causal reaction to the facts already presented. These discourse markers function as specific linking devices, in which coherence is interactive and meaning is located across speakers. Symbolically then, two speakers become one voice by jointly constructing their positions in the story.

After Endang, a third member of the factory group, arrives, the women discuss the events with more animation. It is impossible to discern what, if any, discursive asymmetry might exist among the three women. No one stands out as being in charge, as all take exceptional strides to preserve an equal footing by cotelling a story, a group stance that is essential for the success of their protest.

(22) *Training*

158. SARI: <u>Åpå</u> enek Tony mau nesu-nesu,	Wasn't that sickening Tony's anger earlier,
"sekarang yang nggak masuk nggak pakai surat ijin,	"from now on, anyone who does not come to work and does not have a letter of permission,
<u>*besuk masuk training.*</u>" [hahaha]	[will be] demoted to training." [hahah]
159. LAINE: <u>Training</u>? [hahaha]	Training? [hahaha]
160. SIGAH: <u>Di lebokke nggon training</u> Mbak.	To be sent down to training Mbak

161. ENDANG: *Padahal dia sudah*   Even though she already has
     berpengalaman kok   experience y'know
     <u>dilebokke nggon training.</u>   to be sent down to training.

Sari initiates the story in (22) by using the past-time adverb *mau* (earlier, before) and an orienting evaluation of disgust for Tony's display of anger,[11] followed by a direct quote from Tony, their boss, issuing her ultimatum. Any worker who misses a day and does not have permission will be sent down to "training." I repeat the word "training" in disbelief, to which both Sigah and Endang allo-repeat in Javanese what Sari quotes directly in Indonesian. A pattern is emerging here in which one woman creates a scene through reported speech and the others repeat it in unified evaluation of the insulting implications. Both Tannen (1984, 1987, 1989) and Ishikawa (1991, after Tannen), discuss this type of repetition as joint idea constructions that complete or supplement another's utterance. Tannen (1989:62) regards repetition as one of the features of "high involvement style," and Ishikawa (1991:568–569) shows how allo-repetition, or the repetition of another's words or phrases, represents the shared ideas and stance among the participants. All the occurrences in this speech situation support this view of repetition as an important feature of jointly constructed agreement and support, making them an essential feature of solidarity.

To preserve their perfect unity, the women almost exclusively avoid kinship terms, pronouns, or names throughout their conversations. The absence of these indexes of individuality is highly marked (Joseph Errington, 1988; Keeler, 1984; Wolff and Poedjosoedarmo, 1982:40–46; Wolfowitz, 1991). There are two exceptions, however. In turn 66, Sari says, "*Rådå ora penak he dik*" (it's rather not very nice, is it *dik*), and in turn 114 Sigah uses *Mbak Endang* as a greeting for Endang's entrance. These two occurrences of kin terms show that the women are aware of their status-laden age differences. It assures us that Sari is indeed the eldest, and Sigah is the youngest. Yet the women ignore the kin terms, which serve to separate and rank them, making their avoidance even more significant. Meanwhile, I am frequently addressed by the respectful kin term *Mbak* or *Mbak Len*. As I am the only member of the group who does not share their factory experiences, they may be strengthening their in-group solidarity by framing their stories for me. By directing these utterances to another, they in effect strengthen their coproduced positions as multivocalic and equal in purpose.

The longer they enact these positions, the bolder and the more animated the women become in their empowering solidarity. The following excerpt is an orientation round for story (23):

263. SIGAH: Åpå rådå mumet *saya*   I'm getting a headache.
     Dua hari . . . tiga hari ki,   Two days, three days already,
     tidur di pabrik   sleeping at the factory

264. LAINE: Ah . . . !	Ah . . . !
265. SARI: *Nggak dibayar* . . .	And not paid
266. ALL: Iyaa! Mulih wae! bali!! [haha]	Yea! just go home! go back! [haha]
271. ENDANG: Kerjå *tapi* ora dibayar	To work but not to be paid

In turn 263, Sigah complains about having had to sleep at the factory for three nights, to which Sari adds a comment about not getting paid for any of it. All three women shout out an overlapping chorus of *mulih wae! mbali!* followed by Endang's allo-repetition of Sari's previous utterance. Sari then begins a story frame by returning to her formulaic reported speech to remind us again of the morality of their predicament. Here she presents it within the factory context to show how immoral their disempowerment is.

(23) *All That Crying*

272. SARI: → Jarene *saya nggak mau tahu*	→ And they said "I don't want to know."
Mbayangke we sedih åpå,	Can [you] imagine the sadness, heh,
enek, sing nglakoni [ha ha ha . . .]	[its] disgusting, what [they] did [hahaha]
Direwangi nangis-nangis ora entuk mulih . . .	All that crying and still not allowed to leave . . .
273. SIGAH: Ha.a. nangis neng ngarep lawang,	That's right crying in front of the door,
ora entuk bali tetepan . . .	and still not allowed to leave.
274. LAINE: He.e . . .	He.e . . .
275. ENDANG: Nganti jam telu	Up to 3:00
ngantek aneng kantin anu	there in the canteen, uhm.
"Kowe ki seka ngendi wae to?"	"What are you doing in here?"
"Ngelih pak" ngono.	"[We're] hungry sir" it was said.

These turns present the full impact of the factory scene—young women standing by the locked door, exhausted and frightened, crying and wanting to go home. The women are answered with a firm "I don't want to know about it" in Indonesian. "Get back to work!" Allo-repetition unifies Sari's and Sigah's utterances, and Endang's expands the scene of cruelty and despair to the canteen, where some of the workers had hidden. They were discovered and had to justify not being at their work stations. Endang repeats for her cohorts the words that were spoken on the scene, in effect clarifying again the diverse we-they roles that were being played out here. In her story, the empowered are angry because some workers had stopped work to have lunch, even though lunch was already three hours late.

Yet, whether or not Sari or any of her cohort had taken part in these scenes or how often they may have occurred is not specified. All of the subject positions are left ambiguous. The conarration can become a protest discourse because it constructs an inclusive story frame, in which all are equally subjected to the injustice. Solidarity in the protest discourse means perfect unity, so that none of the distinguishing features of Javanese interaction may be uttered.

The significance of the protest discourse is found in the correspondence of meaning between its discursive form and the psychological and social realities thereby constituted (Ishikawa 1991; van Dijk, 1994). To these women, solidarity is created by sharing the words and the responsibility for their consequences, all of which are achieved through repetition. Jointly constructing the protest stories is what creates their empowering solidarity in terms that have been similarly described elsewhere: "The acts that construct a narrative are also acts that construct a family" (Ochs 1993:295).

This is not a "family discourse" in a Javanese sense, however, because Javanese families are hierarchically ranked and labeled by obligatory vocative kinship terms. In the protest discourse, the "siblings" avoid such distinguishing terms in favor of a highly marked equality. The protest discourse, created through symbolic symmetry and the story round—in which each speaker has an equal position both in the "family" and in the story—are iconic constructions of shared responsibility for the consequences of their words.

Evaluation Tropism

Despite a clear and moral purpose in creating a firm and unified voice in the performance of their protest narratives, it is in the evaluation stances that major differences of character appear. The diverse styles of evaluating the whole experience expose the discursive areas where potential social and cultural diversities become apparent.

Sari's preferred strategy for evaluating the ugliness of the scene is to use reported speech, especially the repetition of the line she evaluates as most cruel and most unjust:

42. SARI: *"Pokoknya saya tidak mau*   "The point is I don't want to know
    tahu."   about it."

Often questions are raised about an experience and the reports of it. The truth of a direct quote is not at issue but rather the action it serves in the narrative. Whether or not the quote is constructed (cf. Tannen 1989) or is the faithful rendering of a past utterance, its frequency and its purpose in the narratives show that the women wave it like a banner. It is an opportunity for the workers to confront and challenge authority. The women have appropriated the voice of their own oppressor in order to fight back (Bakhtin [1934] 1981). Whereas others have said that reported speech (e.g., Besnier 1993; Duranti 1993; Graham 1993; Shuman 1993) is a way for speakers to lessen responsibility for their own words, these women have achieved the opposite. The voice of authority is the voice of lies, injustice, and immorality from which the cohort's just and moral voices can be better heard. But, individually and at work, the women are silent. Collectively and at a distance from authority, they are empowered. Invoking the voice of authority, then, empowers their own voice of resistance. But resistance requires solidarity.

The Javanese protest discourse depends on multiple layers of repetition for its determinacy, which, as suggested by Becker (1984), establishes a topic-chain that creates a density in the interaction. The strategy of repeating the quoted words of the women's oppressors invokes a living enemy that must be fought, and thus affirms the contested positions as two distinct voices. This is what creates the event as protest. The recognition and naming of the enemy is an act of empowerment as it defines the locus of the women's disempowerment as immoral and unjust. Hence, repetition not only creates a highly animated topic-chain (cf. Becker) of conflicting voices, which are extended throughout the conversation, but also achieves the cohort's empowerment through the coconstruction of solidarity in opposition to the frequently named enemy.

Whereas Sari uses reported speech, Sigah turns to other evaluative strategies in story (21):

82. SARI: → Ånå ning wis "*nggak mau tahu*.."
"*Pokoknya*. . . . piye wingi kae jawabane,
"*Peraturan itu dapat diubah*?"

→ There are [some] who just "don't want to know."
"The point is" how'd that go yesterday that response,
"The regulations can always be changed"?

83. SIGAH: *Mana yang* diemut *kalau peraturan-peraturan diubah-ubah*!

What can be done if the regulations are repeatedly changed!

Sigah confirms Sari's recall of the immoral words as she adds and expands to the impact by externally evaluating it (turn 83). Sari repeats the disempowering words while Sigah displays their effectiveness. The women's words function interdependently, so that one turn is not nearly as effective without the other. Sari's reported speech is an internal marker that evokes the words that had wounded her, while Sigah's contribution externally evaluates the wound, expressing its depth and pain. Sigah repeats Sari's quoted words *peraturan* and *diubah* in the reduplicated forms to show how her participant role is to expand, enforce, and evaluationally intensify Sari's disimpassioned utterances. Sigah externally evaluates their situation, while Sari's style of evaluation tends to be internal. Their complementary styles may be a reaction to the other, a part of their personal styles, or a part of the cooperative strategy of unity. To construct equal responsibility, one must be equally positioned and equally involved in the story.

Yet, a potential conflict arises when Sari and Sigah show their differences with regard to rude, aggressive language. Sari and her family have definite urban *priyayi* values despite their poverty, whereas Sigah is more able to express emotion and anger. When Sigah blurts out crude names in reference to one of the bosses, Sari agrees but does not use the same style of language:

59. SIGAH: Kae wong Batak	That [woman] is a Batak[12]
60. LAINE: Såpå kuwi,	who's that
61. SARI: Bu Meri kuwi.	That Bu Meri.
63. SIGAH: Singkek jenenge	[Like a] Chinese[13] it's called
64. SARI: **Enten ngangge** kok ging kok, kok,	There are [who] use, (false start?),
→ *Saya ngak mau tahu*	→ "I don't want to know"
65. SIGAH: Singkek ki elek-elek uwis!	These Chinese they're disgusting and that's that!
66. SARI: Rådå ora penak he Dik, nyambut gawe neng kono ki.	It's rather not very nice is it Dik, working over there.

While Sari does not disagree with Sigah's vulgar references, she cannot repeat them. In turn 64, she switches to *båså*, not to honor her interlocutor, called *Dik* in turn 66, but to distance herself from Sigah's discourse. All that comes out is *kok ging kok, kok*, which has no meaning beyond surprise and disbelief, *kok* being what Errington (1988) calls a psycho-ostensive of surprise. Sari may be just as surprised at her inability to express her anger as she is at the treatment she is forced to endure at the factory. She falls back on her internal style of evaluation by repeating her formulaic reported speech: *saya enggak mau tahu*, made more poignant by the listener's knowledge that this is the most anger Sari is capable of displaying. She caps off the topic by vastly understating her situation:

66. SARI: Rådå ora penak he Dik, nyambut gawe neng kono ki.	It's rather not very nice is it Dik, working over there.

Both Sari and Sigah gradually match their affective stance. Turns 66, 70, and 71 show how Sigah gives up her obscenities and Sari moves toward Sigah's externally evaluated stance. They reclaim unity on middle ground through repetition of the understating *rådå* ("rather"):

66. SARI: <u>Rådå</u> ora penak he Dik, nyambut gawe neng kono ki.	It's rather not very nice is it Dik, working over there.
70. SIGAH: Anu . . . <u>rådå</u> pelit	Hmm, [they're] rather stingy.
71. SARI: <u>Rådå</u> ora percåyå!	[They] rather can't be trusted.

As Sigah becomes more agentic in her evaluation, however, so does Sari.

85. SIGAH: <u>Aku</u> nganti lårå . . .   I am just sick from it all
86. SARI: Sesok <u>aku</u> pindah kok Mbak   Tomorrow I'm going to move
    Len.   y'know Mbak Laine.

In turn 85 Sigah steps out the story's frame to globally evaluate her personal situation. Sari follows suit but without the emotional and physical
intimacy Sigah uses.[14]

The Repositioning: Unity and Its Accomplishments

The stories have revealed that Taman Tirto's management is withholding
salaries; subjecting workers to arbitrary pay cuts; and forcing the women
to work overtime, sometimes locking them in the factory all night.[15] While
hours are doubled, meals and breaks are awarded only to those who
comply. When the women do not come to work or show up late, they
are punished by being demoted to "training" status, despite many years
of experience. No one, according to the stories I heard from workers, has
ever verbally confronted the management, except for the letter incident
Sari describes in (20). Any attempts at discussion are instantly blocked by
pokoknya, saya enggak mau tahu.

Global event clauses in both Sari's and Sigah's utterances are in object-
focus constructions or, in terms of Goffman's framing principal, are specifically nonagent:

40. SARI: Arep maju protes kuwi.   [We] plan to advance the protest.
42. SARI: Yo *kan, kebetulan*   So, y'know, coincidentally,
    sing maju ki aku.   the one who stepped forward was
                                           me.

    . . .

Nganti sakiki ora dibayar tho . . .   Up to now, [salaries] haven't been
                                          paid.
72. SIGAH: *Tapi* nek kon protes ngono   But if ordered to protest Mbak,
    ki Mbak dho wedi   everybody's scared

It would be erroneous of us to view a discursively nonagentic (passive
voice or object focus, as it is sometimes referred to in Indonesian) utterance as iconic to the women's passivity in facing up to their predicament.
They are utterly, and without a doubt, disempowered by their factory
managers.[16] But the women's actions are by no means passive. Sari, Sigah,
Endang, and others have organized meetings, contacted the Department
of Labor, and studied the laws and regulations regarding the treatment of
female factory laborers. In a society that will not openly condone strikes

or even differences of opinion, Sari and her friends are indeed behaving with exceptional boldness. Such resolute behavior requires wide support, and the women must act as a group. Regardless of personal positions, the women must protect their conformity, which they see as their only chance of survival.[17]

In (24), the women are discussing the attack strategy they have been enacting for at least a few weeks, that is, a type of lottery for getting a day off from work.[18] While they may be prevented from any direct interaction with their oppressors, they do have their clandestine discourses, which have led to small accomplishments. The key to the success of these empowering discourses is their unifying solidarity, that is, the equality and preservation of the group.

In the following story round, the women are discussing tomorrow's events, which leads them to evaluate their own roles within the group.

(24) *The Lottery*

248. SIGAH: Pådå-pådå sesuk <u>ora mlebu</u> kan Mbak-Mbake.	Tomorrow everyone won't go to work y'know the Mbak-Mbake.
"*Soalnya saya itu dititipi surat,*	"You see, I have been entrusted with this letter,
karena teman-teman ada keperluan yang penting."	because my friends have an important engagement."
Saya harus sampaikan pada teman-teman yang lain.	I must inform the others.
249. LAINE: Ow . . . ya ya . . .	Ow . . . ya ya . . .
250. SARI: Nek dipikir, aku yå arep <u>ora mlebu</u> neng aku kan kokean sing arep.	If [I] think about it, I too wouldn't go to work. but [if] I [too stay away] y'know too many [won't go in tomorrow].
251. ENDANG: Kan, aku setu wingi wis <u>ora mlebu</u>! Saiki genti aku sing <u>ora mlebu</u>. . . .	Y'know last Saturday I had my chance to stay out! Now my turn has come around again *to* stay out.

As seen in (20), presenting a letter to request release from overtime fails. So the cohort have created a system whereby a predetermined number of women each day have absentee letters given to the management on their behalf. Thus, the workers prevent the rejection of their requests by never appearing for the interaction. In turn 248, Sigah is rehearsing what she will say to the Indonesian-speaking bosses at the factory when the *mbak-mbake* ("sisters") do not show up for work:

248. SIGAH: "*Soalnya saya itu dititipi surat,*	"You see I have been entrusted with this letter,

karena teman-teman ada	because my friends have an impor-
keperluan yang penting."	tant engagement."
Saya harus sampaikan pada	I must inform the others.
teman-teman yang lain.	

Sari also has a role. She must appear tomorrow at the dreaded place to allow others the opportunity to stay home:

250. SARI: Nek dipikir, aku yå arep <u>ora mlebu</u>	If [I] think about it, I too wouldn't go to work.
neng aku kan kakean sing arep.	But [if] I [too stay away], y'know, too many [won't go in tomorrow].

And Endang too, accepts the fairness of the lottery. Tomorrow is her turn to stay away:

251. ENDANG: Kan, aku setu wingi wis <u>ora mlebu!</u>	Y'know last Saturday I had my chance to stay out!
Saiki genti aku sing <u>ora mlebu.</u> . . .	Now, my turn has come around again to stay out.

In these utterances, each speaker presents an agentic description of her activities for the next day. Yet, the contents of each turn displays its firm responsibility to the others through a discursive format that is interactively equal in terms of position, purpose, length, and goal. Story (24) shows that each player knows her role in the performance, and it is exactly this responsibility to the group's unity over all potential independent roles or asymmetries that leads to each small success.

In chapter 2, I quoted Paolo Freire's *Pedagogy of the Oppressed* to find a possible explanation for the role of authoritarian control in the cognitive and behavioral development of the *wong cilik*. Freire described this relationship as one of *prescription* since it "represents the imposition of one individual's choice upon another, transforming the consciousness of the person prescribed to into one that conforms with the prescriber's consciousness. Thus, the behavior of the oppressed is a prescribed behavior, following as it does the guidelines of the oppressor" ([1970] 1993:28–29). We need to go deeper into an oppressed model of humanity to better understand why, as Freire also states, "the oppressed . . . tend themselves to become oppressors" ([1970] 1993:27–28).

Story (25) shows Sari, Sigah, and Endang repositioning themselves in relation to another boss, Meri, a Philippine woman whom they describe as crude, loud, and ill mannered. This text shows how the Javanese social values of refinement and elegance are evoked—not for its role in disempowering the cohort but for the purpose of reviving their self-esteem.

(25) *Meri, Wong Ndeså*

169. SARI: Nek <u>ngomong banter-banter</u> iyå Mbak Len?	When [she] speaks, it's so loud y'know Mbak Len?
170. LAINE: Iyå . . . pådhå wae . . .	O yea, same [as me]
171. ENDANG: <u>Omong-omonge keras</u> suarane. . . .	[Her] speaking voice is so crude
172. SIGAH: Kåyå <u>eneng gunung</u> kae, <u>ora duwe tånggå</u>, hahaha. . . .	Like up in the mountains, with no neighbors, hahah
174. SARI: Kae ki, kae ki, <u>wong ndeså</u>.	That [woman], that [woman], no class,
<u>Neng</u> Filipina <u>gunung ora duwe</u> <u>tånggå</u>,	These Philippine mountain [folk that] have no neighbors,
nek <u>ngomong bengok-bengok</u> neng arep lawang [hahaha]	when [she] speaks [she] screams in front of the door [hahahh]

In this text, the women link their utterances into one unified narrative by repeating and allo-repeating their insulting descriptions of their boss, Meri, coconstructing a cohesive story, rich with imagery of vile, ill-mannered behavior. This coconstructed story vividly demonstrates how these victims of the social order are ready to use any means at their disposal to classify and persecute another. Meri's visible frustration and anger with what she sees as the ignorance and incompetence of her workers become a tool for ridicule because a "proper" Javanese adult must never call such attention to herself. Yet, the public display of social elegance as a celebrated and measurable badge of in-group membership is denied to the cohort because of its own low status as factory workers. Not only Meri is branded vile because of her lack of refinement; so are the *wong ndeså*, or "rural peasants" that Meri is compared to, as were the lowly pedicab drivers at the Stasion Tugu story (7).

If we examine more closely how the women maintain their self-esteem under these difficult conditions, we can extract a scale of social worth based on negative behaviors and classifications. Individuals who display loud or crude actions, as described in (25) and (26), are referred to as *ndeså*. To refer to another as *wong ndeså*, or "peasant," is highly insulting but not crude, as was Sigah's use of the racist terms *singkek* and *wong Batak*. *Singkek* is a vulgar term for ethnic Chinese, who are frequent targets of political separatism, violence, and hatred—partly because of a history of social and economic inequality during the Dutch era; religious differences; and what is said to be the periodic and well-organized incitement of mass hysteria, intended to draw attention away from other social issues.[19] This is easily achieved in a nation internally separated by hundreds of ethnic groups and languages. As we can see by the women's use of ethnic and class slurs in a highly derogatory manner, they certainly do see their own refinement as superior to others', permitting them the recourse to disparage other ethnic groups and powerful individuals, as well as the lower classes, for their crudeness.

While the women are aware of their own oppression, their perception of it is dangerously impaired by a reality that is defined by the "natural" order through which they understand their world (Freire, [1970] 1993). Thus, the women tightly grasp the same system for measuring social worth that permits their own abuse in a cyclic order of oppress-and-be-oppressed. Through the evocation of these Javanese scales of refinement in their stories, we can observe the women actively evaluating and redefining their own and others' social status. Meri, marked as one of the immoral oppressors, is ridiculed for lacking the attributes that should ideally mark her position of power, not for representing power or even abusing it. The oppressiveness of social hierarchy is not at issue here, but the behaviors appropriate for occupying positions of power are.

The cohort coconstruct these humorous pictures of an inappropriate model of power by taking up one another's contribution, repeating and expanding it to achieve their own superior status as refined, Javanese, urban dwellers.

(26) *Tony Nesu*

331. SIGAH: Mbanting lawang | Slamming the door
nggåwå gitik kae | carrying that whip (?)
njuk nek <u>nesu</u> | so when [she's] angry
sikile diunggahke kae [hahaha] | [she] raises her leg like that [hahaha]

332. SARI: La <u>ngomong basa inggris,</u> <u>yå ora dong</u>! | And speaking that English, can't understand any of it!

333. ENDANG: Tony yo judek yo! | That Tony is really hopeless right!
<u>Nesu-nesu nganggo båså</u> | [When she's] furious [she] uses
<u>inggris</u> yå? | English right?
Mbuh <u>ora dong</u> maksude åpå | haven't a clue what she's saying
deke <u>ngomong</u> |
Ning akhire lungå dewe [hahah] | In the end [she] just goes away [hahaha]

La <u>ora dong ha ha aku</u> . . . | I just haven't a clue ha hah
Såpå wae, | Who ever,
la masalahe åpå ora dong. | the problem [I] don't get it hahahah
hahahah |

334. SARI: "Sit.Sit.Sit!" åpå kuwi, | "Shit, shit, shit!" What's that,
Ndremimil kae le <u>ngomong</u> | She really does run off at the mouth
<u>bahasa</u> Inggris | in that English.
<u>Aku ora dong yå</u>! [hahahaha. . . .] | I can't understand any of it! [hahahaha. . . .]

335. SIGAH: *Bola-bali bilang* "no-gut" | Back and forth saying "no-good"
kae |
njuk *pergi* | then, go away

336. LAINE: Jahitane på <u>elek</u>?	Is it that the sewing is bad?
337. ENDANG: Ya *karena* <u>elek</u> *itu!*	Yep, because it's bad!
338. SIGAH: *Karna dia tidak*	Because they don't pay attention
memperhatikan kita	to us
dadine <u>jahitane elek</u>	we mess up the sewing

A good manager ought to "pay attention" to the workers for them to produce, as Sigah informs us in turn 338. Not only is their behavior shockingly inappropriate, but also the managers display none of the paternal attentions expected from someone in power. It seems extremely likely, then, that a manager who is Javanese and refined could easily achieve everything that Meri and Tony could not (Wolf, 1996).

In the safety of their band of conspirators, far from the disempowering realities of the Taman Tirto factory, the three women are able to find humor in the behaviors and words that will again tomorrow cause them pain. By ridiculing those that ridicule them and by intentionally sewing badly whenever a supervisor is not watching, the workers get their small revenge. As in (25), in story (26) the women coconstruct a slapstick comedy routine in which their Philippine bosses, in the starring roles, are ranting and raving, kicking doors, and screaming in a language none of the workers understands. The stories consist of each participant's involvement in a coherently similar turn, which contributes to the whole of the discourse. None of the cohort stands out as separate and none places herself into the story in any exclusive manner. None of this sufficiently empowers the women to overcome their problems either. This type of empowerment is enacted for day-to-day survival and self-esteem. But in terms of their relative real-world positions in the Javanese social order, the women are actively reproducing the very behaviors and discourses that marginalize them.

Conclusions

This chapter has illustrated how a group of young Javanese women was able to reconstruct positions of relative status and power both in their immediate cohort and in the broader community by altering their discursive practices. Their group solidarity and empowerment in relation to their oppressors are artificially created by women who recognized these positions to be strategically linked and fully dependent on a unified base. This illustrates what I call an iconic association between empowerment and solidarity. The power to take on one's oppressor comes from unity— not the kind of unity that is naturally found in sameness of gender, culture, background, experience, or principle, but a solidarity that extends to the creation of a single, unified voice as a protest genre. Power among the disempowered, then, must be free of all the status-distinguishing markers found in normal Javanese daily interaction. Rather than distinguishing the "we" roles, a dichotomous arena of righteous victim and crude oppressor was created and made determinate by each speaker.

The protest discourse was created by story rounds in which participation was kept equal and fully supportive. Similarity of gender, age, social status, and equal access to information about the conflict was not enough. The cohort needed to construct a sameness that was discursively absolute through the avoidance of kinship terms, pronouns, or any of the indexical markers of a social hierarchy. Furthermore, the cohort created solidarity by repeating the voice of the enemy to confirm its immorality. This, in turn, consolidated their own connectedness and righteousness.

Participation in these narratives was linked to shared responsibility. Conceptions of status were avoided to heighten unity through equal footing and equal responsibility for the consequences of the narratives. But, as so much else in relation to Javanese styles of formality, the protest discourse disguised a far more serious problem.

The women had no chance of succeeding in their fight for their legal rights. The Taman Tirto protest stories reveal the repressive powers of discursive practices at this local level. Discursive empowerment could effectively feed the fires of justifiable discontent and burn with the anger wrought by oppression and greed. But the fires were easily extinguished by those whose powers are fully supported by the moral order of roles, rights, and obligations and enhanced through money and connection. Less than two weeks after these events were recorded, the Department of Labor was paid by the factory to drop the case, and the women were promptly fired and blacklisted as trouble-makers. Sari and her friends were unable to find work for two years.

The next two chapters illustrate how the women's families refused a part in the protest discourses, ensuring the unruffled maintenance of the social order.

••• six

Status, Gender, and the Management of Information

This chapter explores issues of gender and access to information in relation to participation. In keeping with the themes of participation and responsibility, we explore discursive styles as they emerge vis-à-vis a speaker's alignment to the main protest narrative. Participants' alignments appear on a much broader scale than that which we have already seen. In the previous chapter, there is full acceptance of the narrative, which includes all the hierarchical implications of topic uptake and development, to the point of negating one's own relational identity. Here we see what the other end of the scale looks like, that is, full rejection of the narrative. Rejection within the Javanese matrix of refinement is not a direct negation of specifically uttered turns or topics; rather it appears as silence: the lack of participation in the discourse. As the conversation develops, refusing a part in the narrative is interpreted as refusing to be aligned with the consequences of the discourse. We see how the factory women are acting quite alone in their protest, not because of the wrongfulness of their case or even the way in which they proceed, which is well within the bounds of legal acceptance. The conflict lies in the fact that responsibility for their actions is incompatible in a community that defines dignity and patient composure as signs of refinement and inner strength. Moreover, responsibility for their actions is too frightening for others to bear in an authoritarian, controlled state that supports hierarchy and development over the health and safety of its workers.

We also bring into the discussion theories of gender in Javanese styles of interaction since Sari's interlocutors are both older males, that is, her father and the father of a coworker. We see how Sari's presentation of information through narrative and her affective stance in these narratives are immensely different from the cooperative, empowering styles described in the previous chapter. In consideration of the gender and age differences in the context of speaking, basic Javanese expectations of behavior compel Sari to be indirect and respectful in her stories. As we soon see, however, this is not the case. Standard assumptions of speech-level ideology cannot explain why Sari would speak much more directly and emotionally in a speech event that classifies her as inferior in status than she did in an interaction with her peers.

In the following texts, Sari is the sole animator for her cohort because the other members refuse the coanimator position.[1] As the solitary animator and as the only speaker with full access to information, Sari is forced to take a principal role, bearing full responsibility for the consequences of her narrative. Yet, despite becoming the sole animator, Sari never emerges as a figure in her stories. The situation is further complicated because of the age and gender differences and the presence of two mature men who have never met before. While most Javanese literature describes the formal requirements of status marking in social interactions (described in chapter 1), few studies have noted gender variations in these acts.

Ward Keeler has shown that Javanese men, on the one hand, are subjected to far greater cultural restrictions than women regarding status, potency, and elevated speech styles. Women, on the other hand, are afforded far greater social latitude precisely because of their inaccessibility to such status. Women are the managers of information and relationships through their flexibility and frankness, as Keeler suggests: "Giving up the forms of high status can afford a certain measure of liberty" (Keeler, 1990:152). Furthermore, Nancy Smith-Hefner (1988) has noted that Javanese women may interact freely with men and enjoy great social mobility. She also finds that it is Javanese men who strive to cultivate politeness for the power and authority it offers, whereas women are more noted for their talkativeness and their control of the day-to-day issues of family and household affairs. Yet, as I suggested in chapter 2, it is also the responsibility of women to create and maintain the foundation upon which male power depends.

Was it precisely because she is a woman and thus not a challenge to status positions that permitted Sari to be more affective and direct in her speech with the men? Why, then, would her interactions with her factory peers display more reserve than this one? The speakers' solidarity was the significant cause of empowerment in the previous chapter, and the building and maintaining of unity required careful monitoring and the restraining of individual positions. In contrast, when she speaks with the men, only Sari has the information relevant to the discussion. This sole access gives her some degree of freedom to speak relatively openly, providing others sanction it. The narrative, then, is anything she can make of it.

This chapter focuses on how Sari manages her situational status in relation to how she tells the story. Her strategy is to present information in a highly controlled manner, intending to win over support from the two men. Support is confirmed by their participation in the narrative. Once she has this support, however minimal, her narrating style changes from relatively respectful and safe to involved and emotional, reflected by changes in speech levels, evaluation, and her own involvement with the storyline. The ways in which the men align themselves to specific aspects of the narrative and reject others reveal where and how they are willing to assume responsibility for the narrative's consequences. But the more involved Sari becomes in the telling of the protest story, the more her male participants reject it.

The ways in which participation is negotiated raises a major question about the boundaries of responsibility, and this, in effect, raises a question about the power of talk. Participation in the narrative displays not only a responsible alignment to the speaking role taken up, that is, a discourse-level involvement, but also one's responsible alignment with the protest and thus a personal share in its consequences. As already discussed, talk is an activity that assigns responsibility, not intention (e.g., Duranti, 1993; Hill and Zepeda, 1993; Ochs, 1988). Talk is an immensely resonant act through which publicly uttered words have a constitutive effect on the world; to say something is to take a position on it, and anything said needs to be accounted for. Thus, participation as status is far less significant an issue here than participation as responsibility.

The speech situation discussed in this chapter, like that in chapters 5 and 7, were all recorded in the front room of the Budi home. Unlike the previous conversation, however, I am not present in this conversation nor in the one to follow. Sari and her cohorts were holding a meeting in the vacant house that belongs to Pak Budi's brother, located directly in front of his own shack. The cohort had called a meeting after work to plan their next protest moves. I had helped Ibu Budi to serve snacks to the cohort, after which I remained in the front house with them. Dhik Sri, one of the workers, had asked her father to pick her up from Sari's home at 7:30 P.M. She thought this would be when the meeting would end, based on her assumption that the workers would be allowed to leave the factory at the usual time. When her father arrived, he found the meeting still underway and his daughter not yet ready to leave.

Negotiating Participant Status

Pak Sri[2] had arrived, and I was the one to greet him and invite him to sit. I also had made and served his tea before any other member of the family came to meet him. Finally, Pak Budi came in and sat down, facing Pak Sri from across the coffee table. I then left to return to the meeting and inform Dhik Sri that her father was here.

In the situation presented here, Pak Budi and Pak Sri, who have never met before, need to negotiate their relative social positions. But since Pak Sri opens with purposeful dialogue—that is, he wants to know why his daughter is not ready to leave—they have no opportunity to appraise each other first. They speak in a level of *kråmå* that signals their relations as strangers but with no *kråmå inggil* words. Although their speech levels slip to *madyå* and even *ngoko*, the men maintain a speech style that displays their caution. Both men speak indirectly, and some utterances have no referential meaning beyond filling in one's turn.

(27) *Picking up My Daughter*

4. PAK SRI: **Kulå** arani   I figured
    nek **bidalipun** jam wolu,   if I left at 8:00,
    nåpå setengah wolu,   or 7:30,
    jam **pinten nikå wau**.   what time was that earlier.
    lare kulå weling,   my child reminded,
    "Pak pethuk stengah wolu."   "Dad pick me up at 7:30."

5. PAK BUDI: **Nembe sami datheng**   They've only just arrived
    lajeng kog anu.   so y'know. uhm,
    tesih **kempal-kempal**.   [they're] still meeting.

6. PAK SRI: **Ngrembag nåpå nggih**,   Discussing what y'know,
    kulå mboten mangertos niki.   I don't understand any of this.

7. PAK BUDI: **Enggih! Menikå mbok**   Oh yes! This well perhaps y'know,
    menawi nggih,
    tuntutan-tuntutan hahaha   demands and all that hahaha

8. PAK SRI: Wow, **ngangge** tuntutan   wow, with demands and all this.
    barang tho **niki**.

9. PAK BUDI: **Pinten-pinten dinten**,   How many days now,
    cah **sekawan**,   four children,
    yen **mboten nggih**,   if not y'know,
    lare gangsal, hahaha   five children, hahahha.

In this text, what is most important is the apparent fact that Dhik Sri had not told her father about her problems at the Taman Tirto factory. Such lack of communication is in keeping with Keeler (1990) and Smith-Hefner (1988): both state that male preoccupations with status and potency traditionally confine mundane events as these to women's discourse. This lack of open, intimate, or personal discussion includes one's own family members.[3]

Pak Sri is concerned with why his daughter is not yet ready to leave despite having reminded him to pick her up at this time. He does not ask directly why his daughter is not ready to go but frames his initial utterances as a story. In this way, he can directly involve his daughter by reconstructing her own words and take the pressure off himself for being early:

4. PAK SRI: **Kulå** arani   I figured
    nek **bidalipun** jam wolu,   if I left at 8:00,
    nåpå setengah wolu,   or 7:30,
    jam **pinten nikå wau**.   what time was that earlier.
    lare kulå weling,   my child reminded,
    "Pak pethuk stengah wolu."   "Dad pick me up at 7:30."

Use of the story and reported-speech format instead of a question permits a more cautious and politely indirect approach to the topic of "picking up his daughter." Within his story, Pak Sri presents himself as a dutiful father, carefully calculating the time between leaving home and reaching the destination to meet his daughter about 15 minutes later than the requested time.

Pak Budi's way of approaching the topic assumes knowledge of the meeting. This was not the case, however. Despite Pak Sri's direct request for clarification (turn 6) about the meeting, Pak Budi also displays an indirect and cautious style of speaking. In consideration of the fact that I never heard Sari talk about the exact factory problem with her family, it is possible that none of them really knew the details. I learned about it when Sari was studying the legal pamphlets in the sitting room. We discussed quite a few of the specific points at that time, but no other people were present. When the Depnaker advisers came, Ibu Budi, several of the Budi daughters and I cooked and served fried noodles and tea to the accumulated group. None of the family members attended the meetings or was seen to be actively interested. As a result, it is difficult to distinguish polite indirectness from lack of knowledge. In either case, the family's behavior with respect to their daughter's crisis should warn us how unusual and sensitive the issue of conflict is for those directly and indirectly involved.

While their speech style does not honor the other, it does distance the men with a protective indirectness. But not entirely. Pak Sri does recognize that *something* is going on when he asks what it is that his daughter is involved with. Pak Sri's utterance in turn 6, as a speech act that requests information, must be taken up by Pak Budi in his role of host:

6. PAK SRI: **Ngrembag nåpå nggih**   Discussing what y'know,
   kulå mboten mangertos niki.   I don't understand any of this.
7. PAK BUDI: **Enggih! Menikå mbok**   Oh yes! This well perhaps y'know,
   menawi nggih,
   tuntutan-tuntutan hahaha   demands and all that hahaha

Pak Budi's answer is not very cooperative since, instead of information, it contains hedges, terms that specifically avoid providing the required information. Hedging is described by Errington as "another face of the allusiveness, indirectness, or what Javanese call the *alus*ness[4] of polite speech" (1988:192). If indirectness is polite and desired among Javanese speakers, Pak Budi's unwillingness to respond in turn 7 becomes increasingly difficult to interpret. The reluctance to assume responsibility for an utterance whose content is controversial may seem very similar to lack of knowledge about the details of the protest in general and, more specifically, the meeting currently taking place in his home.

Turn 7 is extremely vague. Pak Budi's initial, emphatic *enggih!* ("yes!") is not always employed as a sign of agreement in polite Javanese speech.

It is a hedging strategy to give an *appearance* of agreeable harmony where none may, in fact, exist. The demonstrative *menikå* functions as a pronoun, an avoidance of signifying or naming the contested topic that is currently taking place under his care. *Mbok menawi* means "perhaps," and its use directly avoids mentioning the content of the utterance. The second occurrence of *nggih* is a text boundary indexical. I normally gloss final *nggih* as "y'know," but like others in this class of markers, whose function may be no more than to signal the closure of an idea unit, the translation does not always fit. As in Schiffrin's (1987) discussion of "y'know," here *nggih* is a marker of metaknowledge by which the speaker assumes the hearer to know what he is talking about—even if, as in this case, he may not know what is exactly being discussed in his brother's house. Thus, there is a combination of no uptake on Pak Sri's topic (picking up his daughter) in conjunction with the high-pitched intonation, the lack of referentially meaningful content, and the laugh, all of which are cues of topic avoidance and potential sensitivity.

The only meaningful words, the *tuntutan-tuntutan* (demands), are punctuated by a laugh. Pak Sri is concerned only with his daughter's safe arrival home, beyond which he seems to know nothing about the current crisis. He must respond to Pak Budi's uncooperative utterance, so he allo-repeats the only word he can referentially grasp:

7. PAK BUDI: enggih! Menikå mbok	Oh yes! This well, perhaps, y'know,
menawi nggih,	
tuntutan-tuntutan hahaha	demands and all that hahaha
→ 8. PAK SRI: wow, ngangge tuntutan	→ wow, with demands and all, this.
barang to niki.	

Pak Sri's response repeats the new topic as an indirect comment on it, while he does not directly request the information he obviously wants, that is, where his daughter is. The utterance fulfills the participant requirements for dialogue but says nothing else.

Pak Budi's next turn also contains no significant, contextually relevant information. It is a turn filler that strongly hints at *something* going on without ever stating what it is or confessing his own ignorance. Pak Sri's daughter is obviously involved in *something*, and perhaps Pak Sri and Pak Budi have been told no more:

9. PAK BUDI: **pinten-pinten dinten**,	How many days now,
cah **sekawan**,	four children,
yen **mboten nggih**	if not y'know
lare gangsal, hahaha.	five children, hahahha.

This series of turns shows several things, the first being the indirectness through which these Javanese men manage this cautious meeting. Their use of *kråmå* is equally matched with no participant receiving or giving more respect than the other. The speech-level equality however, does not imply any speaker solidarity or intimacy. The interactional complexities rest in their indeterminate relative status, the access and management of requested information that neither really has, the delicate nature of that information (including both the protest or their own ignorance of their daughters' problems), and the fact that these men have never met before. The discussion of personal problems is not public discourse between male strangers in this community, and the planning of a protest is illegal.

Meanwhile, Pak Sri wants to take his daughter home, and no one has yet explained why this is not possible. Sari and Dhik Sri finally emerge from the meeting, and Pak Sri opens the conversation by mentioning Dhik Sri's request to be picked up. Sari is the one to respond, and she immediately begins to describe the factory story by diving directly into the event sequence of a story frame. The protest story is directed in accordance with the participants' responses. Sari's Javanese is in *båså* without honorifics, but her stance is quite direct. She speaks in a *madyå* form of *båså* that will move lower when her affective involvement rises. She is unconcerned with face-saving deference, and she disregards her interlocutor's requests for information by firmly adhering to her own storyline.

(28) *Leaving the Factory*

15. PAK SRI: La mau welinge: hahaha	So the reminder [to be picked up] earlier hahaha
16. SARI: La **wau badhe medal mawon,**	So earlier when [we were] just about to leave,
ndadak di cegat-cegat,	[we were] suddenly prevented
17. PAK SRI: **Sinten ingkang** nyegat-nyegat?	Who was it that prevented [you]?
18. SARI: **Nggih dipun** cegat-cegat. **Mboten angsal medal rumiyen, nåpå**.	Yes, [we were] held up. [We were] not allowed to leave before, what.

Sari orients the story by explaining what had happened just that afternoon in direct response to Pak Sri's immediate interest, that is, picking up his daughter at the Budi home. Both Sari and Pak Sri have a story they wish to tell, and both have posted their own topics. In turn 15, Pak Sri returns to his daughter's request to be picked up, but Sari has a different story to tell. She opens the story by stating her event clause. Event clauses, as discussed in chapter 3, need to contain accessible information. Since the others do not know, Sari must coax her participants into the story frame. Both of their utterances begin with the discourse marker *la*, showing their movement away from a previous topic and initiating a new topical frame. Sari does not directly respond to Pak Sri's interest in picking up his daughter; hence, the initial *la*, showing the topic change. Pak Sri knows nothing at all about his daughter's predicament, or he would have shown his knowledge in response to Sari's event clause. Instead, he requests orientation information.

When Sari states the event clause *ndadak dicegat-cegat*, ([we were] suddenly prevented), Pak Sri asks, "Who was it that prevented [you]?" Sari ignores this question. This is not the orientation she thinks is important here. It would not be proper to blame a superior, so to Sari it does not matter *who* it was. The fact that "[we were] not allowed to leave" is the heart of her issue, as shown by its repetition.

Pak Sri requests further orientation:

19. PAK SRI: Neng endi neng kono åpå neng kene?	Where was this, over there or here?
20. SARI: **Wonten rikå**.	Over there
21. PAK SRI: Wow.	Wow.

Pak Sri shows that he is unfamiliar with the actors and the location of this drama. Since Dhik Sri apparently never told her father about the problems she is facing each day or the even more serious protest she is involved in, Sari must decide how much information to offer. She presents her story's events in a greatly understated fashion to ease its acceptance:

22. SARI: **Dados kedahe medal** jam setengah enem,	So [we] should get out at 5:30,
Nembe medal setengah pitu Pak!	[we] just left at 6:30 sir!

In fact, the women enter the factory at 7:00 A.M. and should work only 7 to 8 hours a day, 6 days a week, with Friday a half day. Getting out at 5:30 means that they have already put in over 10 hours. Sari is avoiding the larger issues here by not actually saying "forced, unpaid overtime."

Sari is willing in certain areas to soften the inherent conflict in her story; she refuses in others. Adherence to the rules of hierarchical respect means not creating conflict. Sari has adapted this rule to mean not calling your enemies by name since they happen to be of higher social rank. But as other participants do not take up any positions in her story, Sari's emotional involvement and her personal and singularly responsible animator's role grow more evident. Her concern in this early part of the conversation is in winning over her audience's support concerning the forced overtime. The ways in which she aligns her story with regard to the overtime can be further developed only if the other participants become more sympathetic and, hence, involved in the telling process.

The nature of "recipient design" explains how story animators may leave out information that may be troubling for some listeners. It also accounts for an animator's role in supplying enough information for a listener to fully understand the point of the story. In this discussion, however, while further complicated by the controversial nature of the story, Sari's story-telling style is an example of what her local cultural knowledge imposes, not how it applies or differs from ideological definitions based on mainstream American expectations. Despite her being the sole participant with access to information, Sari does not perform her animator's role as one in which she must supply full background information. Javanese narratives, as has been argued in chapters 3, 4, and 5, are not meant to fully supply the story. There are no "listeners" because all must ideally become participants.[5] If they refuse or misunderstand their participant roles, Sari is forced to compensate—if she is bold enough. If not, she must change the topic or match the silence.

Sari's father repeats the question—*who* prevented you from leaving?

23. PAK BUDI: Sing nyegat?	Who held [you] up?
24. SARI: Pokoke **diken** lembur **ngaten** lho.	The point is [we were] ordered to work overtime just like that
25. PAK SRI: Wow.	Wow.
26. SARI: **Ken** nglembur **nggih niku**, ndadak di . **niku wau**.	Ordered to work overtime just that, all of a sudden to be . like I said before.
27. PAK BUDI: We: la.	We: la.

Sari speaks directly and with no honorifics, confronting those who keep asking orienting questions she interprets as irrelevant. She ignores them. Her lack of cooperation is based on the nonnegotiability of what she sees as the point of her story. The point is clearly located because of its frequent repetitions (Becker, 1984, 1988). It is not *who* holds them back but the fact that they are frequently and suddenly forced into working overtime with no advanced notice.

Sari's position in such a situation is difficult. While Dhik Sri is sitting next to her in silence, Sari is the only active speaker with access to the information. Meanwhile, she must also consider her social position vis-à-vis her guest and her father. Her strategy is to offer no additional information beyond the basic event clauses until others participate in the story. This is how she reveals what she sees as the central issue, the forced overtime. Her storyline reveals only the events that are immediately relevant:

28. SARI: La **nikå** rak **rencananipun lare-lare**	Just like that don't y'know the group's plan
rak pukul **gangsal nåpå** pukul setengah enem	at around 5:00 or 5:30
ngumpul **ngriki nggih badhe** rapat **nikå**.	to gather over here y'know for the meeting.
29. PAK SRI: Wow	Wow

Sari tells today's events with no evaluation, no reported speech, no personal stance in her own story, and no event clauses that clarify what the women have been forced to deal with. The point she is still trying to get participant support for is the sudden overtime.

Pak Budi comes to his daughter's aid when he externally evaluates the overtime problem by applying well-known and easily acceptable parameters for interpretation:

30. PAK BUDI: **Nikå** *kan*,   Like you know right,
    nyambut damel nikå *kan*,   [we] work, right,
    wolung jam **nikå** *kan*,   for those eight hours, right,
    sampun sanes ukuran.   [this is] already not standard.
31. PAK SRI: **Inggih**, rumongså **kulå**   Yes, I feel also yes
    koq
    nggih **awrat rumaos kulå**.   [this is] serious I think.
32. PAK BUDI: **Enggih:** la **milå nikå**   Yes, [I tell you]
    la **sakngantos** jam setengah wolu   its like up until 7:30 at night.
    ndalu.

Pak Budi approaches the problem from the safest possible grounds, being forced to work more than eight hours per day. His repetition of the Indonesian tag *kan* as a text boundary indexical in turn 30 coaxes involvement because it implies agreement for each of his succession of idea units. Meanwhile, Pak Sri has been forced into agreement in turn 31, where he finally evaluates the situation as serious. Pak Budi then emphasizes the seriousness by adding that the women are frequently held up until quite late, in this case well after dark and after the buses have stopped running. Young women, as we well know, must not roam the streets alone and after dark. Pak Sri also knows this since his very presence in the room is the result of his concern for his daughter's safe trip home.[6]

Sari does not yet embellish her position by describing the withheld wages or the crying women standing in front of the locked door. Instead, she explains only the most recent events, with no evaluation and none of the formulaic reported speech. Sari stresses only the immediate point, the overtime, which Pak Sri has accepted (turn 31). Pak Sri asks for no further information, a sure sign of his discomfort. He takes a safe stance of agreement, buffered behind several layers of protective hedges:

31. PAK SRI: **Inggih**, rumongså **kulå**   Yes, I feel also yes
    koq
    nggih **awrat rumaos kulå**.   [this is] serious I think.

Levels of restraint are apparent in everyone's speech, which is expected in light of the social distinctions that exist between Sari and Pak Sri, the unknown distinctions between the two men, and the sensitive nature of the information. Sari frames her story through event clauses that need to be negotiated as events. Events represent norms and expectations (see chapter 3), not resistance toward the social order and the rejection of the same hierarchical abuse that most members of the community have felt to varying degrees. As long as her event clauses are still under negotiation, that is, she does not have full uptake, she frames them with no affective stance and none of the more shocking facts. The story is simplified and narrowed down to just those clauses immediately relevant to Pak Sri and picking up his daughter. The broader reaches of the story are left for him to request or infer. Pak Budi assists by evaluating the overtime problem in its most expected forms. It is not "standard," which would have made it something that one could easily be aligned to. But it would be obvious to most Javanese that there is a serious problem here, the consequences of which may be extreme.

Pak Sri, meanwhile, is not taking a participant's role in a narrative presented specifically for him. His turns are not actively pursuing more information, nor are they positioning him as taking up any kind of alignment to the events experienced by his own daughter. His absence of demonstrated understanding vis-à-vis the story is similar to Livia Polanyi's description of a listener who makes no comments at the close of a story. Such silence is "a socially salient response indicating embarrassment, confusion, annoyance, lack of understanding, or low esteem for the teller" (1989:49). This brings us back to the issue of responsibility for the discourse. Pak Sri may be listening, but his speaking is distant and will become much more so as Sari's story becomes more emotional.

Narratives of Empowerment

In turn 31, Pak Sri shows a perfunctory acceptance of the overtime problem, which Sari accepts as permission to proceed with her story. Despite such a clearly nonparticipating audience, Sari's own involvement wins her over. She now presents the worker's case through a highly affective stance.

(29) *Getting Home*

33. SARI: **Nikå mawon**	And what's more,
ingkang nDALEMipun tebih-	those whose homes are far away
tebih njih,	y'know,
judek **nikå**.	[they're] desperate.
Arep nangis ora iså.	[They] want to cry but [they] can't.
Sampun mboten komanan bis,	The buses have already stopped running,
ingkang DALEMipun mBantul,	those whose homes are in Bantul,
nikå lho Pak.	what [about them] sir.
34. PAK SRI: La **enggih**.	Oh yes.
35. SARI: **DALEMe** adoh kog Pak	Their homes are so far y'know sir.
Makane njuk malah nrimå	So that's why it's just accepted
malah **mboten** dhå mlebu esuke,	even so no one will go in tomorrow

rak dhå malah anu. to	everyone even whatsit. (false start)
Mesakke.	Its a real shame.
Yen sesuk muni nglembur	When tomorrow [they] say overtime
njuk malah **mboten** dhå mlebu.	then no one's going to take it.

In comparison to her earlier stories with Sigah and Endang, Sari is now highly affective in her storytelling. Since her purpose in telling is very different from that in the previous chapter, her evaluation now uses none of the reported speech she most often used in chapter 5. Here, her goal is to present a clear perspective on the serious implications of the overtime issue, that of being stranded at the factory in light of the shared knowledge about women traveling alone at night. Her affective strategies are the repetition of phrases that stress the distance these women have to travel from the factory:

33. SARI: <u>Nikå</u> mawon   And what's more,
    <u>ingkang ndalemipun tebih-</u>   those whose homes are far away
    <u>tebih</u> njih,   y'know,
    judek <u>nikå</u>.   [they're] desperate.
    Arep nangis ora iså.   [They] want to cry but [they] can't.
    Sampun mboten komanan bis,   The buses have already stopped running,
    <u>ingkang dalemipun</u> mBantul,   those whose homes are in Bantul,
    <u>nikå</u> lho Pak.   what [about them] sir.
34. PAK SRI: La enggih.   Oh yes.
35. SARI: → <u>daleme</u> adoh kog Pak.   Their homes are so far y'know sir.

Her repetition grows more affective as she moves from general, reduplicated *tebih-tebih* ("far away") to the more specific designation of the area many of the workers live in, that is, Bantul.[7] Finally she utters the simple, direct, almost plealike ***DALEMe*** *adoh kog Pak* (Their homes are so far away y'know sir) in *ngoko*. Sari, however, maintains the *kråmå inggil* term ***DALEM*** to be highly honorific of the women she is referring to. While the factory insults them, Sari most certainly will not.

Sari describes the women's predicament by such adjectives as the various terms for distance and the encoded frustration that follows. The second idea unit is also marked by a dramatic level shift into *ngoko*, while only the text boundary indexicals maintain *mbåså*:

33. SARI: Judek **nikå**.   [They're] desperate.
    Arep nangis ora iså.   [They] want to cry but [they] can't.

The women are desperate, in fact, so desperate that they cannot even cry. The issues of travel and safety for women *are* serious; the Department of Labor requires all factories that keep their female workers after dark to supply transportation home. Again, a necessary and humanitarian law exists but is not enforced by anyone with the power to do so. But because their homes are so far away and

| 33. SARI: Sampun mboten komanan bis, | The buses have already stopped running, |

the women are thoroughly trapped again. They cannot go home at night because they cannot afford the expense of the other modes of transportation available, they cannot afford the gossip that brands women who travel at night, and they are afraid of the potential disasters that await women on the streets. Yet, of these three very good reasons for refusing overtime work at the factory, not one is actually mentioned in the story. Silence rarely means insignificance. Here the silence marks shared community knowledge that needs no repetition. Consider what the women had said last week during the conversation among Sari, Sigah, and Endang (see also note 14, chapter 5):

280. ENDANG: Tur nek bengi, yå ora wani Mbak	So then at night, y'know [we're] not brave [enough to go home] Mbak
281. LAINE: He.ee.	He.ee.
282. SIGAH: Ngko nek ditemu uwong piye?	So later if we meet someone [on the streets] then what?
283. ALL: [hahah cilåkå.]	[hahaha disaster]
284. ENDANG: Yå nek sik nemu apik, ora åpå-åpå.	So if [we] run into someone good, no problem.
Nek sik nemu elek,	If [we] run into one who's bad,
285. SIGAH: E.e.	Right.
Nek sik nemu mulih nesu yå?	If [we] run into one who carries a grudge then what?

In more private contexts, in which the women are positioned as equally subject to the dangers of predatory male sexuality, the fear of violence is mentioned. Topics like this rarely arise in conversation, although they are alluded to whenever women need to travel at night.

With all this in mind, the women are forced to accept their plight:

| 35. SARI: Makane njuk malah nrimå. | So that's why it's just accepted. |

Sari's use of the word *nrimå* is symbolic of Javanese acquiescence to one's fate. In terms of Sari's affective stance, and in its cooccurrence with overtime, distance, lack of buses, and the unmentioned cause of it all, *nrimå* strongly marks the women as disempowered victims, subjected to the tyrannical authority of Taman Tirto's management.

With their victimized status firmly established by terms that no father could possibly reject, Sari now shifts her footing to that of the fighter. Her grounds for protest are unarguable, so she can now evaluate, again through repetition, her new confrontational stance:

35. SARI: <u>Malah mboten dhå mlebu</u>   Even so no one will go in tomorrow
    esuke
    rak <u>dhå malah</u> anu. to   everyone even whatsit. (false start)
    Mesakke.   Its a real shame.
    Yen sesuk muni nglembur   If tomorrow [they] say overtime
    njuk <u>malah mboten dhå mlebu</u>.   then no one's going in.

Sari's narrative uses external evaluation, and her stance is direct and to the point and displays a strong conditional:

35. SARI: → Yen sesuk muni nglembur   → If tomorrow [they] say overtime
    njuk malah <u>mboten dhå mlebu</u>.   then no one's going in.

While Sari shows no agent's responsibility by linking a predicate to a central "I," she is, in fact, thoroughly empowered within this context because she has constructed for herself a fully ratified group voice. She uses the abbreviated form of the plural marker *pådhå*, or *dhå*, to signal the existence of the group but not what part of the group or how large it is. As shown in chapter 5, unity is empowering, and by invoking a unified group, the protesters actively empower themselves.

In turn 35, Sari's stance is that of the self-assured fighter, the activist and leader who is perfectly aware of her choices and is prepared to take them. She is showing her empowered stance, especially in defiance of those who attempt to wrongfully abuse her and her cohorts. Her knowledge of her own rights is magnified by her change of frame, in which she steps out of her defiant stance to externally utter *mesakke*, "its a real shame." She shows that she is not defiant by nature but by force. No one should have to endure the indignities thrust upon them, so now, *if* provoked once more, they will fight:

35. SARI: <u>Malah mboten dhå mlebu</u>   Even so no one will go in tomorrow
    esuke
    rak <u>dhå malah</u> anu. to   everyone even whatsit. (false start)
    → Mesakke.   → Its a real shame.
    Yen sesuk muni nglembur   If tomorrow [they] say overtime
    njuk <u>malah mboten dhå mlebu</u>.   then no one's going in.

Sari's status as the sole animator and sole possessor of information, perhaps supported by the gender distinctions, has offered her much more freedom here than she had in chapter 5, where equality and sharedness were the rules. Sari herself lives rather close to the factory and rides a bicycle there in less than 10 minutes, so she does not share the problem of being stranded at the factory at night. But here she is very affective in presenting the group's position, specifically mentioning those that live in Bantul, the district south of Yogyakarta. While not directly inconvenienced herself, she speaks with what seems like a figure's direct involvement:

33. SARI: Judek **nikå**.   [They're] desperate.
    Arep nangis ora iså.   [They] want to cry but [they] can't.

She explains the desperation and tears and lowers her speech style to *ngoko*, further signaling emotional involvement. Yet, her own position in relation to her narrative is ambiguous. Is she a concerned outsider, a mere animator, or is she including herself as a figure? Since Javanese requires no pronominal indexing or subjects, the question needs to be answered from the perspective of participation and the responsibility it implies.

As discussed in chapter 5, Sari's participant role is now one of full responsibility for the discourse in a world where words are as significant as deeds. Both lead to similar consequences.[8] In such a speech situation as this, Sari's ability to get home at night is irrelevant. The fact that she speaks of these objections makes her fully involved and responsible regardless of her own circumstances. While there are no first-person pronouns to index her stance within the story as an agent or even to index the stories as a personal experience, the fact that she is the sole animator indicates her responsibility for that agent's position (cf. Mühlhäusler and Harré, 1990). As Duranti (1988) states, describing a fact about the world has performative ends, and in terms of the consequences for an utterance, the speaker is fully responsible.

This direct implication between participation and responsibility functions for all speakers when all those present are responsible for the shaping and defining of these dangerous utterances. Participation is a collective involvement in which meaning requires uptake. Sari can be bold in her story, however, because she has taken on the responsibilities of her group and is sole animator, although she speaks as "we" not "I." Thus, as already seen in chapter 5 and in other stories shared by these young women, experiences are framed as those of the group. When stories refer to individuals and their actions, these have mainly been found within the equalizing stances of the story round. Instead of orchestrating the coconstruction of a solidarity story with other active participants, as in chapter 5, Sari has the freedom to find her own collective voice.

Sari's position as a collective animator and not one speaking in her own voice allows her a brief moment of escape from the constraints of the dominant discourses (see also Mohanty, 1991a:36–39). We now examine how others try to prevent it.

Responsible Participation as Choice

During Sari's story (29), Pak Sri remained silent except for the occasional obligatory back channel *enggih*. After the story, Pak Sri turned to his daughter (who had been silent up to now) and changed the topic back to how she would get home. This is a conspicuous topic change, and it highlighted Pak Sri's refusal to participate in the protest story. Sari then lightens the tension by changing the key back to the familiar Javanese politeness formula. She mentions to her father the similarities between him and Pak Sri:

43. SARI: Pådhå bapak   Same as you,
    PUTRAne wedok-wedok hahaha   his offspring are [all] girls hahaha

This effectively changes the topical focus to small talk for 13 turns. The topic of children is closed by Pak Budi, using the formulaic politeness phrase:

56. PAK BUDI: **PunUNJUK MÅNGGÅ**   Please help yourself to the drink sir.
    Pak.

It is Pak Sri who returns to the protest story, but he does so in a perfunctory, light-hearted way. He also speaks in *ngoko*, as if only to his daughter and to reject the uncomfortable scene he finds himself in:

57. PAK SRI: Tak kirå rapat åpå kog.   I thought this was a meeting of.
    kåyå arisan,   like savings club,
    wow jebulane rapat//   wow actually it's a meeting//
58. SARI: //Ha.a rapat nasib. hahaha   That's right it's a meeting of fate.
                                          hahaha
59. PAK SRI: Nek **ngaten nggih**:   If that's the case then: that includes//
    termasuk//
60. DHIK SRI: //**Niku ajeng ngrembak** //[We] are about to discuss
    peraturan   regulations
61. PAK SRI: Wow ngono tho.   Wow so that's it.
    Maksutke yå. Yå dhong aku saiki.   It means then yes. now I understand.

Pak Sri now understands, and stating so will close the topic for him. Although he fills a few turns, he says nothing. According to Dhik Sri, her father never mentioned the protest on the trip home nor at home, maintaining instead a meaningful and dignified silence.

Meanwhile, Sari's stance is confident and direct now, and she interrupts Pak Sri to say that the current meeting is a meeting of *fate*. Even Dhik Sri is charged enough to speak. The management of information is made more interesting by Pak Sri's noninvolvement. His distance from the events can demonstrate what is often referred to as a Javanese style of avoiding an emotional shock or unpleasantness. His public demeanor remains refined and untroubled, but he jokes about his own ignorance vis-à-vis the main topic:

| 57. PAK SRI: Tak kirå rapat åpå kog. | I thought this was a meeting of. |
| kåyå arisan | like savings club |

But his silence throughout most of the narrative and his attempts at closing it,

| 61. PAK SRI: Wow ngono tho. | Wow so that's it. |
| Maksutke yå. Yå dhong aku saiki | It means then yes. now I understand |

can also be interpreted as a rejection of the responsibility the words entail.

Sari grows more direct as Pak Sri attempts to distance himself from the interaction.

(30) *Direct Attack*

62. SARI: **Enggih: namung ngrikå**	Yes: just like that
rak taksih kathah anu**nipun**.	don't you know there are still many whatsits.
awake dhewe *dipekerjakan* **ngaten** kog.	they are taken advantage of y'know.
Mboten *sesuai* **kalih** gaji.	[It's] not in accordance with salaries.
63. PAK SRI: Wow, **ngaten njih**.	wow, it's like that yes.
Nek *PT* **niku pancen nggih ngaten nikå**.	If that factory there certainly y'know, sure like that.

Here Sari returns to her protest narrative and offers additional information about salaries. She does not tell Pak Sri that salaries are arbitrarily cut and often withheld. Even without this information, Pak Sri's turn shows politeness, but it also signals no involvement in the narrative. He is not taking up any participant position with regard to the story. From here, he will silently reject the protest story and speak only of bringing his daughter home.

In contrast to Pak Sri's and Dhik Sri's silences, however, Sari and her father discuss the issue in more detail, further revealing ways of negotiating responsibility as participation. This father-daughter discourse displays what Keeler (1984:290) calls "Minimal Madyå."

(31) *Negotiating Moderation*

69. PAK BUDI: Nek gawe *peraturan*	If [you] write up the regulations
ditandatangani kabeh	and have everyone sign it
70. SARI: Ha **nggih**, sing gelem-gelem	Yes, those that are prepared to
nikå.	do so.
la **mboten** mesti gelem he,	but [they] won't necessarily want to.
Angel he golek wong sing iså dijak,	Its hard to find people willing to come along,
Soale **niku** dhå wedi,	The problem is that they're all afraid,
dhå wedi kilangan gawean.	they're all afraid of losing their jobs,
wedi sesuk nek di://	afraid of tomorrow if they are//

71. PAK BUDI: //Nek di *PHK* ngono.	//If they are fired.
Saiki ngono.	Now [you should do] this.
Nek wis usahamu kuwi uwis to,	Your efforts thus far are finished.
dilebokke neng *Pikiran Pembaca*:	Write to Reader's Thoughts.[9]
dirahasia, dirahasiakan oleh	[your names] kept secret, be kept
redaksi,	secret by the editors,
72. SARI: Namung keluhan kog.	But [that's just] complaining though.
73. PAK BUDI: Ha kuwi perjuang ora	Ya but [your] struggle isn't going
dadi-dadi,	anywhere,
wis pirang-pirang ndinå tho?	it's already how many days y'know?
74. SARI: La entek tanggale wong	Time is up for trying to meet [with
ajeng ketemu	them]
mon **mboten saget** kog.	but [we're] just not allowed to y'know.
Malah nek bali,	Even when it's time to go home,
di tekan sore terus kog.	[we] are kept on till late repeatedly
75. PAK BUDI: La kasile nek DEPNAKER	And what about the results of the
ki piye?	Department of Labor?
76. SARI: Ha **nikå** "**mboten** lembur	They say "no night overtime,"
bengi!"	
Sak **nikå mboten** lembur ketuk	Now the issue is still the late
isuk,	overtime,
"Cobå nek diteruske ket."	"[We'll] see if it's continued."
Sak**niku** nglembur ketuk isuk lho	Now, overtime is still the issue
Pak!	y'know Sir.
77. PAK BUDI: Wow, ning saiki,	Wow, but now it seems like
tetep nglembur ketuk jam sångå?	[you] still work overtime until 9:00 P.M.?
78. SARI: Nglembur**ipun** ketuk jam	That overtime it seems is until 6:00,
enem,	
Sesuk *berarti.*	in the morning it means.

In turn 77, Pak Budi mentions working overtime till 9:00 P.M., and Sari corrects him. The buses that offer the women their only affordable route home start up again at 6:00 A.M. Any time the workers are forced to work until after 6:00 P.M., many cannot leave until the next morning. Sari does not even bother to mention their fear of attack.

Pak Budi's attempts to negotiate his responsibility with Sari becomes a one-sided argument. He is urging compromise and strategic bargaining rather than protest or conflict:

69. PAK BUDI: Nek gawe *peraturan*	If [you] write up the regulations
ditandatangani kabeh	and have everyone sign it

Pak Budi is here proposing alternative means to promote orderly dialogue. In turn 69 he suggests drawing up a petition that would list the regulations as presented by the authority. But as we already know from previous conversations (chapter 5),

82. SARI: Ånå ning wis "*nggak mau tahu..*"	There are [some] who just "don't want to know".
"*Pokoknya*" . . . piye wingi kae jawabane,	"The point is," how'd that go yesterday, that response,
"*peraturan itu dapat diubah ?*"	"the regulations can always be changed"?
Ånå peraturan anyar yo ora dikek-i ngerti.	There are new regulations but they are not regarded.

Sari's response does not inform her participants that the authorities have no interest in being accountable for their own rules. They simply "don't want to know about it." Instead, she reminds us that most of the women are afraid of fighting for their legal rights because they will lose their jobs. Whereas she has previously stated defiantly that "no one" will go in to work if the authority once more forces overtime on them,

| 35. SARI: Yen sesuk muni nglembur njuk <u>malah mboten dhå mlebu</u>, | If tomorrow [they] say overtime then no one's going in, |

Now we see again, just as in the previous chapter, that in fact very few of the women will actually support the protest since most are too afraid of loosing their jobs:

70. SARI: Ha **nggih**, sing gelem-gelem **nikå**,	Yes, those that are prepared to do so,
la **mboten** mesti gelem he.	but [they] won't necessarily want to.
Angel he golek wong sing iså dijak,	Its hard to find people willing to come along,
Soale **niku** dhå wedi,	The problem is that they're all afraid,
dhå wedi kilangan gawean.	they're all afraid of losing their jobs,
wedi sesuk nek di://	afraid of tomorrow if they are//
71. PAK BUDI: //Nek di <u>PHK</u> ngono.	//If they are fired.

Pak Budi is himself very well aware of this fear, shown by his completion of Sari's utterance. He knows that most members of this community will not take part in any kind of activity that threatens the harmony of the status quo. This includes fighting for one's own legal rights. So he proposes an alternative strategy:

71. PAK BUDI: Saiki ngono.	Now [you] should do this.
Nek wis usahamu kuwi uwis to.	Your efforts thus far are finished.
Dilebokke neng *Pikiran Pembaca*:	Write to Reader's Thoughts.
dirahasia, dirahasiakan oleh redaksi,	[your names] kept secret, be kept secret by the editors.

72. SARI: Namung keluhan kog.   But [that's just] complaining though.

But this, too, is futile since Sari and her cohort know that there is no one that will come to their aid. Even the Department of Labor, whose job it is to protect and assist workers, is unable to stop the factory from continuing its overtime policies:

75. PAK BUDI: La kasile nek DEPNAKER ki piye?	And what about the results of the Department of Labor?
76. SARI: Ha **nikå "mboten** lembur bengi!"	They say "no night overtime,"
Sak **nikå mboten** lembur ketuk isuk,	now the issue is still the late overtime,
"Cobå nek diteruske ket."	"[we'll] see if it's continued."
Sak**niku** nglembur ketuk isuk lho Pak!	Now, overtime is still the issue y'know Sir!

So she argues, disagrees, challenges, and contradicts each of his suggestions, pointing out its flaws in relation to the factory problem. Pak Budi does not want to support his daughter's protest, far too radical a concept for a civil servant of *priyayi* lineage. He is a prime participant, but his role is to moderate not to take up the narrative. He actively negotiates possibilities, but in the end he, too, falls silent, caught between his own voice of moderation and his daughter's demands for militancy. The tension builds until Pak Sri's silence is finally broken by his humorous exit.

(32) *We're Ready!*

79. PAK BUDI: Wow, sakiki nuntut anune,	Wow, so now demand for whatsit,
80. SARI: Nuntut sing wingi-wingi ngono lho.	Demand what [we said] before like that.
Umpamane, sesuk awake dewe sesuk nåmpå gaji	For example, tomorrow we tomorrow receive our pay
tetep entuk sitik,	and still get too little,
awake dewe wis siap!	we're ready!
81. PAK BUDI: Nek sesuk karo gajine,	When tomorrow with the pay,
we, **mboten nåpå-nåpå nggih**,	wow, it doesn't matter y'know,
Ha nek **mboten** *sesuai* gajine **nggih**,	so if the pay isn't appropriate y'know,
mesakke karyawane.	what a shame for the workers.
82. SARI: Siap omongan,	Prepare the speech,
siap tulisan,	prepare the writing
wektune **mboten wonten** kog **kangge ngrembuk**. [..]	[there's] just no more time for discussion.
Sing **ajeng** mrotes,	Those who will protest
mung **ajeng** metu.	will just walk out

83. PAK BUDI: sing arep diprotes såpå?   Who is it that is protested?
84. SARI: Pak Darsono. **Nggih,**   Pak Darsono. Y'know,
    Sakniki ganti teng Solo   Now [the manager has] moved to
                                             Solo
    Sakniku ganti manager **meleh**   now [they] change the manager again
    dadi **mboten**   so no [protest]

This is as far as any protest discourse is able to go under current conditions. The first question asked by the men in the beginning of this conversation—that is, *who* is responsible for this abuse?—has finally been answered. Knowing who though changes nothing.

At this point, Pak Sri makes his exit. He must also pick up Dhik Sri's older sister. His daughter suggests that he relax first, to which Pak Sri jokingly compares his waiting here to his daughter's forced overtime:

85. PAK SRI: Wow sakrampunge nek   wow, that's the end of this for me.
    ngono aku.
    Wah: ora sah   Wah: it's not necessary
    Mulih aku   I'm going home
    Jam setengah sångå methuk   At 8:30 [I] pick up her sister too
    mbake we
    ngåpå tå?   did you know?
    Perkårå,   [Its a] situation
86. DHIK SRI: Ning **nggih**: ngge leren   In that case yes: rest first.
    riyen.
87. PAK SRI: La iyå.   Oh yes.
    Nek le leren aku ki   If I am resting
    jane tak kirå lembur aku ki   it can be said I think [this is] over
                                         time for me
    wis melek ki rånå   I've already been here far too long
88. DHIK SRI: Ya ampun Bapak! hahaha   Oh good Lord Bapak! hahaha

With these comments, the protest narrative is officially ended. The remaining conversation clarifies how Dhik Sri will get home. Once all is clear, Dhik Sri repeats her previous request as an explanation for her father.

(33) *Pak Sri Departs*
110. DHIK SRI: La aku mung ngugemi   I just support anything you say Pak,
     omonganmu Pak,
     "Aku pethuken jam setengah   "I am to be picked up at 7:30"
     wolu,"
     la **kulå kinten** anu he,   but I thought uhm,
     perusahaane ora ånå rame-rame,   the factory would not be so agitated,
111. PAK BUDI: Hahaha wow.   Hahaha wow.
112. DHIK SRI: **Kulå kinten** biasa   I figure it's usually like this though
     ngaten lho Pak!   Pak!

113. PAK SRI: Yå wis nek ngono aku   That's done then I will leave,
     tak bali,
     ngko ndak, wis ngono åpå piye?   later then, already like that or what?
     Sekirane, hurung bali tak   [I] guess, [if you're] not back I'll
     pethuk yå.   come ok.
     Åpå piye?   How's that?
     Jam sångå.   9:00
     åpå. setengah sepuluh nek   or 9:30 if [you're] not back,
     hurung bali,
     tak pethuk!   I'll come get you!
114. PAK BUDI: Hahaha. **MÅNGGÅ**   Hahaha (Formulaic greeting or leave
     MÅNGGÅ: taking from host)

Dhik Sri allo-repeats her request to be picked up at 7:30 through reported speech followed by a brief explanation of why it failed. Under the current circumstances, it is impossible to know when the workers will be released. Her excuse is a perfect example of why the factory's arbitrariness is such a problem for these women. As he leaves, Pak Sri states that if his daughter is not home by 9:30, he will come and get her. With this closure, Pak Budi gives him his leave.

Conclusions

We have just seen a markedly different framing of the protest narrative in this storytelling situation from that seen in chapter 5. This variation demonstrates some of the multiple stances Javanese speakers may take in relation to contextual factors. By exploring these differences in the framing of narratives and the discursive features that define them in relation to contextual information, a more particularly Javanese conception of participation is beginning to emerge. Such a view is based on meaning, person, and story as highly flexible and dependent on participation for the accomplishment of any speech action.

Participant frameworks are useful but not fully adequate to explain the highly resonant consequences of talk in Java. A long tradition of ascribed hierarchies, combined with claims that talk requires a carefully weighed evaluation of the factors that constitute and are constituted by speech, supports a notion of participation that is not the independent choice of intentioned individuals. In pursuit of this goal, I have followed the work of Duranti (1993, 1988), Hill and Zepeda (1993), Myers and Brenneis (1984), Ochs (1988), and Rosaldo (1982) in proposing a notion of participation as responsible agency. Agency, then, is not an individual act but must account for the constitutive influences of talk on others in the immediate context. Furthermore, talk may not disrupt the harmony of the speech situation or the wider community. Whereas the previous chapter has shown how cooperative participation and interactive relationships are social strategies for sharing responsibility in the construction of meaning, this chapter has shown how such a collective interpretation of responsible agency functions when it leads to conflict. Ideally, participation should be balanced or at least based on clearly demarcated positions, be they hierarchical or not. This chapter has examined what happens when the balance is skewed.

In terms of social norms, any speech situation requires good hosts to make their guests feel comfortable. But such was not the case here. Sari's position in having the information to which none of the men had access and the culmination of a series of events in which she and her cohorts were subjected to undignified silences and cruelty have taken their toll.[10] Unequal access to information, a singular animator's role as a collective agent, and a clear point—to convince others of the righteousness of their protest—firmly empowered Sari. As seen in the previous chapter, by presenting a unified and moral front, Sari pledged to herself, her cohorts, and the two men the morality of the protest. Moral correctness was shown not just in control of the floor but also in a succession of evaluative clauses. In her position as animator for the collective, Sari used mainly external evaluation and intensifiers for enhanced affect, all of which functioned as indexes of group, not personal, involvement.

For the men, however, relative status and self-presentation were important in their cautious, indirect speaking styles, particularly in Pak Sri's firm distance. Despite his own daughter's involvement, Pak Sri rejected a participant's role in a story told for his benefit. He did not question or seek further information about the problem. He did not negotiate any position with respect to it beyond affirming his own ignorance, that is, his rejection of the story, the situation, and its consequences.

This refusal to participate shows his concern for the consequences of the spoken word on his own presentation of self. Sharing in the discourse through participation implies not just taking a stance in the protest and sharing in its responsibility. It also means taking a stand against the norms of the community and confronting the very foundation of social harmony and national stability since these are all tied together in the public discourses. Also frightened by the consequences of his daughter's actions, Pak Budi attempted to reframe the story and its consequences as more moderate, as more *alus*. His attempts demonstrate, however, how participation can be a negotiable and agentic choice even when it fails or falls silent. In these terms, silence is a highly meaningful statement.

seven

Respectful Intimacy and the Production of Identity

This chapter is the final one in the ethnographic trilogy. It presents an additional perspective on the notion of responsible agency and participation by examining Sari's protest narratives in yet another situation. In conjunction with the previous two chapters, these sequences of conversational narratives assist us in clarifying how participation is controlled by a sense of responsibility toward others. *Others* can mean other participants, or it can mean a nonpresent group such as the factory workers, the factory's management, predatory males on the streets at night, the sultan and his faithful *abdi-dalem*, religious organizations and clubs, and the numerous other communities through which the rules of social harmony are enforced. The nonpresent community shapes Sari's voice in a way that makes it a significant aspect of her story and, hence, her identity. We see that Sari's narrated experiences were those of her factory cohort's to the extent at which it became impossible to distinguish individual agency and responsibility. Since we cannot distinguish the speaker from the community in these stories, I have argued that storytelling is a reflection of these communities more so than of the speaker. As we have also seen in theoretical discussions, storytelling is synonymous with constructing identity. We still need to examine more closely what an identity that is not distinct from community looks like. We also investigate the social burdens of adhering to such an identity.

The speech situations we examine here demonstrate how Javanese stories are a cooperative effort through which meaning and identity are constituted as an intersubjective and (mainly) harmonious reality.

Participation Frameworks and Positioning

At this point, we need to look further at theories of participation in order to tie the processes of constructing speech to that of constructing identity. As we have seen in our analyses so far, participant roles are recognized through the linguistic terms that index social or relative position. In Javanese, these linguistic terms include pronouns and kinship terms, as well as the adverbials, level shifts, reported speech, and boundary indexes that are doubly indexical of both the story in the stream of conversation and the speaker in the context of her experiences. I have also added speech styles as an indicator of relative position through topic control and development, the ability to tell a story and its type or style, self or other referencing, and uptake. Taking stories and conversations as a way to create identity, I have suggested that these Javanese women *are* the way they fit into their communities. This is a notion of identity that is very flexible and adaptable because of its "outward" reach, not something that is concrete and unique because it exists "inside."

The way in which social identity is presented in these Javanese stories seems to be different from that in Erving Goffman's concept of footing. Goffman described footing as "the alignment we take up to ourselves and the others present as expressed in the way we manage the production or reception of an utterance. A change in our footing is another way of talking about a change in our frame for events" (1981:128). While I have already shown how speakers do vary their footings, the fact that Goffman sees footing as *controlled* or *managed* by the speaker makes it fundamentally inappropriate. The more we grow aware of community pressures and national ideology, the more we see that these Javanese women do not have the control over their lives, experiences, or even selves that this theory suggests.

The concept of "positioning" emerged as a more dynamic response to footing. In positioning, individuals are "constituted and reconstituted through the various discursive practices in which they participate" (Davies and Harré, 1990:46; see also Davies, 1990; Harré and Gillett, 1994; Harré and van Langenhove, 1991). This theory also ties human identity to language, proposing that speakers as members of various communities must learn how to speak in different social situations. Positioning emphasizes the fluid and interactive natures of social realities in which meanings and identities are jointly produced by the very act of speaking but which all occur in the various social communities people belong to (see also Mead, 1934).

The theory of positioning points to a need to identify the discourses that sustain social hierarchy as relative positions. Initially, we need to understand how speakers are able to dominate others by shaping their contributions and rights of participation in one situation and then to be dominated in another. Then we can tie this fundamental social inequality to identity construction as it is enacted by the speakers themselves. Is it possible to deal with this multiplicity of positions available to Javanese speakers through "cultural" values and social stratification without evaluative terms such as domination?

In Javanese speech situations, the existence of hierarchical values and speech levels provides evidence for what James Scott (1990) has referred to as the "public transcript." Originally inspired by observations among peasant communities in Malaysia, Scott was taken by the contradictions of class relations: "The poor sang one tune when they were in the presence of the rich and another tune when they were among the poor. The rich too spoke one way to the poor and another among themselves" (1990:ix). Yet, Scott's purpose was to delve beyond these surface variations to describe the political conduct of subordinate groups in terms of a dialect of "disguise and surveillance." Scott then describes "hidden transcripts" as the "truth" that emerges in conversations between subordinates, whereas the "public transcripts" are the performances groups enact during interactions with superiors. These metaphorical concepts explain the inherent conflicts in public presentations of deference and loyalty with the clandestine acts of defiance and rebellion.

In terms of Scott's (1990) metaphors, the *kråmå* vocabularies, especially the humbling attributes of *kråmå andhap* and the highly honorific *kråmå inggil*, are a perfect smoke screen from which speakers can reposition themselves when the dominant classes leave, as we see in chapter 5. Here, speech levels function as a metaphor for ways of behaving since we know that the cohort did not speak in formal Javanese to their managers in the factory. Furthermore, how far can we take the cohort's stories to be examples of "hidden transcripts"? Can we describe them as defiant and rebellious when we know how deeply they remained a controllable product of the dominant cultural order?

Speaking and being Javanese results in a perfectly ordered harmonious world, where those of lower rank faithfully attend to the social needs of their betters—in public. But, as we have seen, militancy is strongly pacified among these speakers' own clandestine interactions. In "private," among their own cohort, we can easily see how the hierarchical values Javanese children learn as they acquire language are maintained and extended to all social interactions. This does not mean that there is no resistance in Java since there obviously is. But it is a call to investigate this resistance from a more community-based, interactive level. As we saw in chapter 5, the discourses of resistance need to be learned. If members need to learn each new discourse, we can already see that learning takes place through a kind of cultural "filter" made up of local values. Thus, we need to return to the concept of positioning to understand how that filter may work in creating identities.

We have already seen how Sari, her cohort, and her family are social actors who have learned to function within their world to survive. We saw this by examining how each attempted to deal with Sari's protest at the factory as a moral dilemma by negotiating his or her own position in relation to it. We can say, then, that this crisis was made up of sets of competing discourses, each of which represented the different factions. The factory managers enacted their position of power by silencing their workers as a way to impose unfair demands. The factory could not be held accountable for their words since they had the power to refuse to allow the women to speak. The managers can do this because they know they have the support of the community on several levels: (1) Javanese women are low in the social hierarchy, meaning they should silently accept the fate imposed on them by their superiors; (2) the police, the military, and others in positions of power also hold the same hierarchical social construct; and (3) national ideology proclaims women as heroes because they work in low-paying jobs to assist in the state's development program. Pak Sri and Pak Budi, each with his own version of male refinement and equanimity to maintain, presented their interpretations of the crisis as an active process of negotiating the protest story's development. Both the men gave up because Sari's story was inflexible.

We have also discussed gender ideology and the ways in which language can both reflect and create how others learn to experience their world. Based on all of these points, we can metaphorically describe our social worlds as made up of competing discursive practices, or *positions*. This is where we can locate the power elements that shape conversations. Positioning as a concept argues that the ways in which people participate in conversations have a formative influence on the structure of the mind.

Positioning begins with conversation as a form of social interaction in which the relative positions of the speakers come into contact.[1] Positioning, then, entails two dynamic processes. The first is the constitutive capacity of discourse. This means that one's experience of gender, race, class, a particular profession, or an opinion can only be understood and expressed through knowledge of the discourses associated with such a position.[2] Learning the terms, storylines,[3] metaphors, images, and concepts that a particular position makes relevant is a matter of choosing from among the various images and practices that make up its repertoire.[4] By learning how to speak from the vantage point of a particular subject's position, an individual's sense of self, his or her subjectivity, is formulated (Davies and Harré, 1990).

The second dynamic of positioning involves the interaction of competing positions in the negotiation of meaning as a natural feature of conversations. Conversation involves the negotiation of participants' positions, which is essential for meaning. This implies that people have the capacity to adopt a range of perspectives on objects, events, and states of affairs and are in that sense inhabitants of many possible positions. The strength of positioning as a theory lies in this flexibility: "An individual emerges through the processes of social interaction, not as a relatively fixed end product but as one who is constituted and reconstituted through the various discursive practices in which they participate" (Davies and Harré, 1990:46). These negotiated positions, then, are the ways we are able to speak in conversations that admit us into the interaction as coherent participants. Any social individual thus engages in talk from as many created and re-created positions as are available through that individual's ongoing experiences of interactions and, hence, his or her ongoing experience of self.

But speakers may also be positioned by others, forcing them to accommodate to and contribute to the dominant storylines, the ideologies or discourses that make up cultural knowledge. If the dominant storyline is one of social hierarchy and glorified acquiescence, those who belong to the community must uphold such a position and adapt its values through all their other positions. Those positioned as inferior in the social order in essence have their agency or choices constrained, or *filtered*, by their responsibility to the "harmony" of that order. I have endeavored to identify these relative positions through the autobiographical aspects of conversational storytelling. Through conversations we have observed how speakers "conceive of themselves and of the other participants by seeing what position they take up and in which story, and how they are then positioned" (Davies and Harré, 1990:48).

Examples of positioning in practice also appear when we examine how the social order positions women, such as in the speeches and slogans that praise women for their sacrifices to the state. We see how Sari positioned herself (or was positioned by community factors) in relation to her cohort and how the cohort positioned themselves in relation to other workers and management. Remember, too, how Sari and Atik positioned themselves in relation to Yanti in the starfruit stories, and how the Budi family positioned me in relation to the pedicab drivers at the railway station. Positioning can occur interactively when one person positions another, and it can also be reflexive when people position themselves. Meaning, then, is developed through the reactions of participants in a conversation as members of society, which has a direct tie to concepts of power in the creation of that reality.

The working-class narratives we have analyzed show that positions of power and inequality in Java are enforced from within disempowered and oppressed communities. Among the working-class women whose stories are presented here, conversations are shaped by a social environment of rights and obligations and the sets of responsibilities that coincide with these various positions. To use the term "agent" in conjunction with responsibilities in situations that are clearly stratified; highly constraining vis-à-vis social rights and obligations to the collectivity; and traditionally, habitually, and politically dependent on calm order in interactions means that agency, utterances, or identity has little to do with autonomy. In these contexts, then, the positions speakers may use in a given speech situation are shaped by the relations of dominance that exist among speakers, their community, and their culture. It should be taken for granted that alignments, frames, or roles exist prior to speaking and that these can and often do shape the ways in which people speak.

Introduction to the Conversation

We are currently enjoying a quiet evening at home in conversation with Sari; her older sister, Atik; and their neighbor and long time friend, Yanti.[5] Although the three women are close friends, Yanti is the oldest by a year[6] and has the highest ranking employment and education. She is a junior high school teacher (*Sekolah Menengah Pertama*), whereas Atik works in the administrator's office of the same school. Thus, as we have already seen, Yanti is afforded respectful status within these contexts. My own position in relation to the others does not fall within the usual Javanese domains since I never positioned myself in accordance with the attributes of age, education, and so on. By now, after almost two years of my presence, the women are accustomed to me as a friend and sibling. As mentioned earlier, I have taken up for myself the role of younger sibling, which allows me to serve the others, assist in the house, and remain silent in conversations. In the following conversation, Sari and I were present only briefly. After offering her new version of the protest narrative, Sari and I leave the room for about 20 minutes. Thus we examine the stories told by Atik and Yanti while they were alone in the room as an opportunity to study variations in narrative styles. We investigate interactional status through the way the conversation is managed in terms of topic, uptake, and involvement.

At the time of this conversation, Sari had already been fired from her job at the Taman Tirto garment factory. The firing was sudden and thoroughly unexpected. Just one day before, Sari and her cohorts had met with their representatives from the Department of Labor, who were currently negotiating with management on the workers' behalf. Sari had told me that the meetings were going very well and that the Labor Department's representatives were very encouraging in their advice and support for the workers' case.

As things turned out, however, just one day after meeting with the labor representative, the women went to work as usual but were met at the factory gate by their bosses, supported by a few dozen armed military soldiers. The women were immediately singled out from the hundreds of other workers and informed that they were fired. They received no warning or compensation for the salaries due. Moreover, they were told that they were all officially on record for being trouble-makers and potential Communists. The handful of women who had taken part in the "protest" were now in tears and justifiably terrified. They immediately ran to see their Department of Labor representative. He refused to meet with them, and the workers were asked to leave the building. They politely conceded. When the women tried to meet and speak with their coworkers who had not openly supported the strike, they were again told to go away. Their still-employed friends had been warned not to speak with the protesters or suffer the same fate.

Over the course of the week that followed the firing, the cohort discovered that the factory had paid the Department of Labor to drop the women's case and that they all had been blacklisted.[7] However, none of this information emerges in Sari's factory narrative; instead, she speaks as if nothing had happened.

The factory story is embedded in a sequence of stories that displays the function of dominance in the construction of shared meaning and identity. Despite our knowledge of the "truth," the sequence demonstrates how relationally disempowered Sari is with respect to the other participants, despite the intimacy one would expect between siblings and good friends. Because of her low relational status and the story's deviance from social norms, the protest story is not part of any main storyline. Although Sari manages to slip it into the topic sequence by finding a connection with other topics, the protest narrative is radically shaped to suit the current relational order. In this context we can see specifically what "truth" means within alternative worldviews.

The following protest narrative is the only one of the trilogy to be indexed with a first-person "I." This will illustrate how the properties of pronouns, as indexes of agency or location (Benveniste, 1971) or as indexes of first-person responsibility (Mühlhäusler & Harré, 1990), need to be expanded to include social rank and distance to understand the indexical systems of Javanese narratives.

Repetition in Intimacy and Asymmetry

We have previously looked at topic development in informal Javanese as a "posting" of a nonspecific idea through key words or phrases. This posted phrase can then be taken up, developed, or ignored, depending on the needs and interests of the other participants. Here, we examine further how a story's topic follows a close, relationally coherent sequence in which progression is linked to the repetition and allo-repetition of the posted words in idea units. Excerpt (34) shows how the two text topics of the conversation were introduced. We then see how topic is mediated in line with hierarchical constraints. Atik's topic is Surti's ill father (see also chapter 4), while Yanti is more interested in how Surti will reconcile her strenuous familial duty with her job. The key words here, then, are "hospital" (*rumah sakit*), as the location of Surti's problem, and "work" (*nyambut gawe*), as the center of Yanti's concern.

(34) *Orienting Stories of Work and Pressure*

6. ATIK: Aku mau ngedrop Mbak Sur ning anu,	Earlier, I dropped Mbak Surti at whatsit,
7. SARI : *rumah sakit*	The hospital
8. ATIK: *rumah sakit.* Saiki <u>nunggu Bapake.</u>	The hospital. Now [she's] caring for her father.
9. YANTI: *Orang-orang* saiki nggih, dilebokke <u>rumah sakit</u> njuk sesuk <u>nyambut gawe.</u>	People these days y'know, go into the hospital then they're at work the next day.

10. ATIK: Ngko mbengi jam sewelas   Last night at 11
    aku kan, karo Pak (?)//   I right, and pak (?)//
11. YANTI: Mending <u>nunggu bapakne</u>   It's better to care for her father
    ra sah <u>nyambut gawe</u>. [.]   [she] shouldn't have to work. [.]
12. SARI: Mboten mungkin.   Not possible.
    Jane Mbak Sur yå rådå istirahat sik.   Actually Mbak Sur rests first.
    ora mung mempeng le <u>nyambut</u>   It's not just energy for working.
    <u>gawe</u>.

Atik's two attempts at posting a topic about being at the hospital with Sur (turns 6 and 8 and again in turn 10) remain incomplete because they achieve no uptake from the high-status member, Yanti. Sari supports her elder sister as she completes her utterance for her in 7, which is then allo-repeated, signifying its fit into the sequence. But Yanti's position with regard to the topic is not supportive. In turn 9, Yanti is taking up the general topic of *hospital*, but she has already compounded it with her own interest, that is, *work*. Atik does not respond to Yanti's utterance but continues to orient her own story. Yanti, however, interrupts Atik to give Yanti's conclusive opinion: if Surti needs to be minding her father, she should not be working also:

11. YANTI: Mending <u>nunggu bapakne</u>   It's better to care for her father
    ra sah <u>nyambut gawe</u>. [.]   [she] shouldn't have to work. [.]

Yanti has shown her storyline to be different from Atik's. Sari's role is limited to supporting the others.

The frequency of allo-repetition among these women makes the location of topics and the tracing of their development quite easy. Repetition is iconic of the harmony that is culturally required as a "way of linking the surface patterns of talk with interactional goals, and of understanding how people are linked to each other" (Tannen, 1987:581). Repetition in Javanese is more than a joint idea construction that functions to complete or supplement another's utterance. It also creates coherence through topic chaining (Becker, 1984) which becomes a center around which other terms may focus.

As the manager of the conversational direction, Yanti shifts us away from the topic of Surti's work and health problems. While the next 10 turns discuss the smell of the traditional medicines (*jamu*) I have brought for everyone, Yanti marks the closure of the previous topic, that is, Surti's care of her father while maintaining her job, by posting the next, guarding one's health:[8]

22. YANTI: Lha **nggih**   Yes y'know
    ning mikir awak.   but [you have to] think about your
                                            body [health].

Sari, far more lively and talkative than her older sister, is the first one to respond. She ratifies Yanti's change of topic to work and health, but she adds the related notion of overtime.

(35) *Sari's Factory Story*

23. SARI: **Niki** tho gek jaman ting	In relation to this that time at that
Taman Tirto tu,	Taman Tirto,
nganti nglembur **niku**	that overtime
tekan jam loro bengi barang.	up till 2:00 in the morning and all.

Sari states that she worked overtime at the Taman Tirto garment factory as late as 2:00 A.M. Her subject position does not stress a personal experience but rather contains *niki tho* (in relation to this). Sari links her utterance to Yanti's previously mentioned topic (turn 22) of looking after one's own health, rather than focusing on her own position at it relates to the topic. The demonstrative (*niki*) plus emphasis (*tho*) discursively link Sari's turn to that of Yanti's, configuring her joint construction as dependent. This is a clue that her factory story will explicitly follow the topic determined by Yanti. In the next few turns, we see what Sari interprets as Yanti's topic for Sari's own protest story.

Atik looks to Yanti to ratify her sister's movement of the topic:

24. ATIK: nglembur **nåpå?**	Overtime what?

Atik allo-repeats the word *nglembur* (overtime) and adds a question particle in *madyå: nåpå?*, thus showing that the utterance is not directed to her sister, with whom she would not *mbåså*. Atik is thus requesting Yanti's permission to expand her topic to include overtime as it is connected to guarding one's health at work. Yanti did not speak, so no objection was implied.

Sari is free to return to her story:

25. SARI: Ha nek aku yo wegah!	Well as for me ya forget it!

Sari resumes her story and expresses her personal feelings about overtime when she states, "well as for me ya forget it!" *Wegah* is a strongly evaluative term, showing that Sari is beyond any attempts at persuasion. Her position is final. She shows that she has refused to work overtime, essentially indexing herself as having been in position to reject the factory and not having been positioned to be fired and blacklisted. Furthermore, unlike the two previous chapters, her subject position is marked with an agentic, first-person *aku*, "I."

Her sister responds with an empathetic reply to Sari's previous statement in turn 23:

| 26. ATIK: Jam loro bengi! | 2 o'clock at night! |
| lha kok le ngereh awak . . . | You mean to say the order . . . |

Atik shows support for the topic by allo-repeating the most obvious of her sister's utterances: "2 o'clock at night!" I assume she is aware by now of her sister's problems at the factory, leading me to believe she may well be displaying this empathy for Yanti's benefit. The allo-repetition (turn 26) occurs two turns after Atik ratified Sari's change of topic with Yanti (turn 24) and three turns after the original utterance (turn 23).

Sari continues her story, enhancing her agent's stance in opposition to that of the factory:

27. SARI: Nek **kulå** ngono.	As for me.
Mbok wis nrimå **matur nuwun**,	[They think I'll] just accept [it with a] thank you very much,
ha: mung nggo sepuluh ewu to!	ha: all for just 10,000! [$5.00 a month]

Sari's stance in this turn is very dramatic, with a direct rejection of the powerlessness imposed on her at the factory. This disempowerment is marked discursively by her use of *nrimå*, referring to the general expectation that all low-statused members of the community accept their fates in a dignified silence. Yet her rejection is marked by *Mbok*, a discourse marker that signals conflict at both the discourse and global levels. *Mbok* shows globally that the factory managers expect the imposed overtime to be fully accepted and that any unwillingness will be borne in silence (*trimå*). They trust that their Javanese laborers will *nrimå* exactly as they always do and have done for centuries, even though the salary is clearly not enough for the task. *Mbok* shows at the discursive level also that Sari is displaying a conflict; it signals her sarcasm, encoded by framing her evaluation externally: *Ha: mung nggo sepuluh ewu to!* ("Ha. all for just 10,000!").

In terms of participation structures, Sari has taken on an ideologically agentic stance in relation to her utterances, something not seen before. She presents herself as author, animator, figure, and principal in a set of narrated events that is not at all similar to those we have observed earlier. Sari knows quite well that both Yanti and Atik do not experience overtime problems like hers; thus she does not discuss them, given the framework of coconstructed narratives and her low rank within it. Despite the fact that the other women already know about these work problems, the inclusion of such information would shatter the harmonious boundaries of this speech event. Rather than discuss a known issue that is not shared by other members of the group, she must enforce what is shared—to speak as if she also faced a managable overtime situation.

Sari's version of the protest narrative is not *false* in the same way that the starfruit stories were also not false. Within the social constraints of this community of Javanese women, there are many levels of truths that are judged far more important than an individual's actions or experiences.

Participation and Pronouns

Studies of participation quite often begin with person categories linked to pronouns since pronouns are natural indexes to a participant's framework (Benveniste, 1971; Hanks, 1990; Mühlhäusler and Harré, 1990). Hanks suggests that the establishment and maintenance of participation in talk is mediated through "demonstrative individuation," most clearly seen by pronouns like "I." Urban (1989) has also shown how footing is substantiated through a selection of first-person pronominal positions. Narratives, then, are said to make use of "I" indexes as a way to accomplish a referential projection of self, perception, cognition, and affect away from the current context onto a narrated one.

The Javanese narratives we have seen so far do not demonstrate an exclusive "individuation" but rather inclusion and relationality.[9] Thus, it is more accurate to say that the narrated "I" in these Javanese stories expands notions of referential projection to include a communal self. This is a self that transcends individuality to incorporate contextual values as part of one's own flexibility of being. Self-positioning in this version of Sari's protest story demonstrates this variant on the narrated "I." Her own words position her as in control and able to reject the factory's offenses. This self-positioning is fully agentic, meaning that the subject "I" precedes a predicate that describes a particular action. When "I" is the subject of a clause, the predicate becomes the direct responsibility of that subject in that the "I" is the actor of the predicate. "I"-indexed clauses demonstrate a speaker's recognition of selfhood and individuality since every "I" requires a "you" to distinguish speakers (Benveniste, 1971; Mühlhäusler and Harré, 1990).

In Sari's story, however, these standard versions of an agent's positioning and responsibility fail to include responsibility beyond the boundaries of the utterance. Sari's agentic stance is placing her not only as physically and experientially absorbed in the factory but also as morally responsible for preserving contextual harmony. Her way of adapting the protest narrative to the immediate needs of the situation is to assume a stance best described as a moral responsibility to defend herself from the factory's persecution. If she interprets this moment as requiring a particular type of stance, that, too, is worthy of a fully agentic support. This, then, is the flexibility of responsible agency.

Yet, while neither of the two events discussed in previous chapters revealed agency, that is, first-person stance, on the part of any of the participants,[10] in this case all the women present declare their positions in relation to the common topic, using the "I" form of *kulå*. The *kulå* form of self-indexing is not as directly indexical of its speaker as the *ngoko* form *aku* since it appropriates the *båså* norm of indexing the placement of "I" at a respectful distance from "you." While all occurrences of "I" presume a "you," the Javanese speech levels can serve to lessen the self-indexing values of "I." The indexical properties of the Javanese "I" are able to fluctuate between standard pronominal coordinates of time and place (Benveniste, 1971) and responsibility (Mühlhäusler and Harré, 1990) by exposing the social-hierarchical conditions that speakers create to signify their interactive and relational stances. "I" does not so much index the speaker as it indexes a speaker's relation to the "you," an outward focus that places the "you" as a major player in the framing of a speaker's story. *Kulå* as a symbol of stylistic respect implies a commitment of refined acceptance to the social order, as seen by Sari's refraint from imposing her unharmonious storyline on the current interaction.

Yet, the women's speech styles also display a similar commitment to the social order from the *ngoko* first-person *aku*, which was assumed to indicate a right of self-expression. Such freedom has yet to present itself as a patterned occurrence in this corpus of young women's stories. While the elderly speakers have exhibited autobiographical stories, as already mentioned, their style of presentation permits other speakers a role in the telling. Rarely are any of these stories completed. Although none of them display the elegance of formal, high Javanese, they do show how flexibility of discursive style and social identity firmly supports the refined traits of self-awareness and sensitivity. None of these interactions looses sight of the tacit moral and ethical agreement through which speakers mutually preserve and guard equanimity by relegating self to the higher needs of that social order (e.g., Joseph Errington, 1988).

Sari's agentic "I" stance in this speech event, then, is not a sign of her agency or power in the face of her story-world factory problem. It is a cooperative self-positioning, an acknowledgement of her low status in relation to her real-world interlocutors. Yanti, as the high-status member, often uses the same outwardly indexical *kulå* to mark positions. Hierarchical respect, then, is not found in speech-level indexes since Yanti responds reciprocally. We instead see how variants in speech styles signal contextual empowerment.

Sharedness and Topic

Unlike the speech situations in the two previous chapters, the Taman Tirto protest narrative is not the sole storyline here. The three women lead distinct lives, which are here brought together to assign meaning to shared experience. But their positions are never equal and the assigned values of stories are not equal, and while stories are separately experienced and located, they will be molded to suit the social norms of the group.

But it was Sari nevertheless who initiated the topic of overtime in relation to Yanti's topic of work and health. Sari's completed narrative took up Yanti's topic and will now be taken up by the other participants. Yanti now takes her place in the story round.

(36) *Yanti's Overtime Story*

28. YANTI: Ha **nggih. kulå** tå misale,	O right. And me for example,
tekan jam pitu ngono	up to 7:00 y'know
nek aku wis prei	if I am on holiday
kosik-kosik.	[I can] remember.

Turn 28 takes up the group topic of overtime and health but focuses mainly on overtime. Yanti opens with *Ha nggih*, an affirmative marker of agreement. Such agreement may be directed toward either a previous utterance or perhaps just the topic. Solidarity, as mentioned in previous chapters, is easily simulated with this formulaic marker.

Yanti presents her overtime story by first signaling her acceptance of the topic and by adding, **kulå** *ta misale* ("and me, for example"). The word *misale* ("for example") might or might not signal a true story. It is unique in that "for example" most often functions to signal a frame change into metaphorical stance, a narrative world of fictitious possibilities, as Urban (1989) has found in Shokleng and Berman (1992) in Javanese-Indonesian speakers like these. Yanti however, is more likely to be using "for example" to focus on herself in the group and not the utterance, a kind of "*my* example is this." Such an agentic, self-indexing stance, however, firmly unites her story with the topical flow, showing her solidarity to the group.

Atik, as in the starfruit story, offers her experience last. It cannot compete at all with her sister's but is similar to that which she interprets as Yanti's experience.

(37) *Atik's Overtime Story*

29. ATIK: **Kulå nggih** jam nem,	I y'know [by] 6:00
mpun balik kok //	[I'm] already back [at home]//
30. YANTI: Sing //	What that means //
31. ATIK: //Setengah lima	//4:30

Atik's *kulå nggih* completes the symmetry of the story round, bringing the topic of overtime to its presumed closure. Atik contributes her story, which affirms adherence to the topic and the group harmony. The offering is not very interesting, but it signals the required "I am one of you" or "we are all in this together" bonding.

As Clare Wolfowitz describes, styles of respect in Javanese are forms of politeness that are different from what is usually termed formal speech. Respect does not need to express "social distance, but a positive and asymmetric relationship of marked closeness" (1991:37). The first-person pronoun *kulå* is an example of the respectful style of asymmetric place, as are kinship terms that function as vocatives in utterance final positions. Atik frequently punctuates her turns with *Mbak Yanti*, whereas such respectful vocatives are not reciprocal. Yanti does, though, match or frequently use a higher number of *båså* terms than do the others.

But Yanti had not finished her portion of the story round.

(36) *Yanti's Overtime Story Continued*

32. YANTI: //Kit esuk **nikå**.	That's in the morning that.

Yanti allows Atik enough time to introduce her uneventful offering before she adds very simply, "that's in the morning that [previous statement meant]." Atik's startled response is quite intriguing, especially since it reveals how much shared information actually exists between the women:

33. ATIK: Ket esuk!	In the morning?!
Tenan **nggih** ngrampungke *surat*	Really, o yes, finishing up those
tugas **niku**.	instruction letters.
Wa: **kulå** niku, ngantek . waduh,	Wah: I, . up till . oh wow. [false start]
Akeh banget Mbak Yanti.	That's an awful lot Mbak Yanti.
surat tugas (?)	instruction letters (?)

Atik is shocked by the fact that Yanti works overtime until 7 A.M., but in her amazement she also reveals her familiarity with Mbak Yanti's story. Junior high school teachers would not have a reason to work through the night until morning. Yet, Atik knows without Yanti telling her that the overtime was caused by a need to finish instruction letters. Since this is not a widely recognized part of a teacher's job, there is a strong possibility that Atik already knew this story. But she is shocked by this information, as shown by her false start: "Wah: I. up till . oh wow." (*Wa: kulå niku, ngantek . waduh*). She is shocked because she cannot relate nor compare her own experiences to what she has just heard. All she can add is that those official letters must have been a lot!

It is already well known that Sari's overtime experiences are even more horrendous. By seeing how shocked Atik was at hearing Yanti's story, we can glimpse what communal story rounds are meant to avoid. Because Yanti has opened the way for "shocking" stories, only now does Sari allude to the fact that she, too, has worked overtime until morning, something that has, unlike Yanti's experiences, occurred frequently and without her own consent:

34. SARI: Ha mbok wis nek aku.	Well that's also been the case with me.

She will not compete with Yanti, so she understates her own story by saying that she, too, has worked overtime until morning, giving her cooperative support for Yanti's orientation. Using the marker *mbok*, she again hints at the sarcasm or conflict she conceals in her utterance. But Yanti is the one who is given control of the interactive positions and topics, and thus it is she who is allowed to tell her story:

35. YANTI: **Kulå riyin**	I in the past,
surat tugas **kalih** *korektor.*	instruction letters and corrections.

Yanti explains that in the past (*riyin*) she was responsible for official letters, as well as for correcting exams. It was during this time that she had to work in the office until 7:00 A.M. Atik's uptake of Yanti's story takes the form of a succession of questions about the details of her overtime experience:

36. ATIK: Korektor Mbak Yanti **nggih** melu?	A corrector Mbak Yanti so you did that?
37. YANTI: Korekto anu, korektor IPA **kulå.**	Correc. uhm. IPA corrector, I was
38. ATIK: Korektor **teng ngrikå**.	The correcting over there.
39. YANTI: **Teng pundi**?	Where?
40. ATIK: **Teng** Senopati.	At Senopati.
41. YANTI: O: lha **nggih**.	O yes that's right.
Nek korektor	When there were corrections
kulå teng ngrikå.	I went over there.

In turn 38, Atik utters the elliptical ["you did] the correcting over there," which signals what she interprets as shared information. This is not the case, as Yanti asks, "Where?" Atik then replies, "at Senopati?" which is in fact where Yanti had done her overtime correcting. Since this is not where Yanti actually teaches now, such a statement may prove that Atik had remembered where and what jobs she had done before.

This short sequence again displays a heavy use of allo-repetition:

36. ATIK: <u>Korektor</u> Mbak Yanti nggih melu?	A corrector, Mbak Yanti, so you did that?
37. YANTI: <u>Korekto</u> anu, <u>korektor</u> IPA kulå.	Correc. uhm. IPA corrector, I was
38. ATIK: <u>Korektor</u> <u>teng ngrika</u>.	The correcting over there.
39. YANTI: <u>Teng</u> pundi?	Where?
40. ATIK: <u>Teng</u> Senopati.	At Senopati.
41. YANTI: O: lha nggih.	O yes, that's right.
Nek <u>korektor</u>	When there were corrections
kulå <u>teng ngrikå</u>.	I went over there.

Each turn in the sequence is directly linked to the one preceding it through allo-repetition. Repetition functions here like a thread running through each utterance, tying it to the previous one. The progression is clearly signaled, from the activity of correcting to its location, unifying multiple voices into one coherently patterned discourse chain.

Patterned repetition, as we have seen over and over again in the stories, marks the uptake of a posted topic. The repetition of key words may also serve as a stranglehold that tightly winds each utterance into the next, limiting individual or creative interpretations. While repetition in Javanese discourse reveals the bonds speakers create, it is also a way of creating the appearance of harmonious coherence. Allo-repetition is, then, the ultimate cohesive link. But what speakers do not understand or agree with can be avoided by simply repeating it, creating the appearance of a network of multiple layers of absolute alliance, much like the repetition of slogans and ideological definitions that marks homes, roads, mass media, and minds all over Indonesia. This may be taken up as a habitual discourse of survival in a Java overwhelmed by narrow constraints of community in the negotiation of meaning. Repetition can be a simplifying strategy through which speakers give the impression of relational coherence because it helps them to avoid taking a stance. Evidence does show how repetition of key phrases and discourse styles in the story rounds creates the appearance of alliance. We have also seen how the appearance of alliance can have several strategic purposes, only one of which can be respect for high-statused members.

But more than simply to show a marked interest in mundane information, what Wolfowitz (1991) calls a sense of dramatic interest around the prosaic details of daily life, Atik's elliptical style of request is worth noting, especially as an interpretation cue for positioning or rather marginalizing Sari in the interaction. The mutual ratification sequences, which display group perspective in the shaping of social identity, have repeatedly forced Sari into voluntarily re-creating her interpretations in a much less obtrusive form. The mundane topics of everyday life are easily taken up as controllable and conducive to the maintenance of more important issues, such as determining relative social positions and the similarity of perspective and experience that has come up over and over again in the stories. Such topics, above all, are *safe*. Sari is thus marginalized because her experiences are not shared, nor are they appropriate within the usual, apolitical range of topics normally discussed by this group. Even though Yanti has also worked overtime until morning, hers is by choice and occasional, whereas Sari's was forced and regular. Sari's status as a factory worker places her quite low on the ladder of social positions. But Sari loves to talk and is considered the most sociable and outgoing of the Budi siblings. Thus it is Sari who must take the longest strides to conform to the surrounding contextual requirements.

At this juncture in the conversation, Sari and I left the room. Atik and Yanti then embarked on their own stories, giving us an opportunity to examine several different styles of narrative.

Facing Inequality

By this time, Sari's protest narrative is complete. We have seen how she was forcibly silenced by the cruel and illegal will of those in power in her factory and in the Department of Labor, by her friends at the factory, and by her own family. We have also seen how local discursive practices reflect the community's sets of expectations for young, working-class women. We have seen how the community imposes its rules on its members by following the development of the protest narrative and how speakers positioned themselves in a social conflict. What remains shrouded in silence are the stories that reflect anger and resentment. Even off the record, I never heard these from Sari,[11] although I know for a fact that she suffered from earaches for a long time afterward.

We have caught a few brief glimpses of the ways in which women resolve themselves to their fates in silence because their communities will not accept alternatives. Does this mean that these women do not experience a reflexivity of self through which they attempt to objectively understand themselves as unique individuals, acting and being acted on within their worlds? What can they do when problems mount? Speakers cannot discuss their personal issues because divergence from community expectations is invariably met negatively and harshly, as seen in the rape victims' letters. Speakers must not "shock" others, as this will disrupt harmonious order and reflect badly on them. Young speakers rarely talk about themselves; when they do, they are in positions of relative power, and the stories themselves are not exceptionally private. With so many visible constraints on the storytelling process, can we still view storytelling as a social means of identity construction? If these strongly *other*-centric stories do in fact reflect a speaker's identity, how can we learn to recognize exactly what this definition of identity means?

In the rare privacy of the Budi sitting room, Atik and Yanti were left alone to tell each other their stories. Both of these very long and highly detailed stories deal with problems. Atik's story concerns Pak Surti's illness—see story (11), chapter 4—and Mbak Surti's problems in dealing with the imminent death of her father. Yanti returns to Atik's original topic, Mbak Surti's problems, to lead into her own frustration story. Both of these stories, one referring to Mbak Surti, a nonpresent mutual friend, and the other, Yanti's autobiography, deal with social and familial demands on female children. In both cases, these demands are extremely unfair, and both were met with acquiescence and subsequent illness by the women.

The story about Mbak Surti's problems[12] is oriented in turns 43 through 53, when Atik describes Pak Surti's illness, the expenses borne by the family, and Pak Surti's current physical state. All of these utterances are in response to specific questions from Yanti. Finally, she asks Atik to present her synopsis of the situation.

(38) *Surti's Stress*

53. YANTI: Lha inggih soale?	So then y'know the problem is?
54. ATIK: Soale nggih pripun.	The problem is what.
Tenagane mboten onten.	His energy is gone.
Mbak Sur tambah kuru nikå lho.	Mbak Surti has gotten much thinner y'know.
Kok gumunku	I'm real shocked
"Lho kok mung kowe tå sing mikir?"	"How is it that it's only you who thinks [about Pak Sur]?"
Gumun kulå kalih wong siji nikå.	I'm shocked at that person.
Wong atase nduwe Kangmas,	Above her she has a brother,
nduwe Mbakyu nggih kathah.	[She] has elder sisters y'know plenty.

Yanti has specifically requested information that only Atik has access to, that is, details about the sick man. But the clause's topic, the lost energy, immediately leads to the story's topic, how Surti's vigil beside her sick father is affecting her own health. Atik makes the sudden shift back to Surti's condition in this story, which returns to her main concern at the beginning of this conversation. Earlier, Yanti had not taken up this topic, instead shifting the topic toward work.

Atik's story here shows her personal involvement and concern for Surti's predicament. Yet, in terms of community pressures on conformity, we can see that Atik places all the blame on Surti herself. Her reported speech reconstructs her own words to Surti, but they appear as a reprimand: "Lho kok mung kowe tå sing mikir?" ("How is it that it's only *you* who thinks [about Pak Sur?]") Atik asks, followed by the repetition of her shock. The shock is aimed *at* Surti. It is not in sympathy with her because of the selfish siblings who do not assist in looking after their sick parents. Surti herself causes the shock because she is the one who must make the others share the responsibility.

While Atik's position is indexed to herself—"*I* am shocked"— to the point of repeating the sensation, she is maintaining a dignified distance, both from the story and from Surti's situation, by omitting a great deal of highly personal information that would strengthen a sympathetic stance. Atik omits from her story the fact that Surti is suffering from a fit of serious depression, including nightmares, fainting spells, vomiting, and crying. She also does not state that Ibu Budi was forced to forbid Surti from spending the night at their house because Surti's fits and fainting had caused panic and sleep loss.[13] Because Surti is the only one of her siblings still unmarried, she is alone in her family's house since both parents are in the hospital.[14] What Atik could say compared to what she does say can be interpreted in several ways. Does she not discuss Surti's emotional problems because she does not see them, because they are inappropriate among mutual friends, or because they are taboo topics? Atik discusses the issue in terms of selfishness on the part of Sur's siblings, but the heart of the issue within the story is Surti's acquiescence, the fact that she does what she is expected to do in silence. The personal effects this extreme pressure has had on Surti remain silent issues. Atik's framing of the story eliminates the trouble by describing it as no more than "growing thin," a general clue for unhappiness.

Yanti concludes Atik's discussion of Surti's problem by presenting her own interpretation as the coda:

59. YANTI: Ha wedi tunggu wong lårå   [They're] just afraid to mind a sick
     nggih ngaten lho   person y'know

This conclusion matches her own frustration story perfectly. Yanti takes this element of similarity as a cue to switch to her own story, which she immediately orients.[15]

(39) *Yanti's Stress: Day 1 Preparations*
59. YANTI: Ha wedi tunggu wong lårå   [They're] just afraid to mind a sick
     nggih ngaten lho   person y'know
     Kulå dhek <u>setu</u> wingi awan terus   Last Saturday afternoon I went to the
     ngulon,   west,
     <u>setu</u> tanggal <u>selawe</u>.   Saturday the twenty-fifth.
     <u>Selawe</u> kan, teksih onten   The twenty-fifth right, school was
     sekolahan,   still open,
     <u>selawe</u> karo nem likur.   the twenty-fifth and twenty-sixth.
     Pokoke dinå <u>setu</u> <u>niku</u>.   The point is on Saturday.
     Kulå niku <u>masak</u> kan,   I cooked, right,
     ting nggene kåncå kulå.   over at my friend's place
     <u>Masakke</u> lonthong opor <u>niku</u> lho. [We] cooked *lonthong opor* (a type of
                                              food) right.
     Dadi   So//

Yanti's extreme use of repetition and detail in her orientation is not something we have seen in previous stories. Stories usually emerge either in response to a direct question (Pak Surti's Illness) or as a natural development from a previous utterance and in keeping with the posted topics of the interaction. Yanti's story here seems to have no connection to the topic sequence at all since none of her utterances contain the key phrases. This discrepancy will be remedied but not until she reaches the end of a long sequence made up of multiple stories.

Yanti's freedom to hold the floor is symbolic of her status and is reminiscent of Ibu Asmoro's autobiographical stories. Relationally lower-status participants (such as Atik and Sari) tell stories that are brief and highly accessible, initiated by abstracts or orientations as mutual ratification sequences. These are rarely stories of personal experiences. Each segment of information in the Surti story is offered only in direct response to Yanti's posted topic or direct question. Yanti's stories, in contrast, are of personal experience, shown by her highly individualized orientation. But her stories must still be framed so that they link their contents and purposes to those of the patterns already set by the interaction; that is, they must maintain a clear and accessible point. Freedom to tell a story for the sake of telling a story or for sharing one's personal experiences as a sign of friendship does not seem to be an option in these informal speech situations.

Repetition and Sense Making

Yanti's story covers in extreme detail the events that took place on the twenty-fifth, four weeks before this meeting with Atik. Yet, the topical progression seems to be broken, so the pressure is on Atik to discover how a link is going to be made. Atik requests clarification often in her attempt to find that link and to maintain her supportive place in the story, as Ibu Umaya did in supporting Ibu Asmoro.

The orientation segment evolves from the allo-repetition of the key phrases that index activity, *masak* ("cooking") and the expanse of time, *jam* ("time"). Yanti's story is not consistent (she initially says that she cooked on Saturday in line 59 but changes it to Friday in line 61), and Atik attests to her role as conscientious listener by questioning and checking each point. While the details of pressure and a father's illness (i.e., what ties Yanti's stress story to Atik's story about Surti's stress) are not yet given, this story orientation enhances temporal factors:

60. ATIK: <u>Masak bareng</u>?	Cook all together?
61. YANTI: <u>Masak, masak bareng</u>.	Cook, cook, all together.
<u>Sore</u> mpun <u>masak</u>,	that afternoon [we] had cooked,
<u>jemuah sore</u> nikå lho, wah!	that Friday afternoon, wah!
62. ATIK: <u>Jemuah masak</u>?	On Friday [you] cooked?
63. YANTI: Nggawe lonthong	[We] made *lonthong*
64. ATIK: Mpun mbengi?	Was it already late?
65. YANTI: Nggih tekan <u>jam sångå</u>.	Yes, until 9:00.
<u>Jam sångå</u> terus bali.	At 9:00 [I] went home.
Lha esuk, setu esuk niku,	And then in the morning, that Saturday morning,
<u>jam</u> nem mpun <u>mrikå meleh</u>//	by 6:00 [I] was already there again//
66. ATIK: <u>Mrikå meleh</u>, soale <u>masak</u>//	There again. for the cooking//
67. YANTI: Bali jam setengah sepuluh nikå.	Go back at 9:30
68. ATIK: Lho <u>kanggone jam</u> pinten?	What's that for what time?
69. YANTI: <u>Kanggone jam</u> sewelas.	For 11:00
Njuk niku gek esuk teng kåncå kulå niku	Then next morning to my friend's again
mboten adus barang Dhik,	without even bathing yet Dhik,
Dadi tangi turu njuk <u>masak</u> mrikå,	so wake up and cook over there,
nganti uh,	until uh, (false start)

Kok le pengkuh men tho ki.	don't you know the tenacity of it all.
"Sing gek arep mangan wong akeh"	"So many are going to eat,"
ngoten tak pikir.	that's what I thought.
"O: jan wong mung wong telu	"But O! there's just three doing all
sing <u>masak</u>!"	the cooking!"
70. ATIK: Sing <u>masak</u>?	The ones who cooked?
71. YANTI: Wong mung kulå, Hamidha,	Just me, Hamidha,
Kamujiya	Kamujiya
njuk (?) kemempengen	so (?) energetically
kulå ngrasake "nggih ngoten niku."	I felt "yeah it's just like that."

The orientation segment covers 10 full turns, in which participants clarify the activity and the time span of the events to be discussed.

Repetition functions differently for each speaker. Atik's allo-repetition checks her understanding of the story's details while it signals her involvement in supporting her friend's story. For Yanti, allo-repetition functions externally to the storyline to affirm Atik's understanding, while her own repetition performs internally as a rhetorical device to create a sense of intensive patterning of hard work and exhaustion. Similar to Surti's vigil of minding her father while she keeps her full-time job at the school and does all the housework, Yanti's own vigil concerns her father's illness and several days of very intensive labor in the preparation of a huge feast. Yanti has already told us that school is not on a break, emphasizing these extra teaching activities as on a par with "overtime," and thus a link to a previous topic. She offers an extensive sequence of highly detailed orienting clauses to strengthen the intensity of her task.

Once the orientation pattern is established and taken up, Yanti advances her story into its event and evaluation sections:

YANTI:	a. <u>kanggone jam</u> sewelas.	For 11:00
	b. Njuk niku gek esuk teng kanca kulå niku	then, next morning to my friend's again,
	c. mboten adus barang Dhik,	without even bathing yet, Dhik,
	d. Dadi tangi turu njuk <u>masak</u> mrikå,	So wake up and cook over there,
	e. nganti uh,	until uh, (false start)
	f. Kok le pengkuh men tho ki!	Don't you know the tenacity of it all!
	g. "Sing gek arep mangan wong akeh."	"So many are going to eat,"
	h. ngoten tak pikir.	that's what I thought.
	i. jan wong mung wong telu <u>sing masak</u>!"	"but O! there's just three doing all the cooking!"
70. ATIK:	<u>Sing masak</u>?	The ones who cooked?
YANTI:	j. Wong mung kulå, Hamidha, Kamujiya	Just we three, me, Hamidha, Kamujiya
	k. njuk (?) kemempengen	so (?) energetically

l. kulå ngrasake "nggih ngoten   I felt, "yeah, it's just like that"
niku"

Yanti is carefully re-creating her feelings of overwork and pressure through her internal and external evaluation. Evaluation is internal (g, i, l) as reported speech and unusual event (c; it is extremely unusual for people to leave home without bathing), and external (f, h, k) as comments that display her reflexive observations of the activities. Yet this story is quite unusual in that the reported speech reflects Yanti's own internal thoughts and not a reconstructed dialogue with someone else. The initial event clause presents the activity of going to her friends' house but her use of intensifiers stresses the repetitive action—"Then," "next morning," "again"— and thus internally evaluates the linear and prolonged frame of the event. Yanti also uses the text boundary vocative *Dhik* to shift out of the story frame and stress the idea unit as worthy of being noted. For Javanese to leave home without bathing in the morning is unusual, and for it to be mentioned twice ("wake up," "then cook" entails no bath and no breakfast) shows how pressured Yanti felt. A sense of being overwhelmed is clearly stressed through Yanti's external intensifiers—"the tenacity of it all!"—and her direct speech.

Her responsibility to cook for this religious feast is a clear burden, but it is not one that she would consider rejecting. As she herself states, "yeah, it's just like that" (*nggih ngoten niku*). Like Surti, she is resolved to her fate and does nothing to find assistants in order to lessen the pressure.

After her first full day of preparations, Yanti returns home to find that her father is very ill and has been asking for her:

(40) *Yanti's Stress: Day 2, at Home*

71. YANTI: → Njuk tekan omah	So [I] reached home
Ibu muni "timbali Bapak nganu	Ibu said "[you] were summoned by Bapak uhm.
kok ndredeg" ngoten.	y'know [he's] trembling" she said.
Lha wiwit iku wong//	So that's where it started//

Yanti makes a sudden shift in her location, with no previous warning that this was to take place. Nor has she let on that her story, like Surti's, will involve a daughter's burden and an ill father. As framed for Atik, the length and complex actions of this long story are too much. Atik's questions showed from the start that she could not quite understand the point of Yanti's story. Now, she loses touch again (turn 72) when Yanti changes the location and adds a further level of complicating actions in turn 71 to her highly complex story. Atik questions Yanti's change of story location:

| 72. ATIK: Pripun ta? | What's this? |

From the start, she had been unclear about Yanti's motivation in telling the story. This new level of complicating events further confuses her.

In response to Atik's question, Yanti repeats her mother's words and uses demonstratives of distance (*kae*) that index her previous utterance, the source of her repetition. Atik, however, is still lost:

73. YANTI: Ndredeg le muni ibu   Trembling was what ibu said
    gemeter kae lho Dhik.   he was shivering y'know Dhik.
74. ATIK: Le mbayangke   Imagine
    bali såkå sawalan kae sorene//   coming back from a gathering in the
                                     afternoon//
75. YANTI: Mboten bali sawalan.   Not from a gathering
76. ATIK: Bali masak?   Home from cooking?

Atik has lost some of the essential facts that form the basis of Yanti's story. Again, the corrections to Atik's loss of topic are achieved through repetition and allo-repetition, which index Yanti's alignment to the facts of her own story. Yanti gets Atik back on track in Atik's attempts to make sense of the story before Yanti can continue, leaping right back into her story, a highly detailed account of the events concerning her father:

77. YANTI: Bali masak niku kulå   I returned from cooking
    setengah sepuluh niku njuk ah,   It's 9:30 and so uh.
    kok gemeter, iså gembrobyos nikå The shaking, [how can he] be
    Dhik.   sweating like this Dhik.
    Gembrobyos njuk didemok ngoten   Sweating a lot so I touch like this
    niki
    panis nikå bathuke.   really hot his forehead.
    Langsung kulå kompres nikå.   Right away I [got a] compress.
    A:: mbok teles bes nikå,   Ah: really soaking wet too,
    ngantek kulå, ganteni,   so I changed,
    kulå ganteni kaos ngeten.   I had to change his soaking shirt.
    Njuk Bapak niku kan,   And so Bapak right,
    mungkin tensine mundhak,   maybe his pressure is rising,
    dadine ditakoki mulakna (?) sirahe so [I] asked if that's why (?) his
    iki gek//   head
78. ATIK: Angel   Difficult
79. YANTI: Sirahe wong ngelu kan   The head of a person suffering a
                                     headache,
    rasane abot ngeten lho.   right it feels real heavy y'know.

Yanti describes her father's symptoms and her responses to them in full detail, from intensifying the heat of his forehead to describing the sweat that made her change his shirt. Next she externally describes the painful sensations for people suffering from high blood pressure. Now, and fully in keeping with the earlier theme of the interaction, she goes to work after a full night of sitting with her father.

After school, however, Yanti did not go home but back to her friend's to finish the preparations for that evening's gathering. Sequentially, this movement back to her friend's house occurs after sitting up all night with her father *and* teaching until 11:00 A.M. Spatially, however, it returns to the location of her earlier preparations and takes up the same overworked theme. In line with her exhaustion and the pressure, she describes preparing for the feast in fuller detail than she had previously.

(41) *Yanti's Stress: Day 2*

79. YANTI: Njuk ibu mungel ngene,	So then ibu said this,
"pokoke le sawalan ngko sedhelo wae.	"the point is the gathering later just for a short time.
Tekan sekolahan njuk mulih ngeten."	Go to school then come [straight] home again."
Dadi kulå nikå mangkat sekolah mboten tenang nikå lho.	So I left for school [but] I was not at all calm.
Le ku mangkat nggih mpun jam//	My leaving was then at // (leaving school)
80. ATIK: Sewelas	11:00
81. YANTI: nggih mpun setengah sewelas nikå.	That's right it's already 10:30.
Ngko ning kånå gek mulih	Later there then return
setengah sewelas kulå mlaku,	10:30 I walked
tekan kånå mboten gek mulih langsung,	arriving there but not going home directly,
Langsung niki sakniki gek ditåtå lonthonge,	Directly now [I] organize the *lonthong*
gek diirisi, gek ditåtå teng ngriki niki.	all sliced, then placed over here like so
teng piring ngoten lho.	on the plate just right, y'know
Sambel gorenge kulå nganu,	The *sambal goreng* (food) I uhm.
iwake barang mpun kulå kekke teng mriku ngoten lho	even the meat I placed there and all y'know
Iwake kan, mpun disuwiri ngoten lho.	The meat right, already shredded like so, y'know,
ngko garek ngucuri duduh nikå lho Dhik.	so that leaves pouring the broth y'know Dhik.
Mpun kulå racik kabeh mpun komplit	I had already prepared everything it's complete
Njuk es-e ditatani sisan niki.	Then the ice was arranged also
Njuk ngirisi ager-agere,	Then slice the *agar-agar* (Jello),
buah nikå lho Dhik,	the fruit also y'know Dhik,
Nganggo ager-ager barang	[They] even had *agar-agar*
82. ATIK: Ager-ager barang	Even agar-agar
83. YANTI: Nikå lho Dhik	That's the way it was y'know Dhik
84. ATIK: Dadine kaya mantenan	Like a wedding.

85. YANTI: <u>Kaya mantenan</u>.

Ibu nikå tå sing ngendikani angger
es buah,

lha terus kolang-kaling,

tesih bener Dhik,

Lha iki nggih terus nggepuki es
batu

<u>rampung nikå jam rolas</u>

Teng mpun kulå tinggal <u>mulih</u> kok.

86. ATIK: Mrikå dereng <u>rampung nikå</u>
<u>jam rolas</u>.

87. YANTI: <u>Jam rolase</u> ah, <u>bali</u> wae lah.

Kulå <u>bali</u> sidane.

Like a wedding.

Ibu y'know who said as long as
there's iced fruit,

and then *kolang-kaling* (fruit)

[that's] still right Dhik,

And so then [I] crushed the ice

finishing at twelve o'clock

Then all I had left was to go home.

So [you're] not yet finished by
12:00 P.M.

12:00 ah, just go home.

I went home finally

The participants' coherence is ensured through the allo-repetition of each other's utterances. Each of Atik's turns displays either her allo-repetition of Yanti's last idea or Yanti's allo-repetition of Atik's comment, which functions to simulate a common thread throughout their talk and which (Atik has confessed to me as we analyzed the transcripts) did not really exist. From this base of posted—hence, assumed—unity, Yanti expands her story through ever increasing detail.

Evaluation Strategies and Information

On this second day, though, Yanti describes the events involved in preparing the feast in a different way than before. Her strategy to convey the feeling of extreme overwork is to describe some of the dishes and how they were prepared through temporal and activity-oriented repetition:

a. nggih mpun setengah <u>sewelas</u> nikå.

b. <u>ngko</u> ning <u>kånå</u> <u>gek</u> <u>mulih</u>.

c. Setengah <u>sewelas</u> kulå mlaku,

d. tekan <u>kånå</u> mboten <u>gek</u> <u>mulih</u>
<u>langsung</u>,

e. <u>langsung</u> <u>niki</u> sakniki <u>gek</u> <u>ditåtå</u>

f. lonthonge,

g. <u>gek</u> <u>diirisi</u>, <u>gek</u> <u>ditåtå</u> teng ngriki
niki.

h. teng piring <u>ngoten lho</u>.

i. sambel gorenge kulå nganu.

j. <u>iwake</u> barang <u>mpun kulå</u> kekke
teng mriku <u>ngoten lho.</u>

k. <u>iwake</u> kan mpun disuwiri <u>ngoten</u>
<u>lho.</u>

That's right, it's already 10:30.

later there then return

10:30 I walked

arriving there but not going home
directly

directly now [I] organize the

lonthong

all sliced, then placed over here like
so

on the plate just right y'know.

the *sambal goreng* (food) I uhm.

even the meat I placed there and all
y'know.

the meat, right, already shredded like
so y'know.

l. ngko garek ngucuri duduh nikå   so that leaves pouring the broth
    lho Dhik.   y'know Dhik.
m. mpun kulå racik kabeh mpun   I had already prepared everything,
    komplit   it's complete
n. njuk es-e ditatani sisan niki.   then the ice needs to be prepared also.
o. njuk ngirisi ager-agere,   then slice the agar-agar (Jello),
p. buah nikå lho Dhik.   the fruit also y'know Dhik.
q. nganggo ager-ager barang   [they] even had agar-agar

Again what stands out most is the repetition, which, as a form of evaluation, functions as an internal indexical of story involvement. Yanti's extensive use of repetition (underlined) gives her story a frantic pace, especially in conjunction with her temporally developed details (boldface) and
the repetitive *gek* (indicating a current activity) in conjunction with other
temporal adverbs:

e. **langsung** niki **sakniki gek** ditåtå   directly now [I] then arranged the
f. lonthonge,   lonthong
g. **gek** diirisi, **gek** ditåtå teng ngriki   all sliced, then placed over here like
    niki.   so
h. Teng piring ngoten lho.   On the plate just right

And later she repeated the same actions of slicing and arranging with the
deserts. Here, her temporal markers of repetitive action are specifically
sequential (*njuk*):

n. **njuk** es-e ditatani sisan niki.   then the ice was arranged also
o. **njuk** ngirisi ager-ager   then slice the ager-ager

   The words *gek* and *njuk* signal time sequences internal to the story,
linking each of the events as temporally related. This temporal sequencing is very important to Yanti, as she marks it repeatedly through other
words also. The word *mpun*, which is glossed as "already," refers to a
completed action and is used four times to show the passing of time. An
action is completed *mpun*, and it is directly followed by another action,
signaled by *gek*. The repetition of these adverbials, especially with the
combination of completed to ongoing sequential adverbs, is iconic of the
repetitive and unending nature of her job.
   While Yanti's topic is the food preparation, her use of evaluation shows
that her point is to stress the pressure and the extreme amount of work
she had to do. The person she is trying to impress with this excessive
work is Atik. She achieves this not just by telling the story, and telling it
in that style, but also by using text boundary indexes to highlight the external frame, that is, *ngoten lho* and *nikå lho Dhik*. In Atik's stories from
this same speech situation, Atik mainly uses *nikå* or *niku* to chunk her
idea units (see the Surti story and, in chapter 4, the Pak Surti story). These

differences in indexing interactional frames may reveal an active psychological variation in the speaker's involvement. Yanti's *ngoten lho* and *nikå lho Dhik* as boundary markers in her highly charged story seem to maintain the internal story pressure by also appealing for Atik's support in ways that are not nearly as emphatic in earlier stories.

As a very commonly used discourse marker, *lho* is frequently discussed by Javanese and Indonesian language scholars. Joseph Errington (1988:222) notes that the utterance-final *lho* signals the listener to take heed of the importance of that piece of information. Siegel (1986:27) claims *lho* to be a kind of verbal outlet, a discursive cathartic of surprise whose mention prevents possession by an unwanted feeling. Kuswanti Purwa (1976:115) states that *lho* indexes a discrepancy between reality and expectation—a speaker assumes that a listener knows something that in fact she does not.

Yanti's examples do not seem to fall squarely into any of these classifications. In each case, however, the *lho* does not stand alone but co-occurs with other demonstratives, which in combination have not been mentioned in the literature, despite their formulaic frequency:

81. YANTI: h. Teng piring <u>ngoten lho</u>.	on the plate just right, y'know
j. iwake barang mpun kulå kekke teng mriku <u>ngoten lho</u>	even the meat I placed there and all y'know
k. iwake kan mpun disuwiri <u>ngoten lho,</u>	the meat, right, was already shredded like so, y'know,
l. ngko garek ngucuri duduh <u>nikå lho Dhik</u>.	so that leaves pouring the broth y'know Dhik
p. buah <u>nikå lho Dhik,</u>	the fruit also y'know Dhik
83. YANTI: <u>nikå lho Dhik</u>	That's the way it was, y'know Dhik

These utterance-final discourse phrases all have the same purpose, to signal to the listener that the information presented is thoroughly accessible, as food preparations for parties most definitely are. Thus I translate them as "y'know," the discourse marker of metaknowledge, showing that the talked-about information is shared (Schiffrin, 1987:267–268). Yet with the addition of *lho* there is an added feel of excess, whether from the emotion, the surprise, or some kind of variation from the norm.

In Atik's previous story, too, we find a *nikå lho*, which marks the first idea unit in her Surti story. Atik is marking this clause to stand out a bit from the rest because it introduces a story and because it does discuss something that is in deviance from the harmonious norms of everyday behavior:

54. ATIK: → Mbak Sur tambah kuru <u>nikå lho</u>.	Mbak Surti has gotten much thinner y'know.

Yanti's descriptions of food preparations, from slicing *lonthong* to cutting the *ager-ager*, are all patterned, specific activities and highly accessible to any Javanese woman, as is Atik's mention of a friend who is growing thinner as a sign of stress. These boundary indexicals function as evaluators in highly formulaic ways also when Yanti uses them not only to invite a listener's involvement but also to demand it—*lho.* Yanti's frequent use of these formulaic phrases as event clauses that are segmented by the boundary markers and vocatives demand that the listener share in the experience, again alongside the speaker.

I have claimed repeatedly that Javanese speakers most frequently coconstruct their narratives on topics of mutual accessibility to all present. Yet, Atik's stories about Pak Surti's health problems and Yanti's stories about her action-packed, two-day adventure both display unshared information, but only with regard to specific involvement. The details are all highly accessible. Most significantly for the presentation of the genre, both women repeatedly involve the other in these stories. Yanti has framed her cooking ordeal by repeatedly evoking the events as shared knowledge through a detailed account of each of the dishes, all of which are labeled with the demand for involvement: "you know this; you've been here before." Javanese forms of the discourse marker "y'know" achieve this function.

Back home again, on this second night of Yanti's story, the resolution of the problem is set. It is here that she finds that her father is already well, but she expresses her anger at her brother for being useless.

(41) *Yanti's Stress, The Explanation*

88. ATIK: Njuk pripun niku?
    And then what?

89. YANTI: Tekan ngomah nggih,
    Back at home,

    mpun mpun apik <u>nikå</u> sorene.
    [and it's] already already fine there.

    Ibu <u>niku</u> senengane wedi <u>ngoten</u>
    Ibu is quick to worry y'know Dhik

    <u>lho</u> Dhik Atik.
    Atik.

    <u>Nåpå-nåpå</u> kan,
    Whatever [happens] right,

    mesti kulå njuk kremungsung <u>nikå</u>.
    it has to be me so involved.

    Lha kulå tinggal nggih,
    When I leave y'know,

    mboten onten sik teng omah soale.
    the problem is no one else is home.

    Utari piknik,
    Utari at a picnic,

    Wisnu sekolah,
    Wisnu at school,

    Agus teng Solo,
    Agus at Solo,

    kan Yanto libur,
    but Yanto is free,

    Yanto <u>niku</u> nggih mboten isa
    That Yanto y'know can't do anything.

    <u>nåpå -nåpå</u>.

90. ATIK: <u>Malah</u> anu nggih,
    It's like uhm y'know,

    kåyå Mbak Surti <u>malah, malah,</u>
    it's just like Mbak Surti actually,

In turn 89, Yanti has returned home to the scene where her father was ill on the previous night. But the utterances add new information that serves to round out our understanding of the events; the women do not discuss her father's illness since he is now well. Yanti explains why only she can take care of her father: no one else was home, except for her brother Yanto, who is useless.

As soon as Yanti mentions her brother's characteristic uselessness, Atik responds immediately with the conclusion that Yanti had been working toward:

89. YANTI: <u>Yanto niku</u> nggih mboten   That Yanto y'know can't do anything.
    isa nåpå -nåpå.
90. ATIK: malah anu nggih,   It's like y'know,
    kåyå Mbak Surti malah, malah,   it's just like Mbak Surti, actually

Atik now recognizes the purpose of Yanti's stories and marks her positive alignment with Yanti's topic. Yanti expands on this unity:

91. YANTI: <u>Yanto niku</u> angger nganu   That Yanto as long as whatsit
    "kowe Pluk, Pluk" ngoten <u>niku</u>.   "you're Pluk, Pluk" like that [I said].
    <u>njuk</u> nek carane kåyå ngene ki (?)   then, it's like this (?)
92. ATIK: <u>Kulå nggih</u>.   For me too.
    Sakniki mpun biasa Mbak Yanti.   It's already common Mbak Yanti.
    <u>Kåyå Mbak Surti</u> nikå.   Like Mbak Surti also,
    nikå <u>mboten iså</u> ken meneng   she can't be ordered to keep silent
    ngeten.   like this
93. YANTI: Jan-jane <u>kulå nggih</u>   Truthfully for me too
    <u>mboten iså</u>.   I can't.

In terms of the underlying meaning or intention of this entire, prolonged storytelling event, Atik's presentation of the coda is the positive link between both the women's texts.

For Yanti, fortunately, all turns out relatively well in the end. Her father gets better, the cooking preparations are over in two days, and she gets to have it out with her brother for being useless in the crisis. In Surti's case, however, after months of serious illness, two operations, massive hospital bills, extreme depression and exhaustion, and never getting any support from her siblings, Surti's father died, followed shortly by her mother.[16] Nevertheless, Atik picks up on Yanti's cues and notes the similarities between the two women's experiences: "It's like, y'know, it's just like Mbak Surti." Atik then presents a fitting coda for the series of stories, which successfully ties all of the women together in praise of their outspokenness:

92. ATIK: <u>Kulå nggih</u>   For me too
    sakniki mpun biasa Mbak Yanti.   it's already common, Mbak Yanti.
    kåyå Mbak Surti nikå.   like Mbak Surti also,
    nikå <u>mboten iså</u> ken meneng   [we] can't be ordered to keep silent
    ngeten.   like this
93. YANTI: Jan-jane <u>kulå nggih</u>   Truthfully me too
    <u>mboten iså</u>.   I can't.

Outspokenness needs to be seen in relation to community practices. Initially, we have to place Mbak Yanti's story into its community context as an example of her *setress*. As Atik had told me, she was very confused by the story, not knowing what it meant or what Yanti's point was. She found the details very unusual and even uncomfortable, which she explained like this: *Ya, kudu maklum ya, Mbak Len. Mbak Yanti lagek setress* ("well, [you really] need to understand ya, Mbak Laine. Mbak Yanti was stressed").

Topics of Defiance

Atik's coda implies that both women are able to resist the silences that underlie their basic assumptions of Javanese female identity. The norm is to bear the difficulties in a stoic, disassociated silence. But the women see themselves as being beyond the cultural norm because of what they characterize as outspokenness in the face of gender role inequality. In this sense, they align themselves with Surti in rejecting the silence they evaluate as a negative, although essentially Javanese, trait.

These women are offering the very essence of their cultural conceptions of gender roles and the significance these have in lived experience. We can see how aware they are of their roles in relation to the community, but despite claims of outspokenness, none of them question or challenge these requirements. What they question is merely the fact that the entire burden was placed on them. Meanwhile, how far do these questions reach? In Atik's story, the fault lay not on others for being too lazy to help but rather on Surti herself for not speaking up and demanding help when it was sorely needed. In Yanti's case, too, no one else was able to assist. Even if she had demanded Yanto's help, he was unable to do anything because, as a male, he was not expected to help in familial situations and would not know how. Outspokenness, as we had seen in the protest stories also, ultimately leads to nothing but silence.

In terms of storytelling styles, contesting the broader cultural conceptions in these personalized versions of sense making does show a variation. Textual development here is not founded on the creation and maintenance of *sameness* but is instead based on the speakers' maintenance of parallel text topics and the harmonious display of respect for their differences. In these stories, Yanti is more independent and self-sufficient than Atik, as shown by her underlying interest in work-related issues and personal health, her emotional outpouring, and her ability to take on as much as she did and *tell* about it. In turn, Atik evaluated Yanti's story as a sign of her temporary insanity (*setress*).

Social hierarchy fully shapes Atik's storylines, which are based on ratification from Yanti, to whom she regularly pays her respect. She never takes a personal stance, however, but only alludes to her supporter's role without being too graphic or gossipy. Yanti, in contrast, displays her doubts, emotional involvement, loyalty, confusion, anger, and, in short, a wide range of human emotions from an agentic position. But agency is filtered through sets of local constraints that allow her to resent the pressures within the narrow bounds of this context but not to reject them. Atik's stories, however, are entirely other-related and outspoken only in that they show her indignation at what she sees as unfair play between Surti and her siblings. Yet, at least in Atik's case, I know that a great deal is left unsaid. Also Atik regularly helps to constrain her sister Sari's participation by ensuring that she conforms to the dominant stories. Atik's position is always to remain distant, succinct, concerned, and involved but not confrontational and not critical of women's roles. Outspokenness as a learned position, too, is highly filtered by broader cultural constraints so that it does not threaten the status quo.

Conclusions

This chapter has demonstrated how responsibility to the social order implies the acceptance of sets of rules that determine participation roles and their appropriate styles of interaction. In consideration of such openly acknowledged hierarchical positions, Sari frames her story to suit those of the group. In so doing, she has shown how respect is a social responsibility that is indexed through a speaker's cooperative stance in relation to her interlocutors. This does not, however, interfere with "intimacy."

Of the three speech situations in Part III, only this one does not concern the factory problem. The participants share none of Sari's experiences, and there is no need to create a unified empowerment to fight an oppressor or persuade others to participate in a righteous struggle. The fight is already lost. Yet, we still see a highly constraining group-ratification process that underlies all speaking positions, with the possible exception of the high-status participant. As Duranti explains in a parallel context, "The highly stratified nature of Samoan life forces lower ranking individuals to be more attentive to higher ranking individuals' goals. . . . The higher the rank, the more individualistic the people are allowed to be" (1993:44). Thus, Sari reframes her factory story to omit the controversial protest, which displays quite clearly how her participation is linked to her responsibility to the current situation. Despite her personal tragedies and the intimacy of the situation, her story takes on the characteristics of an uneventful and common choice. She chose not to work overtime—and thus her story ends with the situated story round and the harmony it reciprocally serves intact.

Despite statements that attest to their outspokenness, the women's stories of gender inequality are ultimately framed by the same constraints that create their subordinate roles. Responsibility is still theirs alone, leaving only specific incidents for them to resent. Cultural pressures to conform to these roles are so strongly intact that those who cannot handle the pressure, whether temporarily or in permanent mental illness, fall into the same category of *setress*. Here again, topics of defiance, as well as the resulting illnesses, are best hidden in silence.

• • •eight

Conclusion

Four months before I was to leave Java, I visited the Budis and found the whole family fasting and engaged in a 24-hour prayer vigil (*tirakat*). I immediately joined in to give my support to the cause. Pak Budi informed me that his brothers had decided to sell their land, which meant that the Budi warehouse was to be razed and the family forced to leave. The next evening, after another day of fasting and prayer, the brothers arrived and Pak Budi met them in the front house. The tension in the shabby, old sitting room was unbearable. No one spoke a word until Pak Budi returned, sat down with a sigh, and remained silent. Ibu Budi brought him a glass of tea, and after his first sip he spoke in a soft voice: the Budi's would be given a small parcel of land and money to build a house. With no visible displays of emotion, the family resumed their prayers, now of thanks, and decided to hold a small feast to share their fortune with the community (*slametan*).

Late that night I awoke and saw Ibu Budi sitting alone in the dark on the steps to the sitting room. I sat down next to her and reached for her hand. All she said to me was, "I never imagined I would have a house, Mbak Len," which she repeated several times over. After 30 years of suffering, something wonderful and beyond all their dreams was about to happen. The next day, life went on as usual.

MY APPROACH TO THE STUDY of the Javanese language was shaped by my intimacy and love for the Budi family and for Ibu Asmoro. It was entirely through their trust, affection, and assistance that I was able to record these seemingly ordinary conversations and learn how and where to look for the multiple levels of meanings they conceal. Even the most mundane conversation can reveal a great deal of information about the intimate values, expectations, and meanings that define this community of ordinary Javanese people. My approach was to locate and define patterns of indexical elements as they are used in the conversational narratives women told within their natural social networks. From these patterns of elements, of which speech levels are only one, I saw that meaning is interactively produced and verified by the ways in which it is recognized in actual contexts. This approach, suggested by Pak Budi himself, revealed how ordinary Javanese conversations are socially relevant and highly situated acts of interpretation, a reflection of how meaning is achieved in particular settings. While this style of common Javanese speech may not be the elegant expression of courtly grace the Javanese prefer, the psychological salience of respect and refinement is very clearly a major factor in the preservation of hierarchical values even at this lower end of the socioeconomic and political scale.

My own involvement in these speech situations is extremely deep. Not only did I need intimacy with these people to recognize the "silence" that underlies much of their everyday talk, but I also needed the support of a family to give me, a single foreign woman, credibility in the community. For purely personal reasons, I also needed their friendship. Thus, I have not shied away from the controversial issue of "participant observation" or the myths of objectivity.

To analyze the structure and function of conversational narratives in everyday talk, I had to focus on social groups and the relationships and connections that characterize people in common social settings. Interpretations, like the narratives, tended to stress relationships and not individuals. Consequently, it was the relational aspects of the group in its natural social context that became the focal point of this analysis. I grew to become a member of these groups and thus not only gained access to extremely privileged information but also took part in many of the conversations. Only by becoming a part of the community could I learn to recognize the extent of its hold and, hence, the silences that frame so much of local meaning. Access to shared meaning, as Pak Budi informed me early on, was the key to exposing the meaningful (unsaid) elements of speech. Without this shared information, silences remain hidden as confusing gaps, ellipses, and unknown references. Silence is also concealed by the general "truths" that are uttered for social harmony.

In line with the heavy constraints community places on these women, I have shown that social identity, as reflected in the narrative, is interactively constructed in accordance with the community's definitions of self and other. One mirrors the other, while narrative, as a jointly constructed event, is a lucid indicator of how participants interpret the immediate group, as well as their own positions in that group. Individuality or autonomous definitions of agency are inappropriate here. The narratives are a way for the community to maintain its hierarchical values through awareness and equanimity. They are not a resource for publicly reflecting on and constructing an individual self. The few exceptions in my corpus reflect either the privilege of the elderly or the temporarily "insane" (*nge stress*).

These differences reflect not just differences in the structure and function of narratives but rather differences in cultural expectations, interactional norms and needs, and the underlying conceptions of the individual in society. People need one another, and it is this connectedness—made orderly and harmonious by social stratification—that underlies both story and person. This analysis should clarify some of the ways in which culture, social interaction, and person are interconnected within a Javanese framework of meaning.

To clarify the varying levels of societal pressures that unite in the framing of the stories and the speakers, I divide the book into three parts. Part I sets the scene by presenting the interdisciplinary approach that forms the methodological framework of this study. The Javanese language has a long, rich history of scholarly description, which reaches into such diverse disciplines as history, philosophy, linguistics, anthropology, politics, and more. I chose to focus on the particularities of specific events as the locus of situated meaning. This means that I needed to clarify the communities, beginning with the speakers and my relationship with them and extending to the broader ideological positions that form the foundations of Javaneseness. As a woman, I was also subjected to various types of positionings, which as a foreigner I was able to challenge in certain contexts. It became obvious, however, that my female associates had no such freedoms. While the public discourses preach equality and respect for women, simply getting to know my neighbors in the *kampung* quickly revealed shocking inequities in practice. My way of locating the ideological (and "cultural") framing of gender, in spite of these national discourses, came from the brutal discussion of rape and abandonment as one of the many areas of gender inequality shrouded in silence because women accept their guilt in such crimes.

Part II presents the structural aspects of Javanese narrative and links them directly to social interactional purposes. Chapter 3 applies the segmenting facets of the Labovian model to actual Javanese stories to investigate how this text-based structuring framework can be directly related to the hierarchically based social framework that shapes Javanese contexts. Working from this known surface structure for narratives, I describe how micro-level features are shaped by the macro-structure orientation of the participants. I demonstrate that Javanese stories are not easily distinguishable from the surrounding conversation because they are produced jointly. Thus, the stories are not clearly bounded but fluid and interactive in their progression. The conversational narrative, as I have suggested, is a means through which speakers both construct and reflect their self-other-community relationships, where the fusion of a story into a conversation may be a symbolic representation of how speakers are fused into a community within the immediate context and the wider culture.

Chapter 4 expands on the structuring paradigm by proposing the basic structural elements of Javanese stories to be made up of (1) past-tense adverbial markers, (2) reported speech, (3) shifting speech levels, and

(4) text boundary indexicals. By investigating how these structuring elements function in interactive story contexts, I have shown how each reflects meaning within a Javanese framework of interpretation, supporting the role of the conversational narrative as a significant indicator of self-other-community relationships.

A notion of relationality is significant in storytelling. Participants display their interpretation of the essential aspects of their relationship to others in the immediate context and to those that are referenced through the speech event. Relative status, as the most obvious of these relational qualities, is traditionally assumed to be indexed through speech levels. I show that in informal interactions it is also displayed through vocatives, styles of uptake, repetition, control of topic, and privileged control of meaning.

Whereas Part II explores some of the structural and functional manifestations of Javanese stories, Part III looks closer at stories as social action. The Taman Tirto protest stories are the backdrop for an ethnographic trilogy in which we can follow Sari through three different speech situations. The three situations specify which elements of contextual relations are culturally and socially significant because of how they were discursively indexed.

In the first speech event, Sari is coconstructing narratives with coworkers from the factory. These narratives demonstrate the construction of solidarity, having a strong group orientation, cooperative, coconstructed story rounds, frequent allo-repetition, and mutual ratification of all topics and affective stances. Symmetry is maintained by the marked avoidance of kinship terms, pronouns, *båså*, or any of the indexicals of social hierarchy.

Discourse analysis of symmetric style is supported by ethnographic information, showing that conarration creates group empowerment in a clearly disempowering situation. Factory management has robbed the women of a voice, so they bond together in one unified voice to stand up to their oppressors. The discursive strength of their unified voice fortifies their own assurance as they attempt to share it with others too frightened to test the legality of a notoriously corrupt system. Regardless of their moral righteousness, dangers are inherent in protest stories, in which equal participation becomes synonymous with equal responsibility for the consequences of these words.

In the second situation (chapter 6), Sari is describing to Pak Budi and the father of another coworker the events that led to the protest. While age, job, and gender place Sari lower in status than the men, the unequal access to information defers much of the asymmetry. Although a coworker was present, her silence toward her father and his silence toward Sari illustrate alternative stances vis-à-vis responsibility.

The most prominent discursive index in this speech situation is the type of evaluation used. As solitary animator, Sari uses external evaluation, encoded through the repetition of adjectives and intensifiers, and frame breaks to inject sympathetic comments. In comparison to the internal style of evaluation she used in the previous situation (chapter 5), this suggests that different styles of evaluation achieve different functions. Reported speech appears in stories when contextual constraints require careful self-monitoring. In situations that are more emotional and less guarded, evaluation is of the external type, with adjectives, intensifiers, and frequent frame breaks to inject comments. These variations in the distribution of evaluation styles suggest that reported speech as an internal affect marker is less aggressive, a more refined type of evaluation than the external use of adjectives and intensifiers. In this corpus, the more involved the speaker, the more external evaluation she will use, the opposite of that which Labov (1972, 1984) and Tannen (1989) claim for American speakers. This becomes clearer when placed in conjunction with the social constraints on storytelling. Reported speech indexes other speakers' words and thus involves a speaker with her community. External evaluation indexes the current speaker and the current situation and thus makes a point about both.

Participation structures in chapter 6 also show various ways in which responsibility for the consequences of a story may be negotiated or rejected. In Javanese storytelling, ideally there is no audience as stories are designed to be a group effort. Pak Budi's attempts to moderate his daughter's militancy illustrates his inability to accept the story as is, whereas Pak Sri's refusal to take a participant's role in the story indexes his rejection of it. By comparing these positions to the factory women's solidarity stance, we can see how responsible agency is a matter of choice, demonstrated by the degree with which one participates in the story and, hence, takes up its positions as one's own.

The third situation (chapter 7) reveals the asymmetry of intimacy. Sari is conversing informally with her sister Atik and their friend and neighbor Yanti. This is the event in which Sari displays the most relational deference, suggesting that her responsibility to that group is more salient than her personal tragedies. Her use of a first-person agentic stance in framing this story shows the pronoun to be an index of her responsibility to a relational position in the group. It need not index her responsibility to the predicated events. Agency in these texts functions as an index of choice in being responsible to the group-constructed conception of meaning and harmony.

In this chapter we also see how women respond to gender inequality in their stories. Through what the participants themselves refer to as a type of resistance, we are able to recognize the rejection of a small aspect of inequality. The participants are, in fact, upholding the same ideological constructs that force women to take responsibility for all domestic issues.

Whereas ideological explanations of Javanese social interaction (cårå Jåwå) specify a cultural need to index relational values, the stories here illustrate how relationships are indeed a structuring factor in the constitution of stories and their speakers. The sensitivity to contextual factors

Javanese speakers hold essential is displayed through the various "selves" that can be presented, depending on the group and its particular needs. These stories are just a fragment of the range of potential positions available to Javanese speakers, and they only hint at the broad range of contextual factors of significance to the discursive display of a Javanese sense of self.

Most strikingly significant to Javanese speech-level theories, the hierarchical distinctions deemed the very essence of Javanese discursive identity are played out in many ways, none of which are indexed solely by speech levels. Specific speech styles or actions, such as types of evaluation, repetition, vocatives, back-channel feedback, conarrating, questioning, and aligning topics, are all indexes of respect styles of interaction. Lower-status participants express their respect by supporting the positions and opinions of the higher-status members, who are conversely permitted far more freedom to speak openly. The hierarchical ordering of story contexts is apparent in every one of the interactions, suggesting how essential it still is to a Javanese sense of identity.

The protest genre documented in chapter 5 supports this hierarchical salience through its highly marked, self-conscious avoidance of all the features that shape the social order. This very brief rejection of the dominant ideologies that authorize the women's abuse in the first place becomes even more poignant when one realizes how markedly deviant their protest discourse is. The cohort rejects the hierarchical order and the harmonizing effects it is intended to impose. Those positioned at the bottom of the social order may not challenge it, and legal and moral correctness is not a consideration, as the familial responses to the dilemma—and the failed outcome—attest.

All whose voices appear in the stories are capable of speaking formal styles of Javanese. Yet very few of the interactions show refined *kråmå* speech patterns, with the exception of Ibu Harto (who did follow standard expectations of humility) and Ibu Asmoro, who used *kråmå inggil* as an affective index. Informal speech among ordinary Javanese is mainly expressed through a distribution of *ngoko* and *madyå*, showing that among these speakers, the speech levels are not the essential indexes of hierarchy. But, as this study has shown, all speech does fundamentally index hierarchy. The marked avoidance of any hierarchical indicators in chapter 5 shows how powerful a force they still are in the minds of Javanese speakers.

This study has also raised questions that remain to be further investigated. Part II touches on why the stories of elderly speakers are expected to follow a different system of rules than those of the young women. It is clear from my corpus that elderly Javanese women and men tell many autobiographical stories, whereas the younger, urban women do not seem to have the opportunity to do so, with the exception of clearly designated, brief story rounds. These young women's stories are not a means of self-reflection but a strategy for re-creating a self in harmony with contextual

norms. Variations in presentation may reflect a modern, political influence from education and development or perhaps is indicative of the
privilege of the aged (or perhaps a consequence of their freedom from
modern ideologies because of their illiteracy). Investigation of the broader
repertoires of story types and functions would lead to a vastly better
understanding of the narrative as a speech event, and it would also clarify
some of the rules for participation across age variables. Such a study could
further explain the changes that are currently affecting the Javanese language and the sense of person emerging from them.

This study has indicated alternative ways in which Javanese speakers
use speech levels for the accomplishment of functions other than indexes
of respect, and respect is indexed in ways other than the use of formal
and formulaic speech. This study illustrates the great flexibility with which
the Javanese speech levels—with the inclusion of Indonesian—can be
used for clarification and to ease communicative burdens. In this respect,
speech-level shifts are one of the four structuring elements of narrative.
Speakers are able to index evaluational cues and shifts in frames of expectations and footings in both the story and the context. But we have
only brushed the surface of analytic possibilities, and further studies are
needed to investigate the broader roles of speech levels as indexes of
participation in actual social interaction.

In conclusion, this book has shown that the speaking processes in Java
are a type of interaction in which contextual and relationally salient information is built up through repetition and active participation. Speaking,
in effect, creates a vivid reflection of alignments, perspectives, involve-
ments, and information. Thus narratives have performative consequences.
They empower, silence, re-create, challenge, and threaten those who are
physically within their sphere. Words can control and constrain, but they
can also support, validate, authorize, and console. Language in Javanese
contexts is anything but neutral, and participation and the varying degrees to which it is accomplished are socially charged, highly meaningful
actions. Linguistic analyses must combine discourse processes with social
processes to remove "the mask" that conceals the complex and politically charged dimensions underlying theories of person, meaning, and
social action.

Appendix

(4) *Outwitting Robbers*

159. ASMORO: **Kulå nikå saking kitå ageng,**   I was coming from the big city
    Jalan Harjono,   Harjono Street
    Mas Darto **menikå**   That Mas Darto
    dhå lungå golek wong wedok   and the others had all gone in search of women

160. UMAYA: Eee. . . .   Eee

161. ASMORO: Lha **kulå saking** Tegal Gendu   So I was coming from Tegal Gendu
    mantuk **piyambak**.   going home alone.

162. UMAYA: Wah!   Wah!

163. ASMORO: Jam **kalih dalu**   at 2:00 at night

164. UMAYA: **TINDAK?**   Walking?

165. ASMORO: **Nggih**.   That's right
    Ning **kulå kraos wonten tiang jaler kalih niku**   but I sensed these two men were there
    Kulå lajeng cincing mlayu,   So then I reluctantly started to run
    Arah**ipun tebih kalian** (?)   It was far from (?)
    Lajeng kulå menggok nggen damel kijing **nikå**   Then I turned into the place where they make headstones

166. UMAYA: **Wonten** Pakel?   Is that at Pakel?

167. ASMORO: **Enggih menikå sawek** jam **tigå**   That's right at around 3 o'clock

168. UMAYA: Wow . . .   Wow . . .

(8) *The Injured Toe*

63. UMAYA: **SUGENG?**   [Are you] well?

64. ASMORO: **Nggih, meniko teksih** anu.   Yes, this is still uhm.

Nåpå. — What.
Sawek **nggletek globatipun** — Still clearly wet
Wingi kulå (?) ngaten. — Yesterday I (?) like that.

65. UMAYA: Wow! — Wow!

66. ASMORO: Wong tutup tå — Keep it closed
Lajeng lingkep — Then opened
Lajeng kulå ngatenaken — Then I [treated it] like that

67. UMAYA: Wow. **kengeng menåpå** **nikå?** — What happened?

68. ASMORO: **Dawah** . **kengeng** aspal, — [I] fell, struck the asphalt.
kenging wedhi rak **kenging** — from the sand. then hit the asphalt.
aspal. ha ha . . . — haha

69. UMAYA: **Njih** . . . **njih** . . . — yes yes,

70. ASMORO: **Dados menikå** ketekuk, — So then this bent,
dados balungipun nikå — so then the bone,
ingkang ketekuk **ketingal** — the part that bent was visible.

71. UMAYA: Eee . . . — Eee,

72. ASMORO: **Rahipun** ndledek — The blood just flowed.
mawon

73. UMAYA: Ee.. **pun bektå dateng** — You've been taken to the hospital
Rumah Sakit Bu? — bu?

74. ASMORO: **Pun**. — Yes.
Menikå kulå suntik**ken kaping** **kalih** — I've been injected twice
lajeng mboten patos sakit. — so it doesn't hurt so much.

75. UMAYA: **Nggih, nggih,** — Right, right,

76. ASMORO: Wah . . . karang buyer — I've made a right mess of things.
kulå menikå,
Mlampah-mlampah jam — Walking at 4:00 A.M.,
sekawan,
Lajeng mubeng Kauman **ngilen,** — Then around the Kauman (place) to the west,

Plengkung ngidul, — *Plengkung* (the gate) to the south,
lajeng ngetan, — then east,
La kog mak yer.**ngaten,** — Then y'know [I] got dizzy like so,
Langsung mak buk. — Then [I] collapsed.

77. UMAYA: Eh . . . semaput **nggih** bu? — So you fainted right bu?

78. ASMORO: E: . . . Allah: . . . isih — Ya: allah: I still don't look after
kurang ngrekså tå awakku? — myself do I?
Dibanting — Slammed down
la **ngriki njih,** — and so [it was] here right,
jengking jengking, — flipping overflipping over,
la **ngriki** ketekuk. — and so [it was] bent here.

79. UMAYA: Eh . . . **wonten ingkang** — Where there uhm
anu.
Mboten bu . . . **ingkang** — No bu . . . any (false starts?)

80. ASMORO: **Mboten wonten ingkang sawek** setengah **gangsal**

There were no [people around to help]
It was 4:30 [in the morning]

81. UMAYA: **Njih**

Oh.

82. ASMORO: Wah:. malah **keleresan, lajeng tangi** ki//

Wah:. actually, [I] just woke up//

83. UMAYA: // Kålå mben **RÅMÅ** Mardi **nggih,**
sampun mboten wonten nggih, dawah . . . Kålå wingi//

//day before yesterday Romo Mardi y'know,
is no longer y'know,
[he] fell. Yesterday//

84. ASMORO: //Ow . . . **nggih, anggenipun NYAREke** . . .

//Ow right, the funeral was held

(11) *Pak Surti's Illness*

42. SARI: . . . he . . . he . . . he . . . apa kuwi Mbak Len?

Hehehe. What's that Mbak Len? (we leave the room)

43. YANTI: **Mpun** tek okeh **nggih,**

bulane (?) ting Bethesda?

[They've] already spent a lot [of money] haven't they,
[how many?] months in Bethesda (hospital)?

44. ATIK: [.] Obat niku sepuluh seket lima sedinå.
Seket lima **mpun** entuk rong minggu.
Nggih rong minggunan.

The medicine for 10 is 55 [rupiah] per day.
That 55 has been [going on] for two weeks.
that's right two weeks.

45. YANTI:: Seket lima misale entuk ping sepuluh **mawon mpun**//

55 for example
times 10 is already//

46. ATIK: limangatus seket.

550

47. TANTI:: Sing papat, rorikur.
Mpun entek pitungatusan **nggih?**

times 4 is 22.
It's already cost 700-ish right?

48. ATIK: **Dereng** dokter. [.]

That doesn't include the doctor.

49. YANTI:: **Mboten.**
Nåpå ndhisik-ndhisike **niku mboten** tau *mengeluh*
misale nek buwang *air* nganu,

rasane pegel-pegel **niku nåpå ngaten** tå Bapake?

No.
Before all this,
didn't [he] ever complain,
for example when [he'd] urinate uhm,
he'd feel the pain
wasn't there any of that with her father?

50. ATIK: **Riyin niku mpun** tau **nåpå.**
nggon *saluran kencing* **niku onten** batune,
nate *operasi* nek mbiyen.

In the past the problem was what.

in the urinary tract there was a stone,
it had been operated on.

Ning saiki malah ginjele sing kenå.	But now its the kidney that's affected.
51. YANTI: Lårå.	Painful
52. ATIK: Lorone.	Its painful.
Mung sak**niki** nganu kok Mbak Yanti	But now, [what can I say] Mbak Yanti
mlakune **mboten** iså dadi anu, **nåpå** ngewel gemeter **ngaten** lho.	[he] can't even walk any more, [he] trembles and shakes so.
Mboten kuwat ngangkat awak.	[he's] not even strong enough to lift his body.

(38) *Surti's Stress*

53. YANTI: Lha **inggih** soale?	So then y'know the problem is?
54. ATIK: Soale **nggih** pripun.	The problem is what.
Tenagane **mboten onten**.	His energy is gone.
Mbak Sur tambah kuru **nikå** lho.	Mbak Surti has gotten much thinner y'know.
Kok gumunku	I'm real shocked
"Lho kok mung kowe tå sing mikir?"	"How is it it's only you who thinks [about Pak Sur]?"
Gumun **kulå kalih** wong siji **nikå**.	I'm shocked at that person.
Wong atase nduwe **Kangmas**, nduwe **Mbakyu nggih kathah**.	Above her she has a brother, [She] has elder sisters, y'know, plenty.
55. YANTI: Njuk **sakniki** nunggu **teng pundi**?	So now where is [she] watching [over her father]?
Nikå nggih Mbak Sur thok, **niku**.	That's y'know Mbak Sur [I mean]
56. ATIK: Mbak Sur **kalih Mbakyune** sing mbarep.	Mbak Sur with her eldest sister.
57. YANTI: Sik lanang-lanang **niku** rak nunggu mbengi kudune	And the boys they must be keeping vigil at night
58. ATIK: Sing mbarep mungkin mbengi tekan esuk (?)	The eldest perhaps night till morning

(39) *Yanti's Stress: Day 1: Preparations*

59. YANTI: Ha wedi tunggu wong lårå **nggih ngaten** lho.	[They're] just afraid to mind a sick person y'know.
Kulå dhek setu wingi awan terus ngulon,	Last Saturday afternoon, I went to the west,
setu tanggal selawe,	Saturday the twenty-fifth,
selawe kan **teksih onten** sekolahan,	The twenty-fifth right school was still open,
selawe karå nem likur.	the twenty-fifth and twenty-sixth.
Pokoke dinå setu **niku**.	The point is on Saturday.

Kulå niku masak kan
ting nggene kåncå **kulå**.
Masakke lonthong opor **niku** lho.

Dadi//

60. ATIK: Masak bareng?
61. YANTI: Masak, masak bareng.
    sore **mpun** masak
    Jemuah sore **nikå** lho, wah!
62. ATIK: Jemuah masak?
63. YANTI: Nggawe lonthong
64. ATIK: **Mpun** mbengi?
65. YANTI: **nggih** tekan jam sångå.
    Jam sångå terus bali.
    Lha, esuk, setu esuk **niku**,

    jam nem **mpun mrikå meleh**//
66. ATIK: **Mrikå meleh**, soale masak//
67. YANTI: Bali jam setengah sepuluh
    nikå.
68. ATIK: Lho kanggone jam **pinten**?
69. YANTI: Kanggone jam sewelas.
    Njuk **niku** gek esuk **teng** kåncå
    kulå niku,
    mboten adus barang dik,
    dadi tangi turu njuk masak **mrikå**,
    nganti uh,
    kok le pengkuh men tho ki.
    "Sing gek arep mangan wong
    akeh"
    ngoten tak pikir.
    "O: jan wong mung wong telu
    sing masak!"
70. ATIK: Sing masak?

(40) *Yanti's Stress: Day 2, at Home*
71. YANTI: Wong mung **kulå**, Hamidha,
    Kamujiya
    njuk (?) kemempengen
    Kulå ngrasake "**nggih ngoten
    niku**."
    Njuk tekan omah
    Ibu muni "**TIMBAL**i Bapak nganu,

    kok ndredeg" **ngoten**.
    Lha wiwit iku wong//

I cooked right
over at my friend's place
[We] cooked *lonthong opor* (a type of
food) right.
so//
Cook all together?
Cook, cook, all together,
that afternoon [we] had cooked
that Friday afternoon, wah!
On Friday [you] cooked?
[We] made *lonthong*
Was it already late?
Yes, until 9:00.
At 9:00 [I] went home.
And then, in the morning, that
Saturday morning,
by 6:00 [I] was already there again.//
There again, for the cooking//
Go back at 9:30

What's that, for what time?
For 11:00
Then next morning to my friend's
again,
none [of us] even bathed yet, dhik,
so wake up and cook over there,
until uh, (false start)
don't you know the tenacity of it all!
"So many are going to eat"

that's what I thought.
"But O! there's just three doing all
the cooking!"
The ones who cooked?

Just me, Hamidha,
Kamujiya
so (?) energetically
I felt, "yeah, it's just like that."

So [I] reached home
Ibu said "[I] was summoned by
Bapak uhm.
y'know [he's] trembling" she said.
So that's where it started//

72. ATIK: **Pripun** tå?
What's this?
73. YANTI: Ndredeg le muni Ibu,
gemeter kae lho Dhik
Trembling was what Ibu said,
he was shivering, y'know Dhik.
74. ATIK: Le mbayangke
bali såkå sawalan kae sorene//
Imagine
coming back from a gathering in the afternoon//
75. YANTI: **Mboten** bali sawalan.
Not from a gathering.
76. ATIK: Bali masak?
Home from cooking?
77. YANTI: Bali masak **niku kulå**
setengah sepuluh **niku** njuk ah,
Kok gemeter, iså gembrobyos
nikå dik.
Gembrobyos njuk didemok
ngoten niki
Panis **nikå** bathuke.
Langsung **kulå** kompres **nikå**.
A:: mbok teles bes **nikå**,
ngantek **kulå** ganteni,
kulå ganteni kaos **ngeten**.
Njuk Bapak **niku** kan,
mungkin tensine mundhak,
dadine ditakoki mulaknå (?) **sirahe**
iki gek
I returned from cooking
It's 9:30 and so uh,
The shaking, [how can he] be
sweating like this dik.
sweating a lot so I touch like this

Really hot his forehead.
Right away I [got a] compress,
Ah: really soaking wet too,
so I changed,
I had to change his soaking shirt.
And so Bapak right,
maybe his pressure is rising,
So I asked if that's why (?) his
head . . .
78. ATIK: Angel
Difficult

(41) *Yanti's Stress, Day 2*
79. YANTI: **Sirah**e wong ngelu kan,

rasane abot **ngeten** lho.
Njuk Ibu mungel ngene
"pokoke le sawalan ngko sedhelå
wae.
tekan sekolahan njuk mulih
ngeten."
Dadi **kulå nikå** mangkat sekolah
mboten tenang **nikå** lho.
Le ku mangkat **nggih mpun** jam//
The head of a person suffering a
headache,
right it feels real heavy y'know.
So then Ibu said this
"the point is the gathering later just
for a short time.
go to school then come [straight]
home again."
So I left for school
[but] I was not at all calm
My leaving was then at //
80. ATIK: Sewelas
11:00
81. YANTI: **Nggih mpun** setengah
sewelas **nikå**.
Ngko ning kånå gek mulih.
Setengah sewelas **kulå** mlaku,
tekan kånå **mboten** gek mulih
langsung
Langsung **niki sakniki** gek ditåtå
lonthonge,
That's right it's already 10:30.

Later there than home.
10:30 I walked.
arriving there but not going home
directly
Directly now [I] arrange the *lonthong*

gek diirisi, gek ditåtå **teng ngriki niki**. / all sliced, then placed over here like so

Teng piring **ngoten** lho. / On the plate just right y' know.

Sambel gorenge **kulå** nganu, / the *sambal goreng* (a food) I uhm.

iwake barang **mpun kulå** kekke **teng mriku ngoten** lho / even the meat I placed there and all y'know.

Iwake kan, **mpun** disuwiri **ngoten** lho. / The meat right, already shredded like so y'know,

ngko garek ngucuri duduh **nikå** lho Dik. / so that leaves pouring the broth y'know Dik.

Mpun kulå racik kabeh **mpun** komplit / I had already prepared everything it's complete

njuk es-e ditatani sisan **niki**. / then the ice needs to be arranged also.

Njuk ngirisi ager-agere, / Then slice the agar-agar (Jello),

buah **nikå** lho Dhik, / the fruit also y'know Dhik,

nganggo ager-ager barang. / [they] even had agar-agar.

82. ATIK: Ager-ager barang / Even agar-agar

83. YANTI: **Nikå** lho Dhik / That's the way it was y'know Dhik

84. ATIK: Dadine kaya mantenan / Like a wedding.

85. YANTI: Kaya mantenan. / Like a wedding.

Ibu nikå tå sing **NGENDIKA**ni / Ibu y'know who said as long as

angger es buah, / there's iced fruit,

lha terus kolang-kaling, / and then *kolang-kaling* (a fruit),

tesih bener Dhik, / [that's] still right Dhik,

Lha iki **nggih** terus nggepuki es batu / And so then [I] crushed the ice

rampung **nikå** jam rolas / finishing at twelve o'clock

Teng mpun kulå tinggal mulih kok. / Then all I had left was to go home.

86. ATIK: **Mrikå dereng** rampung **nikå** jam rolas. / So [you're] not yet finished by 12:00 P.M.

(42) *Yanti's Stress: The Explanation*

87. YANTI: Jam rolase ah, bali wae lah, / 12:00 ah, just go home,

Kulå bali sidane. / I went home finally.

88. ATIK: Njuk **pripun niku**? / And then what?

89. YANTI: Tekan ngomah **nggih**, / Back at home,

mpun mpun apik **nikå** sorene. / [and it's] already already fine there.

Ibu **niku** senengane wedi **ngoten** lho Dhi Atik. / Ibu is quick to worry y'know Dhi Atik.

Nåpå-nåpå kan, / Whatever [happens] right,

mesti **kulå** njuk kremungsung **nikå** / it has to be me so (?)

Lha **kulå** tinggal **nggih** / When I leave y'know

mboten onten sik **teng** omah . / the problem is no one else is home.

soale
Utari piknik,   Utari (female name) [is] at a picnic,
Wisnu sekolah,   Wisnu (male name) at school,
Agus **teng** Solo,   Agus (male) at Solo,
kan Yanto libur,   but Yanto (male) [is] free,
Yanto **niku nggih <u>mboten</u>** isa   That Yanto y'know can't do anything.
nåpå -nåpå.

90. ATIK: Malah anu **nggih**,   It's like y'know,
    kåyå Mbak Surti malah, malah   it's just like Mbak Surti really,

91. YANTI: Yanto **niku** angger nganu   That Yanto as long as whatsit,
    "kowe Pluk, Pluk" **ngoten niku**,   "you're Pluk, Pluk" like that [I said],
    njuk nek carane kåyå ngene ki (?)   then it's like this (?)

92. ATIK: **<u>Kulå</u> nggih**,   For me too,
    sak**niki mpun** biasa Mbak Yanti.   It's already common Mbak Yanti
    Kåyå Mbak Surti **nikå**.   Like Mbak Surti also.
    nikå <u>mboten</u> iså **ken** meneng   she can't be ordered to keep silent
    ngeten.   like this.

93. YANTI: Jan-jane **<u>kulå</u> nggih**,   Truthfully me too,
    <u>mboten</u> iså.   I can't.

Notes

1. This direct quote from Pak Budi shows my "double" role in the family. Pak Budi refers to me in two ways: first as *mbak*, which is Javanese for "elder sister," despite the fact that he is much older than me, and then as *anakku*, or "my daughter." *Mbak* shows the respect he feels for me or my position, whereas *anakku* reveals the intimacy.

2. *Weton* involves two dates in the two cyclical measurements for weeks in the Javanese calendar. One is the usual seven-day system, and the other is the five-day Javanese market system: Kliwon, Legi, Pahing, Pon, Wage. My *weton*, for example, is Rabu Kliwon, meaning that I was born on a Wednesday–Kliwon. If any of my younger siblings were born on the same *weton*, according to older Javanese beliefs, I could be at great risk. Thus, ceremonies or even the *tumbal* noted above would be arranged. Today, *tumbal* ceremonies are still practiced in Yogyakarta. The younger child is still symbolically placed in the trash but immediately picked up again and brought back into the home. No change of status is involved.

3. Geertz (1960) divides Javanese society into three parts: *priyayi*; *santri*, the strongly Islamic merchant class (yet see Nancy Florida in Sears, 1996, for a fascinating historical definition of the term); and *abang*, which roughly coincides with the *wong cilik*. Geertz distinguishes each group through its different spiritual practices and socioeconomic status as the basis for linguistic differences. More than 35 years after the publication of Geertz's book, and after 30 years of President Soeharto's restructuring of society according to his own model of modernization, it is difficult to support such divisions.

4. Sari also told me that this was not always the case. In the past, her father did indeed resent his fate. Resentment and frustration took the forms of gambling, drinking, and distancing himself from his family. His neglect naturally placed more pressure on Ibu Budi to care for their six children on her own. Later, Pak Budi realized his errors and turned back to religion and the study of Javanese philosophy as the only true response to his difficulties. In short, the members of the family recognize their suffering as a result of the *nonacceptance* of their fates, whereas acceptance has brought calm and even a degree of prosperity.

5. This exact line originates in news articles, speeches, and posters, from which it becomes an internalized, unquestioned part of the public discourse. See *Bernas*, 21 April 1992, p. 4.

6. See also Diane Wolf's discussion of women in Central Javanese factories in Sears (1996).

7. The argument could easily turn here to a discussion of the Javanese practices of *tirakat*, *upacara*, and *ziarah*, but others have already covered these practices of achieving power and prestige through ritual fasting, sleep deprivation, meditation, and so on. These practices teach the diligent believer humility and serenity despite the chaos. One may also say that fasting glorifies hunger and meditation teaches victims to distance themselves from pain and abuse (personal communication, Father Sara, S.J.). See Keeler (1985) and Pemberton (1989) for discussions of Javanese ritual practices.

8. For more information on the Javanese speech levels, see also Anderson (1990), Geertz (1960), Horne (1961, 1964, 1974), Keeler (1984), Poedjosoedarmo (1968a, 1968b), Soepomo (1986), Suharno (1982), and Uhlenbeck (1970, [1949] 1978).

9. The word *kråmå* is actually spelled in Javanese as <krama> but pronounced [krɔmɔ]. As explained in the transcription segment, I have represented the open syllable <a> as <å> for the benefit of non-Javanese speakers.

10. Personal communication from Romo Barsana Condrapurnama, a well-known local paranormal; *abdi-dalem*; and expert in local philosophy, *gamelan*, and history. Director of Museum Sonobudaya until his retirement, he now runs the Paku Alaman museum.

11. See note 4 and the story at the beginning of this chapter.

12. The exception is Nancy Smith-Hefner's (1989) studies of mother-child interactions.

13. The palace as a source of power in any of these senses is now debatable, but most would still see it as an essential source of cultural power and the center of Javanese refinement and spiritual power, that is, Javanese mysticism.

14. Yogyakarta is known as a university town, containing 36 institutions of higher learning and students from all over Indonesia. Yogyakarta has a population of 3,058,889 as of 1993. Of this number, 42% reside within the city and 58% live in the surrounding rural areas (*Kedaulatan Rakyat*, 5 May 1993, p. 8).

15. This is a difficult statement to explain. Yogyakartans rarely speak Indonesian and foreigners very seldom speak Javanese. Thus, most locals are quite shocked to meet a foreigner with whom they can easily communicate. My linguistic abilities, especially my Javanese humor, gave me celebrity status and an incredible access to conversations of all kinds. If Javanese is the language of intimate communication, thought, self-expression, and "tradition" and Indonesian is more an "official," formal language, it should be assumed that Javanese social relations would be quite different from those in Indonesian. No one needed to change their discursive styles to accommodate me; thus despite my "outsider" status, I was very easy to have around.

16. My language-learning strategy was to speak only Javanese and to graciously apologize to all who spoke to me in Indonesian for my inability to converse in that language. Whoever wished to communicate with me was forced to do so only in Javanese. Additionally, I would read in Javanese for two to three hours a day to strengthen my vocabulary.

17. This use of the word *priyayi* entails a further definition, one shaped by modernity and economic wealth. Since by birth, the Wandos and Budis are all related and, hence, all *priyayi* (i.e., nobility), this use of the term is an evaluation of what the Wandos see as the *economic* basis required for *priyayi* membership. Such a definition includes themselves and rejects the Budis.

18. This is actually because they were too poor to eat meat and thus had a diet mainly of rice, vegetables, and bean curd or tempe, that is, simple "peasant food," low in fat and cholesterol.

19. Indonesia requires all researchers to report regularly in person and in writing to all levels of national and local government. While most regard these registration requirements as a major headache, I actually enjoyed them as an opportunity to test my proficiency in formal Javanese diplomacy. Thus I was never forgotten at subsequent visits, and this "fame" was a huge benefit when the inevitable problems did occur.

20. Her past, however, allows her great prestige among those old enough to remember it. These elderly musicians and performers still pay homage to her through gifts, donations, and occasional marriage proposals.

21. The *abdi-dalem,* for the most part, are rural poor who serve in the *kraton* to be close to, and perchance to absorb, the prestige and power of this spiritual center. The activities I describe are those of the poor, who I actually found much easier to become close to. The wealthy have servants, and visiting them consisted of being honored and served. One could not then help with the cooking or child minding, as such activities take place in the back of the house and away from an outsider's view. Wolfowitz (1991) describes the structure of Javanese homes and their activities as analogous to one's relationship to the family. The deeper into the house one is permitted, the more intimate is one's relationship.

22. Whether this is evidence of the special powers of the sultan and his territory, I leave for readers to decide.

23. I recorded another 87 tapes in a variety of situations between speakers of all ages and genders. These data, of course, cannot all be included in a qualitative study of narrative.

24. This section was developed through the astute guidance of my unnamed reader A, to whom I owe a great deal of debt.

25. Now, it can be said, they are the beneficiaries of New Order patronage, President Soeharto's attempts to wield power through the classic Javanese model.

Chapter Two

1. Mead's philosophy was built around the notion of reflexivity, in which he states that the self is essentially a reflection of a social process going on between the distinguishable phases of the "me" and the "I." In brief, the "I" is "the response of the organism to the attitudes of others," while the "me" is "the organized set of attitudes of others which one assumes" (Mead, 1934:175; Stark, 1996). Through the reflective capacity of these two phases of selfhood, conscious responsibility arises. Reflexivity, then, is an unpredictable struggle between the more conventional social self (me) and the innovative self (I). The response of the "I" involves adaptation, which can affect the self, but it can also affect the social environment that helps to constitute the self.

2. PKK is the primary channel through which the state filters its official ide-ologies to women (see Djajadiningrat-Nieuwenhuis, 1987; Norma Sullivan, 1990, 1994; Suryakusuma, 1996; Weiringa, 1992.)

3. In fact, the hierarchical structure mirrors the position of each member's husband; that is, women acquire position because of their husbands, not be-cause of their own capabilities (Norma Sullivan, 1994).

4. I have recently been told that the 5 points called *Panca Darma Wanita* have been superseded by the 10 points of PKK. PKK's 10 central points are seen everywhere: on signs in front of every government office right down to the level of village heads, called RW and RT, and in relief on gateposts (across from Pancasila) at the entrances to every village and village subsection throughout the country. The 10 points are (1) experience and spread Pancasila; (2) take part in community work activities (*gotong-royong*); (3) take responsibility for food, clothing, and housing; (4) keep order in the household; (5) be concerned with education; (6) possess skills; (7) be knowledgeable in health issues; (8) de-velop a cooperative lifestyle; (9) preserve the environment; and (10) possess healthy intentions.

5. As Norma Sullivan (1994:146) notes, most women will go to enormous trouble to avoid causing their menfolk loss of face. Even the wives of the laziest and most useless men will not talk openly about their lack of responsibility to the family.

6. For example, gender-marked kinship terms are widely used. See the list of such terms in the section on transcriptions.

7. Researchers in the Yogyakarta Balai Penelitian Bahasa (Language Research Center) or at the Post-Graduate Center in Linguistics at Universitas Gadjah Mada knew of no gender studies and could not help in locating dates for their intro-duction.

8. As in the rest of this study, I base my discussion mainly on the city of Yogyakarta, the center of the refinement and hierarchical orderliness that underpin state domination.

9. Although it remains to be investigated, perhaps such perspective may ex-plain the widespread use of the *jilbab* ("head scarf") by local women. By pre-senting a public display of supposedly strong religious beliefs and hiding from view all of her feminine attributes, women are safe. Women activists have in vast numbers turned to the *jilbab* as the way to interact safely in a man's world of intellectual discussion and activism.

10. Sears (1996:37, notes 66, 67) mentions that this celebrated "traditional" dress is in fact an innovation of the 1950s and 1960s.

11. I have reproduced these handwritten letters as accurately as possible, including spelling errors.

12. This is far too complex a topic to discuss here. Those interested in the maintenance of hierarchy at village and *kampung* levels should refer to Guinness (1986), Jay (1969), Sears (1996), John Sullivan (1992), and Norma Sullivan (1994).

13. My interest and knowledge of the informal sector stem from my intimacy with street children from early on in my Java experience. I have continued this association on personal and professional levels, as friend, as researcher, and more recently as a member of the Social Services Department's steering committee on street children. See Berman (1994, 1997).

14. This raises issues of acceptance as consent or as coercion (discussed in Fairclough, 1989, and Herman and Chomsky, 1988). There is a great deal of

evidence in human rights reports to support the latter; see, for example, publications by Amnesty International (Britain) and Human Rights Watch/Asia (United States), and the magazine *Inside Indonesia* (Australia). See also Heryanto (1990) and Berman (forthcoming) for studies that tie a violent history, and thus expectations of violence when disagreement or criticism is expressed publicly, to passive consent now. This book deals mainly with issues of consent.

15. Since returning to Yogyakarta to write this book in 1995, I have been frequently asked to speak at seminars on women's issues. Other speakers are almost exclusively male, as are audience members, discussants, and questioners. The three or four women in a room will inevitably sit in the last row and be present mainly because of their position as "hostess"; that is, in pairs, they will give snacks to the speakers and audience. One will carry the tray while the other, with great formulaic decorum, will hand each person a small box with her right hand while her left crosses the body at a right angle to the outstretched arm, nudging it close to the elbow.

16. Specifically her lack of voice in the selection, impregnation, and divorce process—*dipilih, dikawini, dicerai.*

17. For example, John Searle (1969:21) proposed speech acts as the basic unit of communication, linking "what the speaker means, what the sentence uttered means, [and] what the speaker intends."

18. While evidence for the women I describe here shows strong contrast, Helen Lette (n.d.) describes the narratives she observed from Yogyakartan street toughs as private, and hence threatening, whereas the public domain they were presented into was a known, and hence safe, entity. Thus, the act of transforming these narratives from private to public is the symbolic act of surrendering oneself to the group. Lette is, in essence, insinuating private thoughts and notions of individual experience and identity as unnatural domains for these young men, who never venture far from their cohorts.

19. Berman (forthcoming), Florida (1987), and Pemberton (1989), question the political implications of such "traditions" from different perspectives.

20. And so do a great many others, as seen by the new collection of articles on gender in Indonesia by Laurie Sears (1996), in addition to the authors already mentioned.

Chapter Three

1. Bali is the next island east of Java and is historically and linguistically related to Javanese.

2. Wolfowitz (1991:73–74) discusses the same pattern, which she calls interrogative dialogue.

3. None of the transcripts in this chapter mark for speech levels if they are not salient for the discussion. Instead, the transcripts show repetition (underlined) since this is how a topic is identified. Complete transcripts with speech-level markers are found in the appendix.

4. Actually, as I look over these notes again, my remark that I had seen the festival a year ago is untrue. I had seen it almost 10 years ago on my first trip to Java as a tourist. The fact that I use allo-repetition and maintain agreement with Sari's statements makes the aspects of repetition and community agreement even more salient. I seem to have subconsciously adapted very well to my Javanese role.

5. I should add that I was also scared of the giant, evil-looking puppets—mainly because they were hacked to bits and dripping something bloodlike and thrown into the crowd. At the time, I remember feeling quite nervous and asking my guide how long ago the local people stopped practicing cannibalism.

6. Even though I include myself as one of the speakers here, there will be many more examples to show how such repetition does indeed function in these informal discourses when no foreigners are present.

7. This topic of employment instability for Sari will come up again. Both Atik and Yanti are civil servants (which implies job security) who work in a junior high school.

8. This exact theme of Sari's conformity and status will be investigated again in chapters 5 through 7.

9. See the appendix for the same text marked for speech level.

10. A *becak* is a pedicab. *Becak* drivers tend to be extremely poor and often sleep inside their cabs on the streets or at the station so as not to miss a potential fare. I am a well-known figure among these classes of people, especially homeless children, with whom I have been working since 1991.

11. Sadhar, from Sanata Dharma, is the common name of the university where I taught and had an office from 1991 to 1993.

12. The uses of reported speech are further discussed in the next chapter.

13. This is also why the Budi's insisted I record only friends.

14. As is *abdi-dalem* custom inside the *kraton*, we are barefooted and sit on mats on the ground in a cross-legged position (*silo*).

15. The only exception I saw was when Ibu Sugeng was suffering from what the Javanese fearfully label *nge stress*, a result of "not being in her right mind." See chapter 7.

16. I owe this observation to Clare Wolfowitz.

17. There may be reason to state that this is not a story but a "report," precisely because of its terseness. I shall keep it as a story, however, because of the segments that follow and its use of evaluation.

18. Avoidance of reference can further indicate deference.

19. Even though *gumun* is followed by the pronoun *kulå*, I see this as not being an object focus. Javanese often emphasize an action, emotion, or phrase by fronting it and verbally stressing it (*gumun kulå*.) See the same construction in (1), where Endang says *wedi aku* ("*I* was terrified"), and in (2), where I say *wedi aku* and no one corrects me.

Chapter Four

1. See the introductory section on transcription conventions for translations of Javanese vocatives.

2. Kridå Mardåwå is the culture and arts branch of the *kraton*, responsible for the regular musical performances.

3. I know of no study of discursive time references in Javanese. My understanding of it, based on the coding of several hundred hours of spoken texts, is as a relative marker, not a specific location of precision.

4. I must stress that the texts that make up the data for this study all took place among old friends and family. Nonintimates may not be so direct.

5. Both of these stories are presented in full in the next section.

6. Even now, as I try to locate the dates of the sultans' reigns, I am having difficulty. The highly detailed charts that appear on the back of maps of the city (Yogya) contain all the names of the sultans, wives, concubines, and children, explicitly giving genealogies, but no dates at all.

7. I analyze Yanti's story in more detail in chapter 7. Atik told me that the style reveals her *setress*, how awful an experience Yanti had. There is only one other highly detailed monologue like this in my corpus, which was also described by others present as *setress*. The stress is implicit in the highly detailed, monologic nature of the stories, unusual in informal narratives.

8. Erving Goffman's production formats include an *animator*, one who presents the talk and need not be responsible for it; a *figure*, who is presented through the discourse as a player in the story's world and not in the immediate context of speaking; an *author*, who is the source of the utterance; and a *principal*, who is morally responsible for the beliefs being displayed through the words (see how this relevance is maintained in Schiffrin, 1987; Hill and Irvine, 1993).

9. Note, too, that her numbers do not add up. These are formulaic phrases for her that do not change even though I had heard these stories for four years. There really is no way of determining accuracy if that is what we were after. I tend to follow Bruner (1987) when he states that stories are not necessarily sources of *truth* but rather sources of cultural information. They tell us what these people themselves believe it is important to say and in what contexts.

10. Location in Javanese is done mainly by compass points; that is, turn north (*ngalor*) and so on.

11. I had not known at the time that this working-class *kampung* was famous for its *gali-gali*, or hoodlums and violence. I was an extortion target there and chose to leave. In the heart of Bausasran I also discovered a rather large enclave of extremely poor, abandoned women and children, most of whose husbands had left them for other wives (*madu*). I spent a lot of time with these women, who referred to themselves as my *Mbakyu ireng* or my "black elder sisters." Their stories will appear in a later book.

12. Spatial location in *kampungs* is very important. The *wong gedongan*, or people in stone (good) houses, tend to live on the main streets in or on the boundaries of *kampungs*, whereas the poorer people (*wong cilik*) live in bamboo, wood, or cement houses in the centers, often accessible only through narrow, winding alleys. See Guinness (1986), Murray (1994), John Sullivan (1992), and Norma Sullivan (1994) for further discussion.

13. As it turned out, Yanti never told anyone from our group but me about her marriage until afterward. She had finally resolved on marrying a younger man from her office because, already over 30, she had accepted the fact that there would be no other offers. Thus, she did not invite her own friends and held a small party in her husband's village.

14. There are other reasons, too. Since Indonesian is the language of education and mass media, level switching reconstructs the styles associated with such domains. Modernization and the spread of Indonesian are likely to replace Javanese in generations to come or, at least, non-*ngoko* Javanese.

15. The dilemma is one of crossing social boundaries. As a foreigner, a teacher, and their adopted kin, it frightens them that I would associate with lower-class people. Yet they honor me by resolving the problem when they could have easily left it in silence.

16. Radio Republik Indonesia was the only lucrative alternative employment for musicians. While this story has no date, RRI began on 1 October 1945 and under other names started broadcasting in 1936 (Philip Yampolsky, personal communication). I have reason to believe that Ibu Asmoro speaks about the pre-RRI days when the Dutch regent took a fancy to her voice. The regent, as well as one Hardjowahono, who helped Radio Semarang (a city in north-central Java) get set up, were both in Semarang, which she has said elsewhere is where she was often recorded.

17. The *nikå* form has an oppositional value to both *niki* and *niku* since it alone can appear in *kråmå* utterances. The other two are strictly *madyà*. I owe this observation to Joseph Errington (personal communication).

18. As already mentioned, this study must confine analysis to only the terms that appear in the texts. These are predominantly the various forms of *ki*. Others in this category include vocatives; affirmatives; tags; and *kok, lho, lha, tho, je, wong*, and so on.

19. Note that the prince in Ibu's story does not use any edge markers.

20. The term *Ibu* is a respectful vocative and thus can also fall into this category of edge markers. See Wolfowitz (1991) for further discussion.

21. Yet, in both these examples, there is an underlying conditional, or a general sense of continuity, that is not lexically expressed. In 462, "when" or "if you are not there" has no semantic indicator; and in 470, "when or "if you are going to rehearse" is the same. It is possible that *menikå* has functions as yet unrecognized.

Chapter Five

1. "Natural" oppression is based on a paternal order and enforced through hints and not necessarily blatant violence. "Proper" Javanese would never raise their voices or act in a vulgar manner. For a discussion of female factory workers and "proper" oppression, see Diane Wolf (1992, 1996).

2. Differences between conditions of factory workers in Central Java and Jakarta explain why protests are far more common in one than the other. These Yogya workers, like many of their sisters in rural Java, live at home and thus "don't need the income to live." Wages are seen as "surplus" income (Wolf, 1996). Workers in the larger cities such as Jakarta and Surabaya tend to live in dorms or other paid accommodation, an addition to their need to send money home to the villages. The freedom from direct family influence is probably one of the main reasons for their increased militancy. Melody Kemp's (n.d.; with Sri Kusyuniarti, 1993) studies of health standards in these factories paints a miserable picture of rampant iron deficiency anemia and respiratory and gynecological complaints, as well as problems of insufficient lighting and overcrowding.

3. Note that the women themselves were not permitted to attend these negotiations.

4. Javanese are invariably guarded in speech, especially with strangers. This style of guardedness results in a formulaic speech called *basa basi*. The fact that Sigah did not engage me in *basa basi* but directly entered into a conarrative discourse, albeit after a brief silence, was significant. This indicates that responsibility to the public production of the protest narratives was more important than the exceedingly rare opportunity to conduct a "getting to know you" discourse with a foreigner who speaks Javanese.

5. Since these stories have no specific temporal markers, only relational, it is impossible to know when the overtime and the pay cuts had begun. Scanning previous transcripts with Sari do not help, as the factory is never mentioned. She did not speak about events that conflicted with social norms and expectations.

6. See the note on transcription. There is no *krāmā* speech in this conversation, so underlining here refers to repetition. As usual, the Indonesian language is in italics. Since these women speak mainly Javanese, there is reason to believe that all Indonesian is a repetition of someone else's words.

7. While this amounts only to roughly $12, it is a month's salary in Central Java, but still not enough to live on. To put it into clearer focus, this amount is more than double Ibu Asmoro's palace salary and yet half the minimum requirement.

8. These rounds are very similar in style and function to the mutual ratification stances described in chapter 3. The difference is that here the rounds do not occur before a story; rather all participants tell their story by adapting it to a similar topic, position, and style. The effect creates an iconic unity similar to that seen in the Starfruit Tales. Thus, I use the term *round* somewhat differently from Tannen (1984), who uses it to describe participants who are telling separate stories.

9. Wolf (1996) points out that it is in many respects a better form of exploitation than they are subjected to at home, where they receive no pay and none of the relative freedoms and benefits.

10. This utterance is in *krāmā*, but the speaker is Sari's younger sister, not one of the factory cohort.

11. Note that it is the *anger* that Sari evaluates as disgusting and not the demotion to "training."

12. The Bataks are an ethnic group from northern Sumatra. The Javanese, who tend to see their own refinement as superior to others', frequently condemn other ethnic groups, as well as lower classes, for their crudeness. The Bataks, according to Javanese wisdom, are loud, aggressive thieves who lack refinement.

13. *Singkek* is a derogatory term that refers to a Chinese immigrant who maintains Chinese habits (Echols and Shadily, 1989).

14. While Sari avoids verbalizing her affective stance, she suffers chronic earaches whenever she is upset. During the last several weeks, and several months after the factory problem was over, Sari's left ear was causing her terrible pain. An earache like this does not respond to medical treatment.

15. Some of this is their own decision, an avoidance of a potential *cilākā* (disaster).

280.	ENDANG: Tur nek bengi, yo ora wani Mbak	So then at night, y'know [we're] not brave [enough to go home] Mbak
282.	SIGAH: Ngko nek ditemu uwong, piye?	So later if we meet someone [on the streets], then what?
283.	ALL: [hahah cilākā.]	[hahaha] disaster

As inexpensive transport is not available after 6:00 P.M. in Yogya (they cannot consider a taxi or pedicab), they fear whom they will meet on the streets. These women know that they should not walk the streets at night (see chapter 2). Yet, because of the arbitrary imposition of overtime, they cannot request a family member to meet them. There are no phones in working-class Javanese homes, so requests for pickups have to be well planned.

16. They are also disempowered by a Department of Labor that was paid off by the factory to drop the women's case. They are disempowered by a legal system that did not support their plea for help despite the existence of labor laws. They are disempowered by a system of hierarchical rights and privileges that blacklisted them as trouble-makers, virtually preventing them from working again. Finally, they are disempowered by a social-interactional system that prevents them from discussing these problems since they are not appropriate "events" in the moral order of norms.

17. The following chapters show that this support is internal to the group only and does not involve family members, except in perfunctory ways. Chapter 6 shows that other workers never confided in their parents. At all the meetings I attended, only factory workers appeared; no external family support was visible or discussed.

18. It was the seven-day week that brought Sari's problem to my attention; she herself did not volunteer any information. We had been in the habit of taking a Sunday "picnic," what we called jokingly *ngrampok desã*, or "attacks on rural villages." When Sari could no longer meet me, I asked why.

19. In 1994 there was a huge demonstration for workers' rights in northern Sumatra in which a Chinese businessman was murdered. Many believe that the man was killed by hired thugs for the sole purpose of turning the legitimate issue of worker's rights into one of ethnic inequality since the factory was owned by Chinese. Such purposeful mass manipulation is also said to underlie the recent riots in Java in the wake of the upcoming election in 1997.

Chapter Six

1. This is discussed in part below. Sari is the sole speaker for the group because Dhik Sri will not address her father. She is present but remains silent.

2. *Pak* Sri (as Pak Surti earlier) means "father of Sri" in this context.

3. Kirik Ertanto, an anthropologist with Humana (a foundation that runs the cooperative for homeless children in Yogya), claims that a majority of the social problems in Java today are a result of the "tradition" of noncommunication between parents and children especially fathers' (personal communication). Sari had once told me that she was amazed by the way in which I brought her family together in lively discussion. She said that only when they were still young did their father tell them the kinds of humorous anecdotes and stories he tells when I am present. For me, at least, this verified my double position as a daughter who still required socialization and as a special guest. For the others, communication virtually stopped with maturity. See also Keeler (1990) and Smith-Hefner (1988). This realization raises concerns for my other role as researcher. I have thus attempted to balance analysis between conversations in which I was and was not present.

4. *Alus* is Javanese for "refined," "elegant," "smooth." *Kasar* is the opposite— "crude," "rough," "rude."

5. Yet Dhik Sri is there and *silent*. I do not know Dhik Sri nor her involvement in the protest. It is obvious from the context that she cannot or will not tell her father this story. I am then inclined to agree more with Ertanto (note 3). It is easier for Sari to speak with Pak Sri than it is for Dhik Sri to do it.

6. The question that comes to mind here is how can these overtime problems arise without a father noticing. A possible answer may be that with so much

community pressure on unmarried women to keep themselves "pure," parents rarely need to control their daughters. Daughters, the community, and their peer groups do so themselves. Thus if a daughter comes home late, it is assumed she was attending one of many frequent community meetings, competitions, women's organizations, and so on.

7. Bantul is a rural district just south of Yogyakarta and roughly 3 to 10 kilometers from the factory. This is the same village Ibu Budi would walk home to when she missed her family, as mentioned in chapter 1.

8. Examples are the state's censorship of all media; the frequent ban of books that are not in line with state doctrine; the imprisonment of those who lead student discussion groups, protest, or criticize state actions; and many more limitations on freedom of expression.

9. Pak Budi is referring to something I had done recently. After writing a letter of protest to "Reader's Thoughts" in *Kedaulatan Rakyat*, the local paper, I received an uproar of responses in reference to the issue of violence toward women in the Indonesian cinema. While most were supportive, there were also two death threats from fundamentalist groups. All of these responses I discussed fully with Pak Budi. He was obviously impressed with the attention these letters can achieve.

10. In the nearly two years I had known Sari and had been a constant guest in the Budi home, I had never seen her so outspoken and so animated. Nor was I to see it again. After Sari was fired and blacklisted, she became very quiet and withdrawn. She did not tell me that she had been fired until I dropped by the Budi home one morning to visit her mother and was surprised to see Sari there. Her protest discourses disappeared, even when we visited her old cohorts. In fact, the topic of the factory experience was never raised.

Chapter Seven

1. The term "position" has similarities to Elinor Ochs's (1993) use of "stance" and Erving Goffman's (1981) "footing." I use the term "positioning" because its use is more developed vis-à-vis power.

2. In Mead's (1934) terms this could be the community itself.

3. Storylines are the explicit or implicit parts and characters that make up the story through which a position is understood.

4. In Bakhtin's terms, positioning is a natural feature of language in which the repertoire of discursive positions any individual learns is evidence of the nature of heteroglossia. All these language positions "are specific points of view on the world, forms for conceptualizing the world in words, specific world views, each characterized by its own objects, meanings and values. As such they all may be juxtaposed to one another, mutually supplement one another, contradict one another and be interrelated dialogically" (Bakhtin, [1934] 1981:291-292). Power, or social stratification, is also shaped by differences in the linguistic forms used, each of which conveys meaning. Part of the dialectic nature of "cultural" expectations, dominant groups take advantage of the intentional dimensions of heteroglossia to form their own genre that denotes boundaries and exclusions. Thus, and obvious in modern Java, the dialogism expected in these theories of person are often constricted into a monologue of social and political hierarchy.

5. These are the same three women described in chapters 3 and 4 but at a different time and place.

6. I do not include myself, although I was present, at least partially, for all the recordings.

7. I do not know how they had found out about this. After I had left Java, I received a letter from Sari (6 April 1995) in which she stated that she was now working again in a small tailor shop after nearly two years of forced unemployment. As of 1997, she is still happily employed in this shop, and she even took me there to meet the owners.

8. Texts from this point are marked to show their speech-level shifts.

9. Even those from the elderly *abdi-dalem*, which are much more autobiographical than the stories told by the younger women, narrated a self in relation to others in the story and in the context of speaking. While all storytelling is "recipient designed," the Javanese stories, by virtue of their flexible structure and their propensity to include others in the telling, take notions of "other" orientation to new lengths.

10. There are a few exceptions to this. In each case, the discourse took the form of story rounds in which all participants assumed similar positions. The starfruit stories are a good example of agentic positions that index external harmony, not individual truths.

11. The Budi women were very much in the habit of telling their secrets to me because, as Yati (the third daughter) once said, I am the only safe person they know. She meant that I am enough a part of their world to be easy to talk to but not enough to present a threat by gossiping with others. Most of our secret conversations involved very intimate family issues, such as that in chapter 1, and romance stories.

12. The stress stories are presented in full, with speech-level markings, in the appendix.

13. Ibu Budi herself told me about this, not Atik. When she told me, she was clearly agitated from worry and lack of sleep. While she expressed concern for Sur's troubles, we only discussed them in terms of the selfishness of Sur's siblings. No one else seemed able or willing to help in any deeper way, although we did often sit with Sur in the hospital. Emotional loss of control—called *setress* ("stress") or *ngestress* (verb form)—tends to elicit avoidance and distance, probably because emotional issues are not discussed publicly, and thus the community may simply not know what to do. Psychiatrists are virtually unheard of (except in the Sunday newspaper's write-in columns). Yet, I am fascinated by the overall community obsession with *setress*—and no more—as the most commonly given answer to most social ills. This word is by far the most common graffiti scrawled on Yogyakarta walls (with "vampire" second). For example, one quiet evening at the Budi home, Sari and I were reading the paper (unrecorded conversation). I heard the faint sound of a woman screaming, which continued for some time. I asked Sari what it was, and her response was *tanggane seneng setress Mbak Len* ("the neighbor is usually stressed, Mbak Len"). I was shocked and asked for more information. Sari responded with the word *setress* only. When I pressed her for a reason for the stress, she told me that the young woman had been engaged to be married but shortly before the ceremony, she was attacked and raped. Her fiancé canceled the wedding and broke off the engagement. Ever since, the woman is *setress*; she frequently screams late into the night. I was horrified by this story and asked Sari what has been done for this poor woman. Sari told me that it was not so bad because she is fine during the day. At night, however, her grandmother holds her on her lap like a baby and she'll calm down.

As in Surti's case, the community seems to be at a loss for active responses to variations from social norms. Ideally, women will suppress their emotions and present the expected untroubled demeanor, as Sari had done after her ordeal at the factory.

14. Atik once told me that Surti had not married because she was the only sibling who could take care of the home and her aging parents. Surti's younger sisters had all married, a personal shame for Sur, a sign of her sacrifice, and the cause of much pain and stress.

15. Speech-level markings are available in the appendix and are excerpted where necessary for the discussion. In this section, the Javanese texts are marked for repetition since this is what signals the topics and intertextual development.

16. After her period of mourning and increased illness, Surti found a road out of her predicament. In 1996, when I saw her again, she had married a "friend" because she was pregnant. She hinted to me that the pregnancy was a ploy to land a husband, although she did not love him. She was now quite chubby, a sign of her contentment with motherhood and her new status as a married woman. My request for details about her husband or their relationship was answered only with '*biasa tho*' (the usual).

Bibliography

Anderson, Benedict. 1990. *Language and Power: Exploring Political Cultures in Indonesia*. Ithaca, N.Y.: Cornell University Press.

Bakhtin, Mikhail. [1934] 1981. *The Dialogical Imagination*. Caryl Emerson and Michael Holquist, eds. and trans. Austin: University of Texas Press.

Bateson, Gregory. [1949] 1972. Bali: The value system of a steady state. In *Steps to an Ecology of Mind*, pp. 107–127. New York: Ballentine Books.

Becker, Alton L. 1979. Text-building, epistemology, and aesthetics in Javanese shadow theatre. In *The Imagination of Reality: Essays on Southeast Asian Coherence Systems*, pp. 211–243. Alton L. Becker and Aram A. Yengoyan, eds. Norwood, N.J.: Ablex.

———. 1984. The linguistics of particularity: Interpreting superordination in a Javanese text. In *Proceedings of the Tenth Annual Meeting of the Berkeley Linguistics Society*, pp. 425–436. Berkeley: University of California Press.

———. 1988. Preface: An essay on translating the art of music. In *Karawitan: Source Readings in Javanese Gamelan and Vocal Music*, pp. ix–xx. Michigan Papers for South and Southeast Asia 31, Vol. 1. Ann Arbor: Center for Southeast Asian Studies, University of Michigan.

Becker, Alton L., and I Gusti Ngurah Oka. n.d.. Person in Kawi: Exploration of an elementary semantic dimension.

Benveniste, Emile. 1971a. The nature of pronouns. In *Problems in General Linguistics*, pp. 217–222. Coral Gables, Fla.: University of Miami Press.

———. 1971b. Subjectivity in language. In *Problems in General Linguistics*, pp. 223–230. Coral Gables, Fla.: University of Miami Press.

Berman, Laine. 1992. First person identities in Indonesian conversational narratives. *Journal of Asian Pacific Communication*, Vol. 3, No.1, 3–14.

———. 1994, March. Homeless in Yogyakarta: The remarkable story of GIRLI, a refuge for homeless children. *Inside Indonesia* (Australia), No. 38, 18–21.

———. 1997. The world's first street university. *Inside Indonesia*, No. 50, 11–12.

———. Forthcoming. Strategies of positioning in the discourses of the Indonesian state. In *Positioning Theory: Moral Contexts of Intentional Action*. M. van Langenhove and R. Harré, eds. Oxford: Blackwell.

Bernstein, Basil. [1970] 1972. Social class, language and socialization. In *Language and Social Context*, pp. 157–178. Pier Giglioli, ed. New York: Penguin.

Besnier, Niko. 1993. Reported speech and affect on Nukulaelae atoll. In *Responsibility and Evidence in Oral Discourse*, pp. 161–181. J. H. Hill and J. T. Irvine, eds. Cambridge: Cambridge University Press.

Blackburn, Susan. 1994. Gender interests and Indonesian democracy. In *Democracy in Indonesia 1950s and 1990s*. David Bourchier and John Legge, eds. Monash Papers on Southeast Asia No. 31. Melbourne: Centre for Southeast Asian Studies, Monash University.

Blum-Kulka, Shoshana, and Catherine Snow. 1992. Developing autonomy for tellers, tales, and telling in family narrative events. *Journal of Narrative and Life History*, Vol. 2, No. 3, 187–217.

Bruner, Jerome. 1987. Life as narrative. *Social Research*, Vol. 54, No.1, 11–32.

Burke, Kenneth. 1969. *A Rhetoric of Motives*. Berkeley: University of California Press.

Cameron, Deborah. 1990. *The Feminist Critique of Language: A Reader*. New York: Routledge.

Chafe, Wallace. 1986. How we know things about language: A plea for catholicism. *Language and Linguistics: The Interdependence of Theory, Data, and Application. Georgetown University Round Table on Languages and Linguistics 1986*, pp. 214–225. D. Tannen, ed. Washington, D.C.: Georgetown University Press.

Coates, Jennifer. 1989. Gossip revisited: Language in all-female groups. In *Women in Their Speech Communities*, pp. 94–121. Jennifer Coates and Deborah Cameron, eds. New York: Longman.

Coates, Jennifer, and Deborah Cameron, eds. 1989. *Women in Their Speech Communities*. New York: Longman.

Davies, Bronwyn. 1990. Agency as a form of discursive practice: A classroom scene observed. *British Journal of Sociology of Education*, Vol. 11, No. 3.

Davies, Bronwyn, and Rom Harré. 1990. Positioning: Conversation and the production of selves. *Journal for the Theory of Social Behaviour*, Vol. 20, No. 1, 43–63.

De Waele, J., and Rom Harré. 1979. Autobiography as a psychological method. In *Emerging Strategies in Social Psychological Research*, pp. 177–224. G. Ginsberg, ed. Chichester: John Wiley and Sons.

Djajadiningrat-Nieuwenhuis, Madelon. 1987. Ibuism and Priyayization: Paths to power? In *Indonesian Women in Focus*, pp. 43–51. E. Locher-Scholten and A. Niehof, eds. Dordrecht, Holland: Foris Publications.

Duranti, Alessandro. 1988. Intentions, language, and social action in a Samoan context. *Journal of Pragmatics*, Vol. 12, 13–33.

———. 1993. Intentions, self and responsibility: An essay in Samoan ethnopragmatics. In *Responsibility and Evidence in Oral Discourse*, pp. 24–47. J. H. Hill and J. T. Irvine, eds. Cambridge: Cambridge University Press.

———. 1994. *From Grammar to Politics*. Los Angeles: University of California Press.

Dwiraharjo, Maryono. 1991. Tingkat tutur dalam bahasa Jawa cerminan adab sopan santun berbahasa. Paper presented at Kongress Bahasa Jawa, Semarang.

Echols, John, and Hassan Shadily. 1994 [1961]. *Kamus Indonesia Inggris*. Jakarta: PT Gramedia.

Errington, J. Joseph. 1984. Self and self-conduct among the Javanese priyayi elite. *American Ethnologist*, Vol. 11, 275–290.

————. 1985. *Language and Social Change in Java*. Athens: Ohio University Monographs in International Studies, South East Asia Series No. 65.

————. 1988. *Structure and Style in Javanese*. Philadelphia: University of Pennsylvania Press.

Errington, Shelly. 1990. Recasting sex, gender, and power: A theoretical and regional overview. In *Power and Difference*, pp. 1–58. J. Atkinson and S. Errington, eds. Stanford, Cal.: Stanford University Press.

Fairclough, Norman. 1989. *Language and power*. London: Longman.

Florida, Nancy. 1987, October. Reading the unread in traditional Javanese literature. *Indonesia*, No. 44, 1–15. Ithaca, N.Y.: Cornell Southeast Asia Program.

————. 1996. Sex wars. In *Fantasizing the Feminine in Indonesia*, pp. 207–224. L. Sears, ed. Durham, N.C.: Duke University Press.

Freeman, Rebecca, and Bonnie McElhinny. 1995. Language and gender. In *Sociolinguistics and Language Teaching*, pp. 218–280. Sandra McKay and Nancy Hornberger, eds. Cambridge: Cambridge University Press.

Freire, Paulo. [1970] 1993. *Pedagogy of the Oppressed*. New York: Continuum.

Gal, Susan. 1989. Language and political economy. *Annual Review of Anthropology*, Vol. 18, 345–367.

————. 1992. Language, gender, and power: an anthropological view. In *Locating Power: Proceedings of the Second Berkeley Women and Language Conference*, pp. 153–161. Kira Hallo, Mary Bucholtz, and Birch Moonwoman, eds. Berkeley: University of California Press.

Geertz, Clifford. 1960. *The Religion of Java*. New York: Free Press.

————. 1973. GBHN. *The Interpretation of Cultures: Selected Essays*. New York: Basic Books.

Gilligan, Carol. 1982. *In a Different Voice: Psychological Theory and Women's Development*. Cambridge, Mass.: Harvard University Press.

Goffman, Erving. 1974. *Frame Analysis*. New York: Harper and Row.

————. 1981. Footing. In *Forms of Talk*. Philadelphia: University of Pennsylvania Press.

Graddol, David, and Joan Swann. 1989. *Gender Voices*. Oxford: Basil Blackwell.

Graham, Laura. 1993. A public sphere in Amazonia?: The depersonalized collaborative construction of discourse in Xavante. *American Ethnologist*, Vol. 20, 717–741.

Gramsci, Antonio. 1971. Selections from the Prison Notebooks: Edited and translated by Quintin Hoare and Geoffrey Smith. London: Lawrence and Wishart.

Guinness, Patrick. 1986. *Harmony and Hierarchy in a Javanese Kampung*. Singapore: Oxford University Press.

Gülich, Elizabeth, and Uta Quasthoff. 1985. Narrative analysis. In *Handbook of Discourse Analysis*, Vol. 2, pp. 169–197. Teun van Dijk, ed. London: Academic Press.

Gumperz, John. 1982. *Discourse Strategies*. Cambridge: Cambridge University Press.

Hafidz, Wardah, and Tati Krisnawati. 1989. Perempuan dan pembangunan: studi kebijakan tentang kedudukan perempuan dalam proses pembangunan di Indonesia. Manuscript.

Hanks, William. 1990. *Referential Practice: Language and Lived Space among the Maya*. Chicago: University of Chicago Press.

Harré, Rom. 1984. *Personal Being: A Theory for Individual Psychology*. Cambridge, Mass.: Harvard University Press.

———. 1992. Introduction to new methodologies, the turn to discourse: the second cognitive revolution. *American Behavioral Scientist*, No. 36, 5–8.

———, and Grant Gillett. 1994. *The Discursive Mind*. London: Sage.

Harré, Rom, and van Langenhove, 1991. Varieties of positioning. *Journal for the Theory of Social Behavior*, Vol. 21, No. 4, 393–407.

Hellwig, Tineke. 1987. Rape in two Indonesian pop novels: An analysis of the female image. In *Indonesian Women in Focus*, pp. 240–254. E. Locher-Scholten and A. Niehof, eds. Dordrecht, Holland: Foris Publications.

Herman, Edward, and Chomsky, Noam. 1988. *Manufacturing Consent*. New York: Pantheon.

Heryanto, Ariel. 1990. The making of language: Developmentalism in Indonesia, pp. 40–53. Prisma: The Indonesian Indicator, 50.

Hill, Jane, and Judith Irvine, eds. 1993. *Responsibility and Evidence in Oral Discourse*. Cambridge: Cambridge University Press.

Hill, Jane, and Ofelia Zepeda. 1993. Mrs. Patricio's trouble: The distribution of responsibility in an account of personal experience. In *Responsibility and Evidence in Oral Discourse*, pp. 197–225. J. Hill and J. Irvine, eds. Cambridge: Cambridge University Press.

Horne, Elinor. 1961. *Beginning Javanese*. New Haven, Conn.: Yale University Press.

———. 1964. *Intermediate Javanese*. New Haven, Conn.: Yale University Press.

———. 1974. *Javanese-English Dictionary*. New Haven, Conn.: Yale University Press.

Ishikawa, Minako. 1991. Iconicity in discourse: The case of repetition. *Text*, Vol. 2, No. 4, 553–580.

Jay, Robert. 1969. *Javanese Villagers*. Cambridge: MIT Press.

Jefferson, Gail. 1978. Sequential aspects of storytelling in conversation. *Studies in the Organization of Conversational Interaction*, pp. 219–248. J. Schenkein, ed. New York: Academic Press.

Johnstone, Barbara. 1991. *Stories, Community and Place*. Bloomington: Indiana University Press.

Kalcik, Susan. 1975. ". . . like Ann's gynecologist or the time I was almost raped": Personal narratives in women's rap groups. In *Women and Folklore*, pp. 3–11. C. Farra, ed. Austin: University of Texas Press.

Kaswanti Purwo, H. Bambang. 1976. Presupposition in the Javanese Particles: A Semantic and Syntactic Study. Master's thesis, IKIP Malang.

Keeler, Ward. 1984. *Javanese: A Cultural Approach*. Ohio University SEAsian Series Monograph No. 69. Athens: Ohio University Press.

———. 1985, April 39. Villagers and the exemplary center in Java. *Indonesia*, pp. 111–140.

———. 1987. *Javanese Shadow Plays, Javanese Selves*. Princeton, N.J.: Princeton University Press.

———. 1990. Speaking of gender. In *Power and Difference: Gender in Island Southeast Asia*, pp. 127–152. Jane Atkinson and Shelly Errington, eds. Stanford, Cal.: Stanford University Press.

Kemp, Melody. n.d. The politics of neglect: Indonesian labour standards.

Labov, William. 1972. The transformation of experience in narrative syntax. *Language in the Inner City*, pp. 354–396. Philadelphia: University of Pennsylvania Press.

————. 1984. Intensity. *Meaning, Form, and Use in Context: Linguistic Applications*, pp. 43–70. Deborah Schiffrin, ed. Washington D.C.: Georgetown University Press.

Labov, William, and Joshua Waletsky. 1967. Narrative analysis: Oral versions of personal experience. In *Essays on the Verbal and Visual Arts*, pp. 12–44. J. Helm, ed. Seattle: University of Washington Press.

Lette, Helen. n.d. Comic relief: Carnival and the tactics of resistance.

Levinson, Stephen. 1983. *Pragmatics*. Cambridge: Cambridge University Press.

Linde, Charlotte. 1989. Narrative as a resource for the social constitution of the self. Paper presented at American Anthropological Association, November 1989, Washington, D.C.

————. 1993. *Life Stories: The Creation of Coherence*. New York: Oxford University Press.

Logsdon, Martha. 1985. Women civil servants in Indonesia: Some preliminary observations. *Prisma: The Indonesian Indicator*, No. 37, 68–76.

Lyons, John. 1982. Deixis and subjectivity: Loquor, ergo sum? In *Speech, Place, and Action: Studies in Deixis and Related Topics*, pp. 101–124. R. Jarvella and W. Klein, eds. New York: Wiley.

Mead, George H. 1934. *Mind, Self, and Society: From the Standpoint of a Social Behaviorist*. C. Morris, ed. Chicago: University of Chicago Press.

Mohanty, Chandra. 1991a. Cartographies of struggle: Third world women and the politics of feminism. In *Third World Women and the Politics of Feminism*, pp. 1–47. C. Mohanty, A. Russo, and L. Torres, eds. Bloomington: Indiana University Press.

Mühlhäusler, Peter, and Rom Harré. 1990. *Personal Pronouns*. Oxford: Basil Blackwell.

Mulder, Niels. 1992. *Individual and Society in Java: A Cultural Analysis*. Yogyakarta: Gadjah Mada University Press.

Murry, Alison. 1991. *No Money, No Honey*. Kuala Lumpur: Oxford University Press.

Nichols, Patricia. 1984. Networks and hierarchies: Language and social stratification. In *Language and Power*, pp. 23–42. C. Kramarae, M. Schultz, and W. O'Barr, eds. Beverly Hills, Cal.: Sage.

Ochs, Elinor. 1988. *Culture and Language Development: Language Acquisition and Language Socialization in a Samoan Village*. Cambridge: Cambridge University Press.

————. 1992. Indexing gender. In *Rethinking Context: Language as an Interactive Phenomenon. Studies in the Social and Cultural Foundations of Language 11*, pp. 335–358. A. Duranti and C. Goodwin, eds. Cambridge: Cambridge University Press.

————. 1993. Constructing social identity: A language socialization perspective. *Research on Language and Social Interaction*, Vol. 26, No. 3, 287–306.

————, R. Smith, and C. Taylor. 1988. Detective stories at dinnertime: Problem-solving through co-narration. Paper presented at the American Ethnological Society Annual Meeting, Symposium on Narrative Resources for the Creation of Order and Disorder, St. Louis, Missouri.

O'Connor, Patricia E. 1994. Narratives of Prisoners: A Contribution to the Grammar of Agency. Ph.D. thesis, Georgetown University, Washington, D.C.

Pemberton, John. 1989. The appearance of order: A politics of culture in colonial and postcolonial Java. Ph.D. thesis, Cornell University, Ithaca, NY.

Poedjosoedarmo, Soepomo. 1968a. Index of Javanese terms. *Indonesia*, Vol. 7, 165–190.

———. 1968b. Javanese speech levels. *Indonesia*, Vol. 6, 54–81.

Poerwadarminta, W. 1939. *Baoesastra Djawa*. Batavia: J. B.Wolters' Uitgevers-Maatschaappij.

Polanyi, Livia. 1989. *Telling the American Story: A Structural and Cultural Analysis of Conversational Storytelling*. Cambridge, Mass.: MIT Press.

Polkinghorne, Donald. 1988. *Narrative Knowing and the Human Sciences*. Albany: State University of New York Press.

Rosaldo, Michelle. 1982. The things we do with words: Ilongot speech acts and speech act theory in philosophy. *Language in Society*, Vol. 11, 203–237.

Sacks, Harvey, Emanuel Schegloff, and Gail Jefferson. 1974. A simplest systematics for the organization of turn-taking in conversation. *Language*, Vol. 50, 696–735.

Schegloff, Emanuel.1992. In another context. In *Rethinking Context: Language as an Interactive Phenomenon. Studies in the Social and Cultural Foundations of Language 11*, pp. 191–228. A. Duranti and C. Goodwin, eds. Cambridge: Cambridge University Press.

Schiffrin, Deborah. 1984. How a story says what it means and does. *Text*, Vol. 4, No. 4, 313–346.

———. 1987. *Discourse Markers*. Cambridge: Cambridge University Press.

———. 1994. *Approaches to Discourse*. Cambridge, Mass.: Blackwell.

Scollon, Ron, and Suzanne Scollon. 1981. *Narrative, Literacy and Face in Interethnic Communication. Advances in Discourse Processes*, Vol. VII. Roy Freedle, ed. Norwood, N.J.: Ablex.

Scott, James. 1990. *Domination and the Arts of Resistance*. New Haven, Conn.: Yale University Press.

Searle, John. 1969. *Speech Acts: An Essay in the Philosophy of Language*. Cambridge: Cambridge University Press.

Sears, Laurie. 1996. *Fantasizing the Feminine in Indonesia*. Durham, N.C.: Duke University Press.

Sen, Krishna. 1994. *Indonesian Cinema: Framing the New Order*. London: Zed Books.

Shuman, Amy. 1993. "Get outta my face": Entitlement and authoritative discourse. In *Responsibility and Evidence in Oral Discourse*, pp. 135–160. J. H. Hill and J. T. Irvine, eds. Cambridge: Cambridge University Press.

Siegel, James. 1986. *Solo in the New Order: Language and Hierarchy in an Indonesian City*. Princeton, N.J.: Princeton University Press.

Smith, Dorothy. 1987. *The Everyday World as Problematic: A Feminist Sociology*. Boston: Northeast University Press.

Smith-Hefner, Nancy. 1988. Women and politeness: The Javanese example. *Language in Society*, Vol. 17, 535–554.

———. 1989. The linguistic socialization of Javanese children in two communities. *Anthropological Linguistics*, Vol. 30, No. 2, 166–198.

Soepomo, Gloria. 1986. *Role Structure in Javanese*. Jakarta: NUSA Linguistic Studies of Indonesian and Other Languages in Indonesia, Vol. 24.

Soeroso. 1990. Situasi bahasa Jawa dan pengajaran bahasa Jawa di SMA sebuah tinjauan kasus. Paper presented at Seminar V Antar Pengelola Jurusan/Program Bahasa-Sastra-Budaya Jawa. 15–16 Januari 1990. IKIP Veteran, Sukoharjo.

Sri Kusyuniati, and Melody Kemp. 1993. Behind the factory walls: Occupational health of women industrial workers. Paper presented at the Women in Asia Conference, 1–3 October, Melbourne University.

Stark, Frank. 1996. *Communicative Interaction, Power, and the State: A Method.* Toronto: University of Toronto Press.

Suharno, Ignatius. 1982. *A Descriptive Study of Javanese.* Materials in Languages of Indonesia No.11. W. Stokhof, ed. Pacific Linguistics Series D, No. 45. Canberra: Australian National University.

Sullivan, John. 1992. *Local Government and Community in Java: An Urban Case Study.* Southeast Asian Social Science Monograph. Singapore: Oxford University Press.

Sullivan, Norma. 1990. Gender and politics in Indonesia. In *Why Gender Matters in Southeast Asian Politics*, pp. 61–86. M. Stivens, ed. Clayton, Austr.: Monash CSEAS, Monash University Press.

———. 1994. *Masters and Managers: A Study of Gender Relations in Urban Java.* Women in Asia Series. St Leonards, NSW: Allen and Unwin.

Sunindyo, Saraswati. 1996. Murder, gender and the media: Sexualizing politics and violence. In *Fantasizing the Feminine in Indonesia*, pp. 120–139. L. Sears, ed. Durham, N.C.: Duke University Press.

Suryakusuma, Julia. 1996. The state and sexuality in New Order Indonesia. In *Fantasizing the Feminine in Indonesia*, pp. 92–119. L. Sears, ed. Durham, N.C.: Duke University Press.

Tannen, Deborah. 1983, Fall. "I take out the rock—dok!": How Greek women tell about being molested and create involvement. *Anthropological Linguistics*, pp. 359–374.

———. 1984. *Conversational Style: Analyzing Talk among Friends.* Norwood, N.J.: Ablex.

———. 1987. Repetition in conversation: Towards a poetics of talk. *Language*, Vol. 63, No. 3, 574–605.

———. 1989. *Talking Voices: Repetition, Dialogue, and Imagery in Conversational Discourse.* Cambridge: Cambridge University Press.

———. 1990. You just don't understand: Women and men in conversation. New York: William Morrow and Company, Inc.

Tiwon, Sylvia. 1996. Models and maniacs: Articulating the feminine in Indonesia. In *Fantisizing the Feminine in Indonesia*, pp. 120–139. L. Sears, ed. Durham, N.C.: Duke University Press.

Uhlenbeck, E. M. [1949] 1978. *Studies in Javanese Morphology.* Translation series No. 19. The Hague: Martinus Nijhoff.

———. 1970. The use of respect forms in Javanese. In *Pacific Linguistic Studies in Honour of A. Capell*, pp. 441–466. S. Wurm and D. Laycock, eds. Canberra: Linguistic Circle of Canberra.

Urban, Gregory. 1989. The "I" of discourse. In *Semiotics, Self, and Society*, pp. 27–51. B. Lee and G. Urban, eds. The Hague: Mouton Press.

Van Dijk, Teun. 1984. *Prejudice in Discourse.* Amsterdam: Benjamins.

———. 1993. Principles of critical discourse analysis. *Discourse & Society.* Vol. 4, No. 2, 249–283.

———. 1994. Ideological discourse analysis. Manuscript.

Vygotsky, Lev. 1986. *Thought and Language.* Cambridge, Mass.: MIT Press.

Weiringa, Saskia. 1992, Summer. Ibu or the beast: Gender interests in two Indonesian women's organizations. *Feminist Review*, No. 41.

Wolf, Diane. 1992. *Factory Daughters: Gender, Household Dynamics, and Rural Industrialization in Java*. Berkeley: University of California Press.

―――. 1996. Javanese factory daughters: Gender, the state and industrial capitalism. In *Fantasizing the Feminine in Indonesia*, pp. 140–162. L. Sears, ed. Durham, N.C.: Duke University Press.

Wolff, John, and Soepomo Poedjosoedarmo. 1982. *Communicative Codes in Central Java*. Data Paper No. 116, Southeast Asia Program. Ithaca, N.Y.: Cornell University Press.

Wolfowitz, Clare. 1991. *Language Style and Social Space: Stylistic Choice in Suriname Javanese*. Illinois Studies in Anthropology No. 18. Urbana: University of Illinois Press.

Index

DATE DUE